A HISTORY OF THE DASNAMI NAGA SANNYASIS

JADUNATH SARKAR

A HISTORY OF THE DASNAMI NAGA SANNYASIS

Edited with an Introduction by
ANANDA BHATTACHARYYA

MANOHAR
2018

First published 1958
This edition with new Preface and Introduction 2018

ISBN 978-93-5098-198-6

Published by
Ajay Kumar Jain *for*
Manohar Publishers & Distributors
4753/23 Ansari Road, Daryaganj,
New Delhi 110 002

Typeset by
Ravi Shanker
Delhi 110 055

Printed at
Shri Ganpati Enterprises
Delhi 110 052

To

Professor Rajat Kanta Ray

Contents

Preface to the Second Edition

The cult of the naked Nagas has a long history. The Dasnamis were divided into Gossains and Nagas. The geographical distribution of Sannyasis', *maths* and *akharas* highlighted their area of activities.

The present volume aims to explore new findings which are available in various Archives and repositories in order to fill up the lacuna and shortcomings of Jadunath Sarkar's work on the subject as elaborated in the present introduction. It is unclear as to say why Sir Jadunath did not consult the British East India Company's correspondences, rather, giving much importance to Persian and Marathi sources. In order to demonstrate the idea of *Hindutva* Sir Jadunath glorified the martial valour of the Dasnami Naga Sannyasis. Two-thirds of the book of Sir Jadunath has thrown light on their involvement in warfare and military activities on behalf of the regional powers. While discussing their mercenary activities, Sir Jadunath was also silent about their involvement in the famous palace conspiracy at the Cooch Behar native state. The present introduction as appended with Sir Jadunath's monograph will justify the multi-dimensional aspects of the Dasnami Nagas including their trade and moneylending involvement.

The editor of the present volume is highly indebted to archival officers and staff of the National Archives of India, New Delhi, Jhumur Sengupta, Archivist, of the West Bengal State Archives, Kolkata, Allahabad Regional Archives, U.P. State Archives, Lucknow, Bangladesh National Archives, Dhaka and the various *akhara* organizations for rendering valuable services in retrieving the resources for scholarly purposes. Finally, I would like to thank Sri Ramesh Jain, for agreeing to reprint the book of Jadunath Sarkar.

ANANDA BHATTACHARYYA

Abbreviations

BOR	Board of Revenue at Fort William
BOR (UPSA)	Board of Revenue at Fort William (Uttar Pradesh State Archives, Lucknow)
BOT (Commercial)	Board of Trade (Commercial)
CPC	Calendar of Persian Correspondence
COR	Committee of Revenue
CPRB	Correspondence and Proceedings of the Resident at Benares
CCRP	Controlling Council of Revenue at Patna
DPSR	Duncan Papers and Settlement Records
JCR	Judicial Criminal Proceedings
RDG	Revenue Department, Governor-General in Council, at Fort William
Secret	Secret Committee Proceedings
Select	Select Committee Proceedings

Introduction

ANANDA BHATTACHARYYA

The Dasnami Sannyasis constitute perhaps the most powerful monastic order, which has played an important part in the history of India. The cult of the naked Nagas has a long history. Most of the Nagas belong to the Dasnami group organized by the Shankaracharya, the great of tenth century. They are divided into two sections; the *shastradharis*, who specialize in sacred lore, and the *astradharis*, who bear arms. The Shankaracharyas have combined saintly purity with *shastric* learning and intellectual acumen of the highest degree. At Benares, the Shankaracharya's dynamic exposition of the *shastras* and his persuasive commentary on the *Brahmasutra* and the supernatural genius displayed by such a youthful teacher, created the greatest astonishment among the circle of scholars and devotees who had assembled there from all parts of India. The Shankaracharya passed many years at Sringeri, composing books and teaching his followers, like, Hastamalak, Mandan, Totoka and Padmapad.

Under the circumstances it is prudent to define the connotation of the term Dasnami. Dasnami means ten names, viz., Giri, Puri, Bharati, Aranya, Ban, Saraswati, Tirtha, Ashram, Sagar and Parbat. They were commonly known as Gossains (settled and married Sannyasis) and Nagas (naked). Sources are available about Giri, Puri and Bharati both in official correspondence and census reports. The actual jurisdiction of the Dasnamis can be clearly understood from the official sources preserved in the Archives of West Bengal, National Archives of India, Uttar

Pradesh State Archives,[1] Rajasthan State Archives, Bikaner and Gujarat State Archives. Besides the official sources, it is necessary to consult the Persian and Urdu sources[2] either memoirs or the chronicles, written by the court poets of the regional princedoms. Scholars have also failed to retrieve the Marathi and the Hindi sources, mainly available in the *akharas* and archives[3] widely scattered in various parts of western India. Marathi sources[4] and works of Hindi literature[5] are also useful for understanding the

[1] In Uttar Pradesh there are five Regional Archives, viz., Allahabad, Varanasi, Nainital, Agra and Dehradun. The State Archives of Uttar Pradesh is in Lucknow. The present researcher consulted the primary sources preserved in Allahabad, Varanasi (the Regional Archives) and also the State Archives at Lucknow.

[2] *Tarikh-i-Ahmadshahi* (translated into English by Jadunath Sarkar, 1937), an unpublished manuscript written by an anonymous author, but, by far the fullest and most accurate history of the reign of the Mughal Emperor Ahmad Shah see Khairuddin Muhammad Allahabadi, *Ibratnama*, unpublished manuscript (in Persian); Hari Charan Das, *Chahar Gulzar Shujai* (in Persian), Newal Kishore Press, Lucknow, n.d.; Ghulam Ali Naqvi, *Imad-us-Sadat*, Newal Kishore Press, Lucknow, n.d.

[3] Private Archives of Raghubir Singh, Sitamau, preserves a large number of *Akhbarats* which have been used in preparing this note. Jadunath Sarkar consulted the *Akhbarats* in writing his masterpiece on the history of the Dasnami Nagas (for details see J.N. Sarkar, *Persian Records of Maratha History, Parasnis Collection, Delhi Affairs (1761-1788)*, Bombay Printing Press, Bombay, 1953.

[4] *Readings in History of the Hindustan, 1732-1744*; Marathi Sources, Sitamau, 1941 (unpublished); and Hari Gir and Prithwi Gir, *Gosavi Vatyacha Sampradaya* (in Marathi), Yeotmal, Baroda Press, 1931; G.S. Sardesai, ed., *Selections from the Peshwa Daftar*, Central Press, Bombay, 1930-4; and idem., *Historical Papers Relating to Mahadji Sindiā* (unpublished papers from Marathi to English), Alijah Darbar Press, Gwalior, 1937 with a Foreword by Jadunath Sarkar.

[5] Besides the *akhara* records of Mahanirvani, Juna and Atal the contemporary published literature, viz., Padmakar, *Himmat Bahadur Virudavali* (in Hindi), ed. Lala Bhagavanadin, Varanasi Nagari Pracharani Sabha, Varanasi, 1908; Sudan, *Sujan Charita*, ed. Radhakrishnadas, Varanasi Nagari Pracharani Sabha, Varanasi, 1923 and Moti Chandra,

history of the Dasnami Sannyasis. The importance of the *akhara* records are considered as useful source materials to arrive at a clear understanding of the subject.

The Marathi, Persian and English sources clearly indicate that they belonged to present-day Uttar Pradesh, especially Awadh, Prayag, Mirzapur, Varanasi, Jhansi, Punjab, Maharashtra, Gujarat, and Rajasthan. In Bengal, particularly in Dinajpur and Malda in the mid-nineteenth century a group of Gossains were found. *The Census Report* classified 187 Sannyasis in Dinajpur and 843 Gossains in Malda who were basically from the Giri suborder and engaged in trade.[6] Oral sources are other important resources for understanding the identity, culture and activities of the Dasnami Naga Sannyasis.[7] Besides the religious endowments, the resident Sannyasis acquired valuable properties all-over India, including in various parts of Bengal, particularly Mymensingh and Sherpur in Bagura districts and earned their livelihood principally by moneylending, trade and mercenary activities. Even during my fieldwork undertaken on different occasions large landed properties held by the Sannyasis of the Giri sect were found in the districts of Bagura, Malda, Rangpur and Mymensingh.[8] The zamindar of Sherpur in Bagura granted a large area of land to Chandan Giri Sannyasis. This area presently is known to the local people as Subarnar Char.

Due to the non-availability of abundant source materials it is very difficult to reach the conclusion that when exactly the

---

Kashi ka Itihas, Hindi Grantha-Ratnakar, Bombay, 1962, deserve special mention.

[6] W.W. Hunter, *A Statistical Account of Bengal, Districts of Maldah, Rangpur and Dinajpur*, vol. VII, John Murray, London, 1876: 44, 376-9.

[7] Interviews had been undertaken with the *mahants* of various *akharas* of Uttar Pradesh and Malda in West Bengal. The oral sources, either in the form of testimony, interviews taken with the present day Sannyasis would compliment the colonial records and the vernacular literature.

[8] Jamalpur, popularly known as Sannyasiganj (according to oral tradition), due to their settlement in that area for a long period where they also carried on business and moneylending.

Dasnamis began their ascent in Indian history. The Dasnami Sannyasis were so militant that their fighting propensity was a basic characteristic of them. The Mughal Emperor Akbar in 1567 witnessed a fight between the armed Sannyasis of 'Giri' and 'Puri' suborders at Thaneshwar. The basic reason for entering into armed conflict was over the collection of contribution from the pilgrims who had come there to bathe in the sacred river on a Kumbh Jog, when the sun enters the Zodiac sign of Capricorn (Makar). J.N. Farquhar[9] thought that the traditional account of the revival of the armed Sannyasis began in the mid-sixteenth century when both the Sannyasis and Fakirs went about with arms and took part in frequent warfare. He also said when there was no warfare they were involved into armed conflict with each other. Farquhar accused the Fakirs for attacking and killing the Sannyasis 'as representatives of Hinduism'. He also said, 'as ascetics, these Fakirs held a privileged position and were thus protected from violence and also from interference on the part of the Government' [Muhammedan]. He also went on to say that the Sannyasis being oppressed and hunted by the Muslims felt the need for their own protection. Madhusudan Saraswati, a renowned Sannyasi famous for his learning and scholarship met Emperor Akbar and enquired of him 'whether anything could be done for the protection of the ancient order to which he belonged'. Raja Birbal being instructed by Mughal emperor Akbar advised Madhusudan Saraswati to initiate a large number of non-Brahmins for strengthening their order and also to keep arms for fighting against Malang Fakirs. He also said it was the turning point when the Sannyasis began to keep arms and some of them seized lands and settled down.

Thus were many Kshatriyas, Vaishyas, and, says J.N. Farquhar, 'multitudes of Shudras at a later date' admitted into the order. It is said that half of the Bharatis refused to accept this and went to

[9] J.N. Farquhar, 'The Organization of the Sannyasis of Vedanta', *Journal of the Royal Asiatic Society of Great Britain and Ireland'*, Cambridge University Press, London, July 1925: 479-86.

Sringeri to remain 'pure'. The recruitment of Nagas into organized fighting units appears to have occurred around the time of Akbar's reign, although it is unlikely to have been in response to attacks by Sufis. Nearly all of the recorded conflicts between bands of ascetics have been between factions of Hindus, in most instances between Vaishnava – Ramanandi *vairagis/bairagi* and Shaiva – Dasnami Sannyasis (also known as Gosains) at *melas* (festivals) over bathing priorities for particular *akharas*. The Ramanandis and the Dasnamis are the largest of the 60 or so extant *sadhu* sects in India and Nepal, and also those with the greatest number of Nagas.

The evidence indicates that organized Naga military activity originally flourished under state patronage. During the latter half of the sixteenth century and the early part of the seventeenth century, a number of bands of fighting ascetics formed into *akharas* with sectarian names and identities. These armies were of mercenaries who often largely disbanded during cessations of conflict and during harvest times, when many of the men would return home to attend to agricultural duties. The formation of mercenary Naga armies occurred largely in parallel with the constitution of a formal and distinct identity for many of the currently recognizable sects of *sadhus*, including the Ramanandis and Dasnamis. Several commentators (e.g. Orr, 1940) have maintained that members of the Nath sect (Nath Sampradaya) have at times constituted elements of Naga armies, but there seems to be no substantial evidence to support this assertion. It is most likely that observers mistakenly identified either Ramanandis or Dasnamis as Naths.

From the late sixteenth century until the early decades of the nineteenth century, many prominent regional regents recruited bands of Nagas to fight in interregional struggles for power. The Mughal emperor Aurangzīb authorized in 1692/3 five Ramanandi commanders and their armies to move without hindrance. The British officer lieutenant-colonel Valentine Blacker included '*gossyes*' (i.e. Gosains) in his account of the rise of infantry forces in India in the 1700s, comparing them in proficiency to Afghan and

Jat Sikh *khalsa* troops (the Sikh order, or brotherhood, known as the Khalsa, was, according to tradition, founded by Guru Gobind Singh, and its troops were drawn almost entirely from the Jat caste of north-western cultivators). They were particularly renowned for their nocturnal guerrilla operations: naked, some-times slippery with oil, and dangerous with the dagger. The disposition of regents to employ Naga armies may have also been partly due to their reputation for 'supernatural' yogic abilities, and the consequent potential apprehension of adversaries, and to several historical legal statutes that either restricted or annulled the ability of states to prosecute them, being of religious orders, for crimes committed. In 1763, Prithvi Narayan Shah, king of Gorkha and the founder of modern Nepal, was engaged in a campaign to extend his empire into the Kathmandu Valley. His chief advisor and strategist was a Nath *siddha* named Bhagvantnath, who used his influence to negotiate various matrimonial and military alliances between Gorkha and some of the other 45 kingdoms of western Nepal. During Prithvi Narayan's attack on the village of Saga, his Gorkhalese troops were confronted by 500 Nagas – under the leadership of Gulabram – who were fighting on behalf of one of his opponents, Jayaprakash Malla, king of Kathmandu. All the Nagas were slaughtered by the Ghorkhalese army, though Gulabram escaped. During the 1780s, about 700 Nagas died in battle in another Himalayan province, Kumaon. A total of 1,400 Nagas had been enlisted, with the promise of substantial financial rewards, by King Mohan Chand in his unsuccessful attempt to recapture his seat in Almora, from which he had been deposed by his rival, Harsdev Joshi, king of the neighbouring Himalayan province, Garhwal.

It may be assumed that the Dasnamis came into prominence during the decline of the Mughal Empire. The gradual decline of central authority and the rise of regional kingdoms helped the Dasnamis to act independently and thus their fortunes began to change rapidly till they faced stiff opposition of the English East India Company. This political instability encouraged the Dasnamis wandering all over India to become more militant and they began to act as semi-independent chieftains in the form of roving war bands. D.H.A. Kolff,[10] B.S. Cohn[11] and C.A. Bayly,[12] though in a limited way, mentioned only the Dasnamis' trading network which was facilitated by their mercenary activities. Since the Dasnamis were highly trained in arms and warfare through their *akhara* based organization under the leadership of respective *mahants* they chose to act as mercenaries in the service of the regional powers. Side by side they continued their ascetic way of life by attending the religious fairs and festivals like Kumbha Mela,[13] Ganga Sagar Island on the last day of *Pous Sankranti* (Bengali month corresponding 14/15 January), fair held at Janakpur in Nepal in connection with the birth anniversary of Ram and Sita, the legendary protagonists of *Ramayana* or in other similar types of religious congregation. During the Kumbha Mela, Niranjani, Juna and Atal Akharas would be present and take out processions with arms and ammunition.[14] Chandranath Sitakund, the famous shrine, situated in the Sitakund range of Chittagong Hill Tracts was also a centre of religious congregation of Dasnami Sannyasis. It appears that Maharaja Mudoji Bhonsle permitted Moti Giri

[10] 'Sannyasi Trader – Soldiers', *Indian Economic and Social History Review*, vol. VIII, New Delhi, 1971: 213-20.

[11] Cohn's (B.S. Cohn, 'The Role of Gosains in the Economy of 18th and 19th Century Upper India', *Indian Economic and Social History Review*, no. 4, New Delhi, 1964: 175-83) insufficient approach failed to satisfy the aspirations of the researchers if anyone comes across the archival resources and the district records in an all-India level. There should be an improved version on the trading and moneylending activities of the Dasnami *naga* Sannyasis not only in upper India but also in other parts of India. Cohn even did not mention the significance and importance of the records of the Allahabad Regional Archives, Allahabad and U.P. State Archives, Lucknow.

[12] C.A. Bayly, *Rulers, Townsmen and Bazars: North Indian Society in the Age of British Expansion, 1770-1870*, Oxford University Press, New Delhi, 1998 (rpt.): 126-7.

[13] The Makar Kumbha bath at Allahabad, when the sun enters the Zodiac sign of Capricorn (Makar); the Mesh Kumbha bath at Hardwar and the Singha Kumbha bath at Trimbak.

[14] Gir & Gir, 1931: 173-4.

and Sumer Giri, two remarkable Gossains to visit that place.[15] In Kumbha Mela the Gossains entered into bloody warfare. As W.W. Wilson has shown that a party of them also attacked Col. Goddard's troops in their march between Dorawal and Hirapur in 1780. It was a famous conflict of Hardwar where Bairagi Nagas were also involved. The participation of Jogis and Vaishnavas were indicated. The leader of the Shaiva party was Dhokal Giri who was the spiritual guide of Anup Giri *alias* Himmat Bahadur, a Gosain and in that fierce warfare 2,000 Bairagis were killed.[16]

The Gossains particularly the Puri suborder was very dominant in the province of Malwa and adjoining districts during the early decades of nineteenth century. Their total strength was nearly 2,000 where they enjoyed *inam* land.[17] The Gossains controlled the entire region of Anupshehr (situated on the west bank of the Ganges). J.C. Williams even when he was compiling the *District Census Handbook of Uttar Pradesh* particularly the district Barabanki in 1869 estimated the total strength as 3391. They were mostly found in the tahsils of Nawabganj and Ramnagar.[18] In Sirsa the Gossains also formed a separate caste. In that locality generally the Giri, Puri and Tirtha suborder of the Dasnamis were frequently found. In Baroda in the late nineteenth century the Gossains, particularly the Atit[19] sub-order of them was distributed indicating the number of males and females including

[15] *Calendar of Persian Correspondence,* Imperial Record Department (renamed as National Archives of India), Office of the Supdt. Govt. Printing, Calcutta, 1907-69: 15.

[16] W.W. Wilson, *Hindu Religions*; or *An Account of the Various Religious Sects of India*, The Society for the Resucitation of the Indian Literature, Calcutta, 1899: 154.

[17] Durgaprasad Bhattacharya, and Bibhabati Bhattacharya, eds., *Report on Population Estimates of India, 1820-1830*, Secretariat Press, New Delhi, 1963: 36-88.

[18] John Williams, *A Historical Account of the Rise and Progress of the Bengal Native Infantry from the Formation in 1757 to 1796*, John Murray, London, 1817: 15.

[19] In Benares the Gossains were commonly known as Atit.

married and widowers. The total strength was 10,221 out of which total male persons were 5,787 and females 4,434. They were mostly scattered in Amreli, Navsari, Baroda and Baroda city. In early twentieth century their strength extended even up to Amritsar, Lahore, Karachi and Rangoon. *The Census Report* of 1931 throws light on their occupation and means of livelihood as they did in those areas.[20] Indore, Gwalior, Bhopal, Bundelkhand and Baghelkhand, Western Malwa and Guna were the major strongholds of the Dasnamis including Nagas, Gossains and Puri suborders. Hyderabad proper and Rajputana was not free from their operations. The Sannyasis found in Sindh followed nominally the profession of living by alms, and wander about the country from shrine to shrine but some of them were traders, moneylenders, cattle-breeders and bead-sellers. It was also observed that the Sannyasis found in the Deccan used to render their services as guards at temples or as retainers of prosperous Hindu households.[21]

The total number of Gossains in Indian perspective were enormous out of which Giris were 9,643, Puri 6,236, Bharati 1,463, Ban 386 and Aranya 36. Table I will indicate the existence of the Gossains in Bombay presidency as it appears from the census report. There is no indication about their exact territorial strength in northern India or upper India either in the census report or in district census handbook

The Dasnamis as the disciples of the Shankaracharya were controlled by four *maths,*[22] viz., Shringeri, Joshi, Sharada and

[20] J.H. Hutton, ed., *Census of India, 1931*, vol. I, part I, *Report*, Office of the Registrar General, New Delhi, 1932: 408-9.

[21] J.A. Baines, *Imperial Census of 1881*: *Operation and Results in the Presidency of Bombay including Sind,* vol. I, Bombay Central Press, Bombay, 1882: 133.

[22] Shyamlal Mallick, *Charidham Bhraman* (in Bengali), Mahendra Library, Calcutta, 1331 BS: 1-17; G.S. Ghurye, *Indian Sadhus: A Sociological Survey,* 2nd edn., Popular Prakashan, Bombay, 1964: 67-8; James Hastings, *Encyclopedia of Religion and Ethics*, 1981: 192-3; M.A. Sherring, *Hindu*

TABLE I: DISTRIBUTION OF THE SANNYASIS IN BOMBAY PRESIDENCY

Class	*Group*	*Caste*	*No. of Sub-division turned*	*Total Strength*		*Territorial Distribution*			
				Male	*Female*	*Gujarat*	*Deccan*	*Kankan*	*Karnataka*
Professional	Devotees	Atit	XXXXXXX	9132	7163	16266	XX	XX	XX
-Do-	-Do-	Bharati	XXXXXXXX	51	48	2	X	97	X
-Do-	-Do-	Gosavi	63	21213	49	7008	23202	6296	2229
-Do-	-Do-	Ban	X	60	44	X	104	X	X
-Do-	-Do-	Bharati	X	3	4	7	X	X	X
-Do-	-Do-	Giri	X	3031	2691	298	5287	137	X
-Do-	-Do-	Parbat	X	5	18	X	X	23	X
-Do-	-Do-	Puri	X	927	832	98	1543	118	X
						Ahmbd	Surat	P.M.	N.S.
-Do-	-Do-	Atit	X	9114	7152	1060	X	6	15183
-Do-	-Do-	Gosavi	X	3989	3019	1284	386	561	1978
-Do-	-Do-	Bharati	X	3	4	X	4	X	X
-Do-	-Do-	Giri	X	156	142	X	158	X	X
-Do-	-Do-	Puri	X	65	33	X	53	X	X

Source: W.W. Drew, *Census of Bombay and its Feudatories*, vol. VIII, part II, *Imperial Tables*, Bombay General Press, 1892: 188-9, 194-5, 206-7. The *Census Report* also highlighted that the Dasanamis became educated since 1891.

Govardhan (see Appendix 1). As Atkinson[23] said: 'These people became the heads of the Dasnami or "ten-named mendicants" and anyone joining the fraternity adopts one of these names. They are ruled by an assembly called *Dasnama* composed of the representatives of ten divisions, which has a complete control over all the *maths* of the order.' In fact the Ukhi Math was founded by the Kedarnath order of Shankaracharya with the principal *math* of the north, viz., the Joshi Math. The following extracts from Sister Nivedita's *Northern Tirthas* traces the military character of the Sannyasis in charge of monasteries back to the date of their establishment. 'Ukhi Math was originally granted to the subject of military service by the old kings of Garhwal of the same line as the present family.... The present Raoul [*Mahanta*] is set to be over hundred and twenty-fifth in succession'.[24] The Giri suborder was originally meant to wander in the mountain with the Joshi Math as its headquarters. In course of time Benares became their *de facto* headquarters because of its commercial and religious importance to the Sannyasis. By the close of the eighteenth century there were *maths* also in Mirzapur, Poona, Nagpur, Gwalior, and Bengal, which helped the trading activities of the Sannyasis.

Although the *math* was originally a religious organization, subsequently they became centres of commercial and trading activities where goods could be stored and business conducted.[25] In Bihar the Dasnamis operated their activities through the *maths* established in Bodh Gaya. The Bodh Gaya Math came into existence in AD 1590 (fasli year 997) and controlled by the Gossain

---

Tribes and Castes as Represented in Benares, Trubner & Co., London, 1872: 258.

[23] E.T. Atkinson, ed., *Statistical, Descriptive and Historical Account of the North-Western Provinces of India*, vol. 1, Government Press, Lucknow, 1874.

[24] Cited in J.M. Ghosh, *Sannyasi and Fakir Raiders in Bengal*, Bengal Secretariat Press, Calcutta, 1930: 12.

[25] Francis Buchanan-Hamilton, *An Account of the District of Purnea in 1809-1810* (edited from the Buchanan MSS in the India Office Library, Bihar and Orissa Research Society, Patna, 1928): 81.

Ghamandi Giri whose immediate successor was Chaitanya Giri.[26] This *math* came into existence in the second half of fifteenth century. They were patronized by the Mughal monarchs. A large tract of land was given for the daily maintenance and livelihood of the Sannyasis.

The Tarakeshwar Math in Bengal had a trading network with centres in different parts of Maharashtra.[27] The *math* established at Ghusuri in Howrah (Bengal) under the patronage of Warren Hastings at the request of the sixth Panchen Lama of Tibet had trade relations with Tibet and the *math* at Ramna in Dacca with Joshi Math.[28] There were similar organizational links through *maths* between Bihar and the rest of India.[29] This

[26] He became the *mahant* in AD 1615. Mahant Chaitnya Giri was famous for his learning, piety and spent his time in worship and religious devotion. There is a detailed list of the *mahants* of the Bodh Gaya in the report produced by Grierson. The successor of Chaitanya Giri was Hemnarayan Giri who was a great Sanskrit scholar and collected a large library of original Sanskrit manuscript. He built a large house in Benares for the benefit of the people (Anugraha Narayan Singh, *Brief History of the Bodh-Gaya Math*, Bengal Secretariat Press, Calcutta, 1893: 2-18).

[27] E. Morinis, *Pilgrimage in the Hindu Tradition: A Case Study of West Bengal* (South Asian Studies Series), Oxford University Press, Delhi, 1984: 91.

[28] A.H. Dani, *Dacca: A Record of its Changing Fortunes*, Mrs. S.S. Dani, Dacca, 1956: 120; Haridas Basu, *Dhakar Katha* (in Bengali), Haridas Vasu, Koltabazar, Dacca, 1331 BS/AD 1924. In order to understand the nature of the Sannyasis' involvement in mundane affairs scholar should consult Ananda Bhattacharyya, *Dasnami Sannyasis in Worldly and Soldierly Activities* (Kunal Books, New Delhi, 2014); Gour Das Bysack, 'Notes on a Buddhist Monastery at Bhot Bagan in Howrah', *Journal of the Asiatic Society of Bengal*, Asiatic Society, Calcutta, 1890: 50-100; S.C. Sircar, 'A Note on Puran Gir Gossain', *Bengal Past and Present*, vol. XLIII (Calcutta Historical Society, Calcutta, 1932); Haripada Sengupta and Murari Mohan Chattopadhyay, *Tarakeswarer Mohantalila* (in Bengali), 3 parts, 1923, part I: 4; L.S.S. O'Malley and S.K. Chakraborty, *Bengal District Gazetteer, Howrah*, Bengal Secretariat Press, Calcutta, 1909: 152-4.

[29] Francis Buchanan-Hamilton, *An Account of the District of Sahabad in*

closely interlinked *maths* in various regions played a crucial role in the development of the organization of the Sannyasis all over India. They used to assemble at their respective *maths* to take important administrative decisions, for example, the election to the *panchayat* (assembly).

There were six well-known and principal *akharas*, namely Juna, Mahanirvani, Niranjani, Atal, Avahan and Agni. The Hindi term *akhara* means 'wrestling arena', from which *akhariya* derives, meaning 'master fighter', 'skilled manoevrer', or 'strategist'. There is a network of *akharas* throughout India, particularly in the north, where men train in wrestling and other methods of fighting. *Akharas* specialize in various techniques of fitness and combat, which include the use of weights, clubs, and maces. Various *akharas* came into existence in the pre-Mughal period in Jaipur, Jodhpur and some other parts of Rajasthan[30] and at Prayag,[31] but its principal centre is now in Benares. Mahanirvani was founded in the Siddheshwar temple at Kund Gaud, in Chotanagpur. Niranjani Akhara is believed to have been founded in AD 904 at Mandavi in Kutch.[32] Its principal centre is at Prayag but it has branches at Nasik, Ujjain, Benares, Hardwar and Udaipur. *Akharas* also existed at Lokmanpur in Bhagalpur. Siddhi Giris Mathiya (*math*) situated at Awadh was mainly under the control of Juna Akhara. Their activities covered a wide region from Awadh to the Deccan through this *math*.

1812-13, Bihar and Orissa Research Society, Patna, 1934: 52-140. In Bihar, Buchanan-Hamilton saw a number of *maths* during his survey of different parts of Bengal and Bihar in Lakshmi Kunda and Suraj Kunda and also in *thana* Biloti of the district Shahabad and Karanjiya, Tibothee, Mohaniya and Ramgarh division in Bihar. A *math* was also established at Bodh Gaya in Bihar under the patronage of Akbar. Anugraha Narayan Singh, *A Brief History on Bodh Gaya Math* (Bengal Secretariat Press, Calcutta, 1863).

[30] Ghurye, op. cit.: 67-8.

[31] During his visit to upper India in 1989, the present author was told that these *akharas* at present are to be found mainly in Benares, Allahabad and Hardwar.

[32] Ghurye, op. cit.: 104.

THE DASANAMI SANNYASI AKHARAS

The leading *akharas*, in terms of members and property, are the Niranjani and Juna. The Juna has the largest number of Nagas and is believed to be the oldest of the *akharas*. Members of the *akharas* are also affiliated to one or another of 52 (or 51) *marhis*, which are subdivisions of the *akharas*. The system of *marhi* organization is further organized in a system of eight *davas* (section, claim). Within each *akhara*, there is a hierarchy of authority – *mahant*, *sri mahant*, and *mahamandaleshvara* – and (nominally) at the apex there are the *śankaracaryas*. The *mahamandaleshvaras* usually live in their own *maths* or *ashrams* and generally have little practical involvement in the daily operation of the *akhara*, except when they preside over initiation rituals and become involved in administrative issues. In all *akharas* (including those of the Ramanandis, Udasis, and Nirmals), each of which has an administrative body (*panch* or *panchayat*), there is usually a *sabhapati* (president), and beneath *mahants,* there is a hierarchy of other elected functionaries: *karbaris* (assistants), *thanapatis* (property managers), *sachivs* (secretaries), *pujaris* (who perform ritual worship), *kotvals* (guards), and *kotharis*/*bhandaris* (who manage daily supplies).

The main venue for initiations, elections to positions within the *akhara*, and administrative discussions is Kumbh Melas. The Dasnami *akharas* administer up to a hundred institutions, including temples, *maths*, and *ashrams*. Each of the Dasnami Akharas has a tutelary deity, namely, Karttikeya (Niranjani), Dattatreya Akharas (Juna), Kapil Muni (Mahanirvani), Surya (Ananda), Siddh Ganesh (Avahan), Adi Ganesh (Atal), and Gayatri (Agni). The Nagas of each Dasnami Akhara revere the *bhala*, which is a 5 to 7-meter-long javelin engraved with the sign of the respective deity of the *akhara*. It is carried at the front of the arrival (*pesvai*) and 'royal' bathing processions (*sahi snan*) at *melas* by the chief *mahant* or by Nagas. The *bhala* is usually kept at the headquarters of the *akhara* that it represents, but during *melas*, it is planted in the ground near the temporary shrine of the tutelary deity, at the center of the *akhara's* camping area. The members of six of the seven Dasnami Akharas, apart from the Agni Akhara, take one of the 'ten names', but members of the Agni Akhara take one of the four following names: Svarupa, Prakasha, Ananda, or Chaitanya. These are what are known as *brahmachari* (orthodox Brahman undergoing religious studentship and chastity) names, which are the same four names given to members of the other main wing of the Sannyasis, the *dandis*.

The Sannyasi Akharas, to which nagas belong, function independently from other Sannyasi organizations, those pertaining to the other branches of the Dasanami order, comprising *dandis* and *paramahansás*. *Dandis* are orthodox Brahmans and carry a stick (*danda*). They frequent their own *maths* and *ashrams* and have no organizational connection to the *akharas*. Their link to the *akharas* is only in respect to their common belief in the foundation of their order by Shankaracharya. Paramahansas are affiliated with one or another of the *akharas* but usually live independently in their own *maths*. The Dasnami Sannyasi order claims descent from the philosopher Shankaracharya (*c.*700 CE), through four disciples who, according to tradition, were established in four monasteries (*pithas*) at four places in India (in the north, south, east, and west); the five incumbent Shankaracharyas – two in the south – claim descent from these disciples. However, the tradition of the founding of four monasteries most probably dates from not earlier than the late sixteenth century. The founding of the Dasnami Akharas is difficult to discern. According to traditions among the Dasanamis – one of which is recorded in an influential account by Jadunath Sarkar, which has been reiterated with anomalies in several subsequent publications – the first *akhara* to be founded was Avahan (AD 547) followed by Atal (AD 646) Mahanirvani (AD 749), Ananda (AD 856), Niranjani (AD 904), Agni (AD 1136), and Juna (AD 1156). In other sources the founding year of the Agni Akhara is given as AD 1370. However, Sir Jadunath adds one thousand years to some of the founding dates, which produces many inconsistencies. Notwithstanding accounts stating a greater antiquity, it seems probable that it was during the latter decades of the sixteenth century and the early decades of the seventeenth century that the Dasnami Sannyasi Akharas first formed, a time when diverse lineages of both monastic and militant renunciates coalesced into a sect with a distinct identity, sectarian history, and founding *guru*, namely Shankaracharya.

As has already been said, that the Dasnami Naga Sannyasis were not ethnic Bengalis, but had come to Bengal from various parts of India, particularly the north-west. Uttar Pradesh was a centre for them. I had the occasion to interview the *mahants* of the *akharas* of Dasnami Nagas. In this context, my detailed interview with the *mahants* of *akharas* situated in Allahabad and Benares may be mentioned. The *mahants* and the disciples of Juna and Atal Akharas were very militant. Sir Jadunath has shown how the Atal Akharas produced so many fighting mendicants who were experts in the art of warfare. In Benares, the Niranjani Akhara is situated at Sivala Ghat, Avahan Akhara at Dashaswamedh Ghat, Niranjani, Juna and Mahanirvani are situated on the banks of river Baruna near Sivala Ghat and Hanuman Ghat. Anand Akhara is presently under the jurisdiction of Niranjani Akhara whereas Atal is under the control of Mahanirvani and Avahan is under Juna. Agni Akhara is situated at Rajghat and Anand Akhara at Kapildhara at Benares. According to the *mahants* of those *akharas* it may be said that Niranjani, Juna and Mahanirvani are the oldest and came into existence around the same time. But the Niranjani Akhara possessed enormous wealth and prosperity in comparison to the others. It is learnt from discussion with them that one Digambar Prasad Giri, attached to Niranjani Akhara, had 20,000 *bighas* of land in his possession at Benares. They had also established a market there from which they used to collect rent per month. They admitted that they were not merely ascetics but used to attend religious pilgrimage in addition to their other activities. They used to offer hospitality, food and shelter to their brethren particularly during the religious pilgrimage which continued for more than seven days. They were of opinion that their ancestors were permitted to keep revolvers, guns and other weapons for security of their treasure. This tradition is continued even today. They were so proud of their tradition that they brought out some weapons to show which according to them were used during the period of insurgency against the colonial rule in the second half of eighteenth century Bengal. Two types of flags, namely black and *gerua*, popularly known as Bhairo Prakash and Surya Prakash, are flown on the roof of the *akhara*. This corroborates the opinion of Sir Jadunath[33] that the Sannyasis, particularly, the Nagas maintained a celibate life. Arthur Steale[34] and M.A. Sherring[35] also support this opinion. They admitted that celibacy is the primary condition for *akhara* life. Married persons could not stay in the *akhara*. These *akharas* also provided shelter to the wandering mendicants. The Sannyasis' wearing of *rudraksha* and coral beads is also evident from those residing in the Juna Akhara. The branches of Juna Akhara are situated in Gujarat, Nasik and Hardwar. They also admitted that they had no political affiliation. Even their habit of taking *bhang* (hemp), *ganja* (opium) and hard liquor as we find in the Mohsin Fani's[36] account is also prevalent till today.

The Dasnami Sannyasis of Niranjani Akhara of Benares admitted that in order to keep their body fit they perform physical training. The present *mahants* of Niranjani Akhara were Hardeo Puri and Sundar Giri. They had close links with the Niranjani and Juna Akharas situated at Daraganj in Allahabad. The *akhara* situated at Hardwar was controlled by Mahants Jogender Giri and Narayan Puri of Niranjani Akhara. In Hardwar, Mahants Sankar

[33] Jadunath Sarkar, *A History of the Dasnami Naga Sannyasis* (hereafter *Dasnami*), Panchayati Mahanirvani Akhara, Allahabad, n.d.

[34] Arthur Steale, *The Law and Custom of Hindoo Castes*, W.H. Allen & Co., Lonodn, 1868.

[35] M.A. Sherring, *The Tribes and Castes as Represented in Benares*, Trubner & Co., London, 1872.

[36] *The Dabistan or School of Manners*, translated from the original Persian, with notes and illustrations, ed. David Shea and Anthony Troyer, Oriental Translation Fund of Great Britain and Ireland, Paris, 1843.

Bharati and Bhagirathi Giri also had a considerable influence over the *akharas*. It appears from the discussion of them that they used to compete with each other particularly during their bathing ceremony at Kumbha Mela. It is surprising that Niranjani Akhara established its branches in UK, USA, Sri Lanka and even in some Islamic countries like Pakistan. They even today used to recruit Brahmins, Kshatriyas, Vaishyas and Shudras in order to continue their traditional existence. Generally the *mahant* appears to be the supreme head of the *akharas* and is appointed for six years. Presently the designation of *mahant* has been converted to secretary. The secretary performs his office with an assembly popularly known as *panchayat* consisting of not less than eleven members for taking decisions on disputes particularly for determining the legal heirs and successors of *mahantship*. The decision taken by the assembly had to be agreed by all the members of the *akhara*. They admitted that this tradition is followed even today as it was framed during the time of the Shankaracharya.

Besides Benares, Allahabad was also a major stronghold of Dasnami *nagas*.[37] The discussion with the *mahants* of the Dasnami *akharas* at Daraganj in Allahabad throw light that the old records pertaining to their *akharas* might be available at Hardwar. In Hardwar it is situated at Mayapuri, Kankhal whose *mahant* was Brij Kishen Puri. They had enormous wealth and rent-free land and the adjacent area of that locality was controlled by them. They even established some shops and markets from where they used to collect rent.

Another interview was conducted[38] with the *mahants* of Mahanirvani Akhara, Daraganj, Allahabad. From the outside the *akhara* looks like a fort. According to them it had history of three hundred years. According to local tradition the *akhara*

[37] This survey was conducted on 11 December 1998 with Pandit Uday Shankar Dubey and Kashi Prasad Tripathi of Allahabad Hindi Sahitya Sammelan.

[38] On 11 December 1998 at 1 pm along with Uday Shankar Dubey and Kashi Prasad Tripathi.

came into existence during the Mughal period. The architectural pattern of the *akhara* indicates the Mughal form of architecture and sculpture. There are nearly four hundred rooms along with a large courtyard where the disciples were taking physical training in arms. From the discussion conducted with Omkar Puri, the then *mahant*, it is learnt that this *akhara* was a rent-free land up to the middle half of the British period. They have also a *panchayat* or a Board of Trustees for taking decisions on several issues. The *mahants* of the Mahanirvani Akhara also admitted that their ancestors were in the habit of rendering service as soldiers on behalf of the Indian powers. They also remember the celebrated Gossain brothers Himmat Bahadur and Umrao Giri of the early eighteenth century. Their photographs were hanging in the walls of *akhara*. They used to pay their homage to these celebrated Gossains for their warlike activities. It is revealed from the interviews taken with them that they used to attend religious fairs at Ganga Sagar and Kumbha Mela on the fixed day in every year and used to keep contact with the other *maths* and *akharas* situated in various parts of India and abroad. According to the rule of *Dasnam* assembly, they maintained celibacy particularly those who were residing in *akhara*. The married Sannyasis were generally not permitted to live in the *akharas*. The present *mahant* of that *akhara* stated that elections for creation of a new governing body used to take place every six years.

The Avahan Akhara situated at Dashaswamedh Ghat, Benares, was controlled by Mahants Brahma Puri and Badri Puri. The resourceful persons of the *akhara* went outside for collection of rent from the lands (40-45,000 *bighas*) which were given to different shopkeepers on a contractual basis. I was surprised to see a militant Naga Sannyasi standing in front of the Avahan Akhara at Dashaswamedh Ghat, whose physical presence resembled those of the rebel Sannyasis of eighteenth century Bengal. That Naga Sannyasi was a *kaupindhari* (wearer of loincloth). Though, the *akhara* was very small in appearance, but, it had an underground structure where their armory was loacted. They admitted that even today they were engaged in trade particularly in jewellery which was an old profession for them. The present researcher also met the *mahants* of Agni and Anand Akharas situated at Rajghat in Benares. They used to publish their *akhara* literature regularly. This literature throws light of their past history and also their present day activities.

There was a sharp distinction between the resident Sannyasis and the Nagas while the former were permitted to marry, but Nagas were celibates. The married Sannyasis leading a settled life was known as Gossains.[39] The resident Sannyasis lived in *maths*, wore full dresses of orange and blue cloth where as the Nagas lived in *akharas* and they wore a *kaupin*, smear ashes on their body and used shackles of iron chains. This trend is noticeable even today as the author witnessed it among the Nagas of Avahan Akhara situated in Benares.

To become a Sannyasi not only entails renouncing one's family name and former caste identity in a rite of renunciation but also results in acquiring a new identity and a new name as a member of a recognizable renunciate sect. The rite to become a Dasnami Sannyasi is performed in two stages: the first is the *panch guru sanskar*, when the initiate acquires five *gurus*, and the second initiation is the *viraja homa* (the rite of purification), which is usually performed at a Kumbh Mela, when the initiate performs his own funeral rites, thereby relieving any family member of future responsibility in that regard. Once initiated as a *sadhu*, the initiate may then perform a subsequent rite to become a Naga in an *akhara* (which in some *akharas* entails the tend on in the penis being broken, to ensure celibacy). The processes of becoming a Naga are similar for Ramanandis, the first initiation being the *panch sanskar diksha*, which is almost identical to that performed by – Srivaisnavas (with whom the Ramanandis have a complex historical connection). A second ritual is required to become a

[39] John Williams, *A Historical Account of the Rise and Progress of the Bengal Native Infantry from the Formation in 1757 to 1796*, John Murray, London, 1817: 118; *Gazetteer of the Province of Oudh*, vol. I: *North Western Provinces and Oudh*, Government Press, Allahabad, 1877: xxiv.

tyagi and a third ritual is traditionally required to become a Naga, but in recent decades Nagas have been initiated without their first becoming *tyagi*.

At Kumbh Melas one may see the camps of the 13 *akharas* extant in South Asia. The Shaiva Naths also have institutions in several places in India and Nepal but camp separately from the 13 *akharas* and are not within the organization of *akharas* pertaining to the other Shaiva and Vaishnava sects. Seven of the 13 *akharas* are Shaiva Dasnami Sannyasi Akharas. Three *akharas* of the 13 are of the Vaishnava Ramanandi Sampraday, which are referred to as *anis* (army corps) in Vaishnava terminology, *akhara* being a subdivision of an *ani*. The Dadupanth (Dadu Dayal) also has an *akhara*, which has an affiliation with the Ramanandis. The other three of the 13 *akharas* are affiliated with the Sikh tradition. Two are Udasi ('detached'; *sadhus*), namely, the Bara (large) Panchayati Udasi Akhara, and the Chhota (small) or Naya (new) Panchayati Udasi Akhara; the third of the Sikh-affiliated *akhara* is the Nirmal Panchayati Akhara. Although historically involved in the Sikh movement, these three *akharas* function as independent organizations. All 13 *akharas* have administrative offices, particularly in the cities of Benares, Prayag (Allahabad) and Hardwar (for the Dasnamis), Ayodhya (for the Ramanandis), and Punjab state (for the Udasis). Overseeing the activities of all 13 *akharas* is an organization, the Akhil Bharatiya Akhara Parishad, which is based in Hardwar and meets to decide on practical and policy issues.

The Gossains used to perform the *Vijaya* ceremony just after their initiation, implying that they must not be involved with their wives and families.[40] After becoming a Gossain he must give away all his earthly possession except a *kaupin,* a staff (*danda*) and a water pot (*kamandal).*[41] The Gossains would also admit female in their orders in conformity with the males. They were neither selected nor purchased. They were included in the order by way

[40] Sherring, *Hindu Tribes and Castes as Represented in Benares*: 256-7.

[41] Sarkar, *Dasnami*: 67.

of discretion.[42] A Gossain belonging to Giri suborder could not marry a woman of his own suborder but could select anyone of the other suborders. Though the people belonging to inferior castes were recruited but they could not rise to the position to which Brahmins and Rajputs belong. Even the higher caste people did not touch the food cooked by the lower group of people.[43] Here also virulent casteism prevailed as in other areas of Hindu society. The Dasnamis also entered into marriage life with Brahmins and followed the profession of cultivation. In their social life the Dasnamis generally nominated the *chelas* as their legal successors. The widows were also entitled to have maintenance. Secular Gossains generally did not engage themselves in cultivation. In their dress they used turban and *dhoti*. The Dasnamis were the worshippers of Shiva because they were Shaivaites. As Shiva himself wears a rosary of *rudraksha* seeds, every Sannyasi does the same. A *rudraksha* is said to have the greatest sanctity and mystic power. Besides Shiva, Hanuman also was one of the chief deities worshipped by the Dasnamis and Kanphata Jogis.[44] Umrao Giri, the brother of Anup Giri had six sons of his own and three illegitimate children. The Dasnamis were in the habit of keeping concubines. The family of Umrao Giri was popularly known as Gossains of Rasdhania and of Himmat Bahadur as Bandawala.[45] After initiation into the Dasnami order a disciple generally would lose his old caste and enter a new order. Celibacy was the primary condition of the Dasnami order. When a Dasnami settled down, 'he remains therefore a Gossain by name and adds a new caste to the society'.[46] Some of them lived in small societies and possessed

[42] Steale, *The Law and Customs of the Hindu Castes*: 438.

[43] James Hastings, ed., *Encyclopedia of Religion and Ethics*, New York, 1981, vol. VI: 192-3.

[44] Padmakar, 1908: 18; Peter van der Veer, *Gods on Earth: Management of Religious Experience and Identity in a North Indian Pilgrimage Centre,* Oxford University Press, New Delhi, 1989: 149-50.

[45] *Gazetteer of the Province of Oudh*, vol. I: *Allahabad*, North Western Provinces and Oudh, Government Press, Allahabad, 1877: xxiv.

[46] 'Narrative of a Journey to Srinagar', *Asiatic Annual Registrar* (VI), Baptist Mission Press, Serampore, 1799: 315.

considerable wealth. The Gossains of Balarampur Pargana were merchants of jewellery. The famous Gossain merchant of this locality was Moti Giri who had a large house in that region. They used to trade in jewels, spices, gold and asafoetida. The chief trade was conducted between Nawabganj and Bengal. The religious fairs held at Hardwar were mainly controlled by the Gossains under the leadership of the *mahants*. The role of *mahants* may be summarized in this way: 'These *Mehunts* (abbots) meet in Council daily, hear and decide upon all complaints brought either against individuals or of a nature tending to disturb the public tranquility, and the well management of this immense multitude.' In central India the Sannyasis used to operate their trade since the pre-colonial period. The famous Gossain Kaushal Giri was a moneylender who lent the amount of Rs. 42,789 to Rana Sujan Singh, Daulat Singh and Bhao Singh of Gargunga in the year 1855 *samvat.*[47] In 1806 Anup Giri's assignments in Bundelkhand were exchanged for a territory of the Kanpur district (Rasdhan) yielding a revenue of Rs. 1,35,000 a year. The family of Umrao Giri and Kanchan Giri received pensions till 1807.[48]

The descendants of Anup Giri and Umrao Giri were located in various places of north India, viz., Fatehpur, Kanpur, Panna, Naogaon and Bundelkhand. It is very difficult to say when these Sannyasis and Fakirs began to keep arms. Religious reformer Kabir found them in the fifteenth century and denounced them for their habit of committing violence and extortion. Kabir's disdain is fully reflected in his own writings. Some portions of the translation may be mentioned in this context:[49]

> Never have I seen such yogis, Brother.
> They wander mindless and negligent

[47] Gir & Gir, 1931: 265.

[48] E.T. Atkinson, ed., *Statistical, Descriptive and Historical Account of the North-Western Provinces of India*, vol. 1, Government Press, Lucknow, 1874: 41.

[49] Linda Hess and Sukhdeva Sinha, *Bijak Kabir*, translated by Linda Hess and Sukhdeva Sinha, essays and notes by Linda Hess, Oxford University Press, New York, 2002.

Proclaiming the way of Mahadeva.
For this they are called great mahants
To markets and bazaars they bring their meditation,
False siddhas, lovers of maya.
When did Dattatreya attack a fort?
When did Sukadeva join with gunners?
When did Narada fire a musket?
When did Vyasadeva sound a battle cry?
These make war, slow-witted.
Are they ascetics or archers?
Become unattached, greed is their mind's resolve.
Wearing gold they shame their profession,
Collecting stallions and mares and
Acquiring villages they go about as tax collectors.

In spite of such differences both of them possessed a militant outlook, frequently indulged in warlike activities and involved in economic and political activities. Only those Naga Sannyasis who were attached to particular *akharas* could be the inmates of their respective *akharas*. A Naga's specific status depended on his *akhara* and was not connected to the particular order of the Dasnamis he belonged to.[50] The Sannyasis deposited their cash and wealth with the common fund of the *maths*, from which the *gurus* and *mahants* would advance money to the *chelas* (disciples) to carry on trade and other economic activities.[51] The *akharas* were the storehouses of arms and weapons and produced fighters to combat enemies. Even a majority of the insurgent Sannyasis belonged to the *akharas*. Jadunath Sarkar has shown how the Atal and Avahan Akharas produced various heroes during the later Mughal period.[52]

The following explains the activities of the Dasnami Sannyasis with special reference to their relations with the regional powers, local *zamindars* (local rulers) and the common people. The nature of their relations with various strata of the state and society

[50] Ghurye, op. cit.: 103.
[51] Steale, *The Law and Custom of the Hindu Castes*: 435-7.
[52] Sarkar, *Dasnami Sannyasi*: 90.

developed in a two-way process. They rendered services to the regional powers of India; in return, they enjoyed the latter's respect and favours such as *jagirs* (large tracts of land), pensions, and titles.

In the popular imagination, the Dasnami Sannyasis, the participants of anti-colonial resistance in Bengal, which is popularly known as Sannyasi Rebellion, were the people of Bengal. But this is a wrong assumption. This religious group originated outside Bengal, particularly, in northern and western India. These areas were the major strongholds of the Sannyasis. Even central India and parts of the Deccan were the centres of activities of the Dasnamis. In order to establish the group identities of the Dasnamis we have to identify the geographical locations of their *maths, akharas*. They not only used to reside there but also operated from there. It is also necessary to mention in this context, the exact geography of north-west India consisting of Allahabad, Mirzapur, and Benares, a part of Bundelkhand, Punjab, Gujarat, Rajasthan and Maharashtra, where Dasnami Sannyasis were very much dominant. From the north-western region they used to enter Bengal and Bihar for the purposes of pilgrimage, trade and moneylending. Bengal and Bihar were simply their hunting grounds for extorting contributions in the name of religious charity from the rural people and the zamindars.[53] This explains

[53] Jamini Mohan Ghosh, *Sannyasis in Mymensingh*, Pranballabh Sen, Dacca, 1923; *Sannyasi and Fakir Raiders in Bengal*, Bengal Secretariat Press Calcutta, 1930. The recent edited work by Ananda Bhattacharyya, *Sannyasi and Fakir Rebellion: Jamini Mohan Ghosh Revisited*, Manohar, New Delhi, 2013, analyses the existing myth about the nature of the rebellion including their origin, identity and relations with the East India Company. A.N. Chandra, *The Sannyasi Rebellion in Bengal*, Aruna Prakashani, Calcutta, 1977; Suprakash Roy, *Bharater Krishok Bidroho O Ganatantrick Sangram* (in Bengali), DNBA Brothers, Calcutta, 1966; Suranjan Chatterjee, 'A New Reflection on Sannyasi, Fakir and Peasant War', *Economic and Political Weekly*, January 1984: PE2-13; Atis Dasgupta, *The Fakirs and Sannyasi Uprisings*, K.P. Bagchi & Co., Calcutta, 1992. The author sharply contradicts the existing myth. See Ananda Bhattacharyya, 'The Peripatetic

why the Dasnamis performed activities as traders, moneylenders and mercenary soldiers in those regions since the Mughal period.[54] Though the Dasnamis were very much known as freewheeling foragers[55] in Bengal in the second half of the eighteenth century, they did not commit any violent activities in their places of residence.

Before I address my major points, I will briefly acquaint the reader with some of the existing literature on the Sannyasis. Contemporary scholars writing in English have generated misunderstandings that I hope to eliminate in my introductory note. It is ironic that David N. Lorenzen[56] and William Pinch[57] in their works seem to have failed to consult the various sources of invaluable importance available in various archives,[58] Collectorate Record Room,[59] monasteries,[60] and oral testimonies[61] left by

---

Sannyasis: A Challenge to Peasant Stability and Colonial Rule'? *Indian Historical Review*, vol. 41.1: 47-66.

[54] For details in this aspect scholar should consult Ananda Bhattacharyya, 'Dasnami Sannyasis: Polity and Economy', *Studies in History*, August 2014, vol. 30, no. 2: 151-77.

[55] This term echoes Ranajit Guha's explanation in his masterpiece (*A Rule of Property for Bengal: An Essay on the Idea of Permanent Settlement* (2nd revd. edn., Orient Longman, New Delhi, 1982) but later on he was silent in his subaltern thesis (*An Elementary Aspect of Peasant Insurgency in Colonial India*, Oxford University Press, New Delhi, 1992). It is surprising to the social scientist why Guha was silent about portraying the characterization of the Sannyasi rebellion. The contradiction is found in his later work.

[56] D.N. Lorenzen, 'Warrior Ascetics in Indian History', *Journal of the American Oriental Society*, vol. 98, New Haven, Boston, 1978: 61-75.

[57] William Pinch, *Warrior Ascetics and Indian Empire*, South Asian Edition, Cambridge University Press, New Delhi, 2006.

[58] West Bengal State Archives, National Archives of India, New Delhi, Allahabad Regional Archives, Allahabad and U.P. State Archives, Lucknow.

[59] Collectorate Records of Murshidabad, Malda, Dinajpur, Dhaka and Mymensingh.

[60] *Akhara* Records of Niranjani, Juna, Atal, and Avahan Akharas of Benares, Allahabad and Hardwar.

[61] Oral Testimonies taken between 1990-2 from the *mahants* of the

the disciples and *mahants* belonging to the Dasnami order. Lorenzen's entire thesis is speculation based on secondary literature. He even failed to relate the rise and growth of ascetics. He had come to the conclusion that 'warrior ascetics or monks who became a significant political and military presence in north India from about the fifteenth century' and 'continued until the early decades of the nineteenth century'. But Lorenzen failed to point out how the Dasnami Nagas had become so significant. He mainly relied on secondary sources such as the published works or narratives of Farquhar,[62] Orr,[63] Ghurye and Jamini Mohan Ghosh. Lorenzen's claim that the main purpose of his article was to review the general history of military-cum-religious movements in medieval India and to analyse the complex character of that movement that culminated in the Sannyasi Rebellion appears to be a misconception, if the primary sources of West Bengal State Archives, National Archives of India and Bangladesh National Archives, Dhaka, are thoroughly consulted. Lorenzen himself admitted the importance of primary documents for a fresh discussion on the subject. But in spite of this, close to two-thirds of his paper dealt with the evolution of the warrior groups in ancient India with which the Dasnami Sannyasis had no relationship. There are a couple of references from the ninth to twelfth centuries, to Shaiva *mathas* containing armouries for the storage of weapons of war. In a frequently cited reference to fighting ascetics in the mid-sixteenth-century *Bijak* of Kabir is poured on *yogis*, *siddhas* (another name for *yogis*), *mahants* (chiefs/superiors), and ascetics who resort to arms, keep women, and collect property and taxes. An entourage of (perhaps) three thousand, which included armed *yogis* in service to a *yogi* king

---

akharas, viz., Mahanirvani, Niranjani, Juna, Atal, Avahan, Agni and Anand.

62 J.N. Farquhar, 'The Organization of the Sannyasis of Vedanta', *Journal of the Royal Asiatic Society of Great Britain and Ireland*, 1925: 479-86.

63 W.G. Orr, 'Armed Religious Ascetics in Northern India', *The Bulletin of the John Rylands Library*, no. 25, Manchester, 1940: 78-98.

in conflict with a ruler in Gujarat, is described by Ludovico di Varthema of Bologna the early sixteenth century in what may be the first account by a European of a contingent of armed ascetics. William Pinch outlined a detailed narrative of the armed *yogis* and their encounters with other religious groups, excluding the Dasnamis, Bairagis, and Nathpanthis in an all-India perspective and, in order to demonstrate this, he quoted the well-known accounts of Badauni,[64] Pietro Della Valle,[65] Duarte Barbosa,[66] Peter Mundy,[67] and Francois Bernier.[68] But he failed to mention how the complex relationship evolved between Dasnami Nagas and other Hindu religious ascetics and also with the Muslim Fakirs.[69] For the symbiotic relationship between monks and nuns on the one hand and lay followers on the other Monika has discussed in detail in her another works.[70] Pinch claimed that he had traced the rise of the warrior ascetics since AD 1500 and depicted the narrative of a 'killer yogi', and from there he skipped over to the career of Rajendra Giri, Anup Giri and Umrao Giri

[64] *Muntakhab-ut-Tawarikh*, vol. II, tr. W.H. Lowe, rpt., Cosmo Publication, New Delhi, 1990: 94.

[65] Pietro Della Valle, *The Pilgrim: The Travels of Pietro Della Valle*, abridged edition, tr. G. Bull Hutchinson, London, 1989: 238.

[66] Duarte Barbosa, *A Description of the Coasts of East Africa and Malabar in the Beginning of the Sixteenth Century,* notes and preface by Henry E.J. Stanley, Hakluyt Society, London, 1866: 99-100.

[67] *Travels of Peter Mundy in Europe and Asia, 1608-1667*, vol. II: *Travels in Asia, 1603-1614*, ed. R.C. Temple, Hakluyt Society, London, 1914: 176-8.

[68] A. Constable, ed., *Travels in the Mogul Empire, 1656-1668*; a revised edition based upon Irving Brock's tr., S. Chand, Delhi, 1968.

[69] Ananda Bhattacharyya, 'Reconsidering Sannyasi Rebellion', *Social Scientist*, vol. 40, nos. 3-4, March-April 2012: 81-101.

[70] Monika Thiel-Horstmann, *Symbiotic Antimony: The Social Organisation of a North Indian Sect,* Canberra, Australian National University, 1986 and also M. Thiel-Hortsmann, 'The Example in Dadupanthi Homletics', in *Tellings and Texts: Music, Literature and Performance in North India*, ed. Francesca Orsini and Katherine Butler Schofield, Open Book Publishers, Cambridge, 2015: 31-59.

the famous Gossain monks, from AD 1730 until 1804, obviously leaving a long gap between the sixteenth and eighteenth centuries. Pinch did not consult the Persian and Marathi sources to identify the growth of asceticism and the role of Sannyasis in the Mughal period, and then suddenly jumped into the Sannyasis' appearance in the Maratha camp without explaining why and how the Naga forces were recruited by the Marathas.[71] The Sannyasis used to wander in various parts of India in search of services as mercenary soldiers since the Mughal period and thus they were recruited by the regional powers frequently, including the Marathas. Pinch's work provides ample evidence of an Indian ascetic who was not a monk in the proper sense and far from the concept of non-violence (*ahimsa*). Both Lorenzen and Pinch frequently referred to the fight between Giri and Puri suborders that Akbar, the Great Mughal king, had witnessed at Thaneshwar in AD 1567. They mainly relied on Badauni's translated version of Elliot and Dowson[72] and accounts given by Farquhar. In order to situate the Dasnami Sannyasis in an all-India perspective it is essential to consult the Persian and Marathi records.[73] Pinch even failed

[71] T.D. Broughton, *Letters Written in a Mahratta Camp during the Year 1809, etc.*, John Murray, London, 1813: 129-30.

[72] Nizamuddin Ahmad, *Tabakat-i-Akbari*, translated by Elliot and Dowson, *The History of India as Told By its Own Historians,* vol. V, S. Gupta, Delhi, 1990 (rpt.): 538.

[73] Dealing with the subject scholar should not only consult Persian but also Marathi sources such as the *Calendar of Persian Correspondence*, vols. I-XI, Office of the Supdt., Govt. Printing, Calcutta, 1907-69; *Tarikh-i-Ahmadshahi*, written by an anonymous writer and translated by Jadunath Sarkar; Khair-ud-din Allahabadi's *Ibratnama* (tr. Jadunath Sarkar); Hari Charan Das, *Chahar-Gulzar Sujai* (in Persian), Lucknow, Newal Kishore Press, n.d. Similarly, so far as the Marathi sources are concerned, Hari Gir, and Prithwi Gir, *Gosavi Vatyacha Sampradaya*, vol. 1, Baroda Press, Yeotmal, 1931; G.S. Sardesai, *Selections from the Peshwa Duftar*, Central Press, Bombay, 1930-4 and *Akhbarat* (preserved in Raghubir Singh Library, Sitamau, translated by Jadunath Sarkar, 1941), *Readings in Maratha History*; *Readings in History of the Hindusthan, 1782-1789*, Sitamau, are the basic sources for understanding the Sannyasis' mercenary, trading and

to narrate the *akhara*-based organization of the Naga Sannyasis. Furthermore, the appearance of Anup Giri with his 20,000 armed followers in the 1700s as viewed by Pinch is incorrect in the sense that Anup Giri and Umrao Giri were given the rank of 4,000 *zat* and 3,000 *sawar* by the government of Awadh. In addition, Asaf-ud-daullah, the Nawab of Awadh, had given them the privilege of maintaining 2,200 soldiers under their command.[74] This inaccuracy becomes clear if the life sketch of Anup Giri is compared with the work of Jadunath Sarkar.[75] Pinch relies on Varthema,[76] whose account is similar to that of Abul Fazl. The existence of armed Sannyasis expert in wrestling is shown in *Ain-i-Akbari*[77] and Tavernier's account that 'they were well armed, the majority with bows and arrows, some with muskets, and the remainders with short pikes'. A similar account is available in Abbe Carre.[78] Besides Anup Giri, when Pinch was describing Rajendra Giri's service under Safdar Jang in 1751 he mainly relied on Orr. In order to understand Rajendra Giri's influence among the Turani nobles and upon Safdar Jang, the wazir of Awadh, the

---

moneylending activities and their relations with the Maratha chieftains such as Mahadji Sindhia, the Rohillas and Mirza Nazaf Khan, the Regent of Delhi.

[74] Harper to Council, late October 1768, Select; Bristow to Hastings, Secret, dated 1 July 1776, no. 4; Foreign (Misc.), vol. 41 A: 142. But Davies (C.C. Davies, *Warren Hastings and Oudh*: Oxford University Press, Oxford 1939: 89) considered that the total strength of the two Sannyasi brothers was 10,000 foot soldiers and 9,000 horsemen.

[75] Sarkar, *Dasnami*: 156-246.

[76] *Travels of Ludivico di Varthema (1503-1508)*, trans. and ed. John Winter Jones, notes and introduction by George Perry Badger, Hakluyt Society, London: 111-12. Elliot and Dowson, *The History of India as Told by its Own Historians*, vol. 3, S. Gupta Delhi, 1990, rpt.: 538.

[77] Abu'l Fazl, *Ain-i-Akbari*, vol. III, tr. H. Blochmann and H.S. Jarret, with corrections by Jadunath Sarkar, Asiatic Society, Calcutta, 1927-49: 263, 428.

[78] Barthelmy Carre, *The Travels of the Abbe Carre in India and the Near East, 1672-1674*, Hakluyt Society, London, 1947: 457.

translated version of *Tarikh-i-Ahmadshahi* in addition with other sources[79] should be thoroughly consulted.

Similar discrepancy is also found in the account of Ghurye. Even Pinch's detailed analysis about the existence of armed ascetics in Rajputana had already been recorded by Jadunath Sarkar and Monika Thiel-Horstmann.[80] These are important in the sense that their works were prepared on the basis of documents available in the Rajasthan State Archives, Bikaner. In order to understand the Sannyasis' influence in an all-India perspective and to establish the credibility of my argument, it is essential to show how they were patronized by the Indian powers. Besides Rajendra Giri, the Sannyasis under Anup Giri were given an allowance for their subsistence. A list of such beneficiaries has been shown in Table II.

It was Anup Giri who was given an allowance of Rs. 98,000 annually by the Government of Awadh for the maintenance of his soldiers, including their payment. Moreover, Anup Giri and Umrao Giri were sanctioned Rs. 49,000 as additional favour.[81] It appears that this privilege was previously enjoyed by the Maratha Generals attached to the armies of Awadh. For his military achievement in the operation at Dig in March 1786 Anup Giri was given Rs. 20,000 by Mahadji Sindhia as an allowance for the maintenance of his retinue.[82] And it was he who after realization of tribute from the Raja of Jaipur in 1781 received an offer of

[79] C.A. Silberrad, 'A Contribution to the History of Western Bundelkhand', *Journal of the Asiatic Society of Bengal*, vol. IXXI, part II, Asiatic Society, Calcutta, 1902: 99-135; Sudan, *Sujan Charita* (in Hindi), ed. Radhakrishnadas, Varanasi Nagari Pracharini Sabha, Varanasi, 1923 (2nd edn.): 191-6; Ghulam Husan (pen-name Samin), 'Ashraf-e-Usmani', a Persian manuscript translated into English by William Irvine in *Indian Antiquary*, vol. 36, March 1907, Bombay: 66-70.

[80] Monica Thiel-Hortsmann, 'Soldiers of God; Soldiers of Fortune: A Chapter of Indian Religion and Military History', unpublished Occasional Paper.

[81] Ghulam Ali Naqvi, *Imad-us-Sadat*: 102.

[82] Jadunath Sarkar, 'Readings in History of Hindusthan, 1782-1789', Sitamau, 1941: 132 (unpublished).

TABLE II: PARTICULARS OF THE SANNYASIS AS BENEFICIARIES

Sl. No.	*Name of the Person*	*Place*	*Amount*
1.	Puran Giri	Ghazipore	34-14-0
2.	Sheoram Giri	Benares	11-13-0
3.	Bisram Giri	Benares	31-14-0
4.	Bucktawar Giri	Benares	17-10-0
5.	Jawala Giri	Benares	4-8-0
6.	Deo Puri	Benares	11-13-0
7.	Ram Giri	Benares	29-10-0
8.	Mangal Giri	Benares	11-13-0
9.	Ramchandra Giri	Benares	11-13-0
10.	Rukbeer Giri	Benares	17-7-0

Sources: List of Pensioners in Zilla Benares: Duncan Papers and Settlement Records, 1792, vol. 145, p. 143; Registrar of persons admitted in the Benares Moolky Treasury: RDG, 29 October 1792: 453-7.

maintaining a force of 5,000 soldiers. At the time of conquering Bundelkhand for Ali Bahadur, Anup Giri maintained a force of 3,000 artillery and 2,000 cavalry.[83]

Moreover, the status and prestige enjoyed by the Sannyasis characterized their importance to the regional powers. The titles 'Rajendra' and 'Himmat Bahadur' reveal the prestige enjoyed by the two Naga commanders in the army of the Awadh government. Rajendra Giri's original name was Inder Giri. The title, Rajendra, he earned from the Maratha chief as a recognition of his services.[84] Furthermore, Safdar Jang, conferred on Rajendra Giri the extraordinary privilege of not bowing in his presence and

[83] William Franklin, *Military Memoirs of George Thomas*, John Stockdale, London, 1805, Appendix iii: 270.

[84] William Irvine, 'The Bangas Nawabs of Farrukhabad: A Chronicle 1713-1857', *Journal of the Asiatic Society of Bengal*, no. 1, pt. 1, Calcutta, 1879: 124-34; Hari Gir, op. cit.: 238; Padmakar, op. cit.: 14.

of beating his kettledrum.[85] This honour was actually enjoyed by the highest rank in the Mughal peerage.[86] All the above evidence shows how inadequate and sometimes even incorrect have been the narratives of Lorenzen and Pinch. Thus, a fresh investigation into the activities of the Dasnamis is called for in view of the new findings.

Besides pension, the Sannyasis were also given large tracts of land in various parts of north India. It seems that the regional powers used to bestow their patronage either for rendering military services or to provide them with land for maintaining their religious way of life. Their landholding capacity particularly in Uttar Pradesh is shown in Table III.

Besides the Sannyasis residing in Awadh were also given a large tracts of land which is shown in Table IV.

The Dasnamis continued their military activities unhindered by either the common people or the pre-colonial powers. But after the rise of the British power in Bengal, the Company's government began to view with disfavour and also to oppose some of their activities as objectionable. It was, however, not easy for the Company's government to suppress the Dasnamis because they, equipped with military and political experience, proved to be redoubtable opponents.

RELATIONS WITH THE REGIONAL POWERS

The soldierly activities of the Dasnamis had developed by a two way process. In lieu of their services they enjoyed respect and favours of the regional powers by enjoying *jagirs*, pensions and titles. In this way they had become the semi-independent chiefs and king-makers particularly during the period of Mughal decline. Monika Horstmann identified them as an order who 'exhibit a

[85] A.L. Srivastava, *The First Two Nawabs of Oudh*, Lucknow, Upper India Publishing House, 1933: 162-3.

[86] Jadunath Sarkar, *Fall of the Mughal Empire*, Orient Longman, Bombay, 1971, vol. 1: 307-8.

TABLE III: ACCOUNT OF LANDS & JAGIRS HELD BY DASANAMIS IN PARGANA GURHAH, KANPUR (U.P.)

Name of the Village	*Name of grantees*	Bighas *of land cultivated by each persons*	*Purity* zamin *or fallowed land held by each persons*	*Total* bighas *held by each person*	*Rates of each* bigha	*Number of persons holding Krishnarpan lands*	*Medium Jumma*
Barrow	Swadhan Giri	10	23	25	10	2	
Kythoreah	Sadhoo Giri	3	2	5	X	X	
Deheree	Awaden Giri	105	20	125	1	X	105
Rampoor	Bhowan Giri	25	X	25	1	1	25
Bughownah	Onpoona Giri	150	150	300	112	X	8
Mahadenooah	Bhowan Giri	35	X	35	X	X	X
Nerhayee	Sowan Bharati	75	26	101	12	1	36.6
Neelkuntpoor	Bhowan Giri	5	10	15	12	1	5
Mahareen	Mahee Bharati	5	10	15	1	1	5
Koytholee	Jobraj Bharati	20	5	25	1	2	20

Source: Decennial Settlement of the Pargana of Gurhah in district of Gazipur, 18 April 1790. CPRB, 1 September 1790, vol. 34: 36, 41.

TABLE IV: DASNAMI AS A LANDHOLDER

Sl. No.	*Name of the Landholders*	*Name of the Villages*
1.	Gobind Giri	Jaurunpoor
2.	Badal Giri	Jaurunpoor
3.	Bisram Bharati	Tajpur
4.	Nirmal Giri	Sooraroobund
5.	Hira Giri	Hussenpoorah
6.	Doolar Giri	Doorjunpur
7.	Ganga Giri	Inderpur
8.	Domun Giri	Gopalpur
9.	Bhababooty Giri	Akhaur
10.	Ranjit Giri	Taluk Dighaur
11.	Jeet Giri	Basantpur
12.	Golab Puri	Beerpur (Chowrasi)
13.	Mokum Giri	Rampur & Mujegawan (Chowsa)
14.	Payem Giri	Mogree (Burhar Agoree)
15.	Dusa Giri	Parsia (Ejeh Ghur)
16.	Jubraj Bharati	Koysholee
17.	Bhown Giri	Neelkantpur
18.	Bhiro Giri	Kullianpur (Amorah)
19.	Raghunath Giri	Benichak (Sohmpur)

Source: SPDR, vol. XXX, 15 June 1790, no. 17; vol. XXXIII, April 1793, pp. 118-32; CPRB, 1 September 1790, vol. XXXIV, pp. 36-41; SPDR, vol. XXXII, 1792, p. 143; BOR (UPSA), 16 August 1803, nos. 66-7. See RDG, 29 October 1792, pp. 454-7.

mixture of the religious with the violently mundane, and existed in vast numbers during the period of social and political upheaval; they have an ideology . . . and traits of their lifestyle namely the religious and mundane ones'.[87] Their involvement with the

[87] Monika-Thiel Horstmann, 'Soldiers of God; Soldiers of Fortune: A Chapter of Indian Religion and Military History', unpublished paper. Monika discussed the dual identity of the Nagas of the Dadupanthi sect of

government of Awadh for the three preceding generations helped them to establish their suzerainty over the Hanuman hills near Faizabad, through their oldest institution, Sidhigiris Mathiya (monastery), situated in Awadh. This monastic involvement also helped them to engage with the Nawabs of Awadh, like Shuja-ud-Daullah and his son Asaf-ud-Daullah for nearly two decades. The mercenary activities of the Dasnami Sannyasis has been explained in detail in J.N. Sarkar's unpublished English translation from the Marathi source material that the Sannyasis joined with Ramkrishna Mahant, a Vaishnava Gossain who looted camps scattered in various parts of Bharatpur.[88] The central argument of the present introductory note would be to show how the Dasnamis had been able to amass liquid cash that they invested in the field of trade and moneylending. There were some Sannyasis, particularly, the Giri suborder, who joined with their armed retainers, the Nawabs of Awadh, the Jat Raja of Bharatpur, the Rajas of Benares, Kumaon and Bundelkhand, Mahadji Sindhia, the Maratha chieftain and also the Rajas of Jaipur, Jodhpur and Jaisalmer. In this context it will be worthwhile to mention some of the Dasnami leaders who were very famous since the early years of eighteenth century. They were Gossain Rajendra Giri, Anup Giri *alias* Himmat Bahadur, Moti Giri, Beni Giri, Puran Puri, Puran Giri and others. Sir Jadunath paid a high tribute to these celebrated Gossains for their war-like activities. Poet Padmakar, contemporary of Anup Giri and a private tutor of None Arjun Singh (who later became the Regent of Banda), compared Anup Giri with Raja Harishchandra of our ancient India. Some passages of *Himmat Bahadur Virudabali* depicting the multi-dimensional qualities and characters of Himmat Bahadur translated by Pinch (1998) may be cited here:

Rajasthan as devotees and militant monks (M. Thiel-Horstmann, 'On the Dual Identity of Nagas', in D.L. Eck and F. Mallison, eds., *Devotion Divine: Bhakti Traditions from the Regions of India* (*Studies in Honour of Charlotte Vaudeville*), Groningen, 1991: 255-72.

[88] Sarkar, 1947: 15; Khairuddin, n.d.: 86; Sarkar, 1953: nos. 135-7.

'Himmat Bahadur is a great king, incomparable in his excellent benevolence.
He is generous, brave and compassionate, [but] to his amassed enemies he is death itself.
He humiliates his enemies and scorches them in their jungle hideaways.
He shows his long armed compassion for the poor during religious sacrifices.
He gives endowments to support *dharma*, and in the clothing that covers Hindu shame.
He is the embodiment of radiant splendor, but an insatiable demon when his anger is provoked.
He is as true to his word as Harishchandra, [and] is ever the source of bliss.
He is the enemy of sadness, constantly engaged in sacrificial rites.
The lamp of his own sect blazes radiantly, [he is] the most valiant protector of the earth.
To the class of poets he is like the sun to the lotus, [and] is full of benign moral conduct.
He is extremely knowledgeable, [and] always puts forth a serene countenance.
When he sees the needy he is compassionate, when destroying evil he is merciless.
He is a remarkable horseman and an unsurpassed archer.
He chants Siva *bhajans* with such excellence and equanimity – no one can compare.
Himmat Bahadur is a powerful king; his army's presence immediately destroys his foe.
His occupation is world conquest; he is notorious in the lands of his enemies.
And after briefly describing the Rajput army, Padmakar returned to the praise of Anup Giri:
Now I'll sing of an army that all the *Thakurs* [Rajput landlords] have heard of.
Near the massive Ajaygarh fort, united they are fearsome.
Whence the conch shell is blown, [can be seen] his mighty sword.
The incessant beat of the kettledrum scatters his enemies like so many snorting pigs.

The following ode to the goddess from *Shiva Purana* captures the sentiment based 'Smeared with the mire of demon blood and fat, ablaze with rays'.[89]

The historical enquiry begins with an examination of their role as mercenary soldiers on behalf of the regional powers. Such was their success as mercenary soldiers that regional powers even entrusted them with service in the field of civil and military administration. Their alignment with the state power increased their strength and resources. They also began to act as semi-independent chiefs and warlords. The Dasnami Sannyasis thus not only grew in strength and position but amassed large tracts of rent-free land. The resources derived from land and monetary privileges sanctioned by the Indian powers helped them to extend their influence in the economy. An important branch of the activities of the Dasnamis was investment in trade and moneylending. It appears that the Dasnamis, though of a religious background, were involved in multifarious activities in addition to their normal duties of per-forming religious pilgrimage. The multidimensional nature of their activities began to decline after the establishment of colonial rule in Bengal Presidency in the early nineteenth century, though they continued their trade and economic activities until the mid-nineteenth century. The surprising fact is that though the power and strength of the Sannyasis, both in the economy and politics, declined they still existed as a religious group. Their existence is recorded in the census reports, and their presence is still noticed in the *akharas* and *maths* where they maintain a luxurious lifestyle.

Naturally, the question may arise why the Dasnamis were recruited as soldiers in the northern and western India on a large scale. At the same time it is questioned why their activities as mercenary soldiers and also in the field of civil administration were quite limited in Bengal as compared to northern and

[89] Cited in William R. Pinch, 'Who was Himmat Bahadur? Gosains, Rajputs and the British in Bundelkhand, 1800', *Indian Economic and Social History Review*, 35, 3, 1998: 293-335.

western India. It appears that their activities in the field of polity and economy comprised a wide region in northern India from Awadh, Prayag (Allahabad), centring round Lucknow, Jhansi, Bundelkhand to the Deccan Plateau. It even extended as far as to Punjab, Simla and Kangra hills where they were in the habit of doing trade and moneylending at an exorbitant rate of interest.[90]

The Sannyasis' role as mercenaries in the armies of central, northern, western and eastern India was significant. An early example of their mercenary activity in north India was their participation in two battles: one between Prithviraj Chauhan, the Rajput ruler (AD 1190-2) and Mohammad Ghori in AD 1191 at Narayangarh (near Panipat) and the other between the Rajput ruler and Chandel Raj of Bundelkhand near Mahoba.[91] The Sannyasis' involvement in warfare seems to have increased in the seventeenth century when Bir Singh Deo of Orcha built a fort he had garrisoned with the help from the Sannyasis.[92] Under the leadership of Rajendra Giri the Sannyasis settled in Jhansi (1730-50). Their mercenary role seems to have increased during the early eighteenth century, their leadership was assumed by Raja Rajendra Giri Gossain who had been a great patron of Naro Shankar, the Maratha chief (1730-50) of Jhansi. Since his power and position became a threat to the Marathas in Bundelkhand, Rajendra Giri was expelled from his possession by the Maratha chief in 1749-50 and went to Allahabad for joining with the armies of Safdar Jang (1739-54), the *wazir* of Awadh. Rajendra Giri also used to go on pilgrimage to the holy Prayag. In course of his pilgrimage he also went on fighting with his opponents. Rajendra Giri took the side of Safdar Jang when the latter was engaged in war with the Afghan chief Ahmad Khan Bangash of Farukhabad in 1750.[93]

[90] Denzil Ibbetson, *Punjab Castes, Being a Report of the Chapter on 'The Races, Castes and Tribes of the People'*, vol. II, Superintendent Government Printing, Lahore, 1916: 303.

[91] Hari Gir and Prithwi Gir, op. cit.: 6.

[92] Silberrad, op. cit.

[93] Naqvi, op. cit., 64; A.L. Srivastava, *Shuja-ud-Daulah (1765-1775),*

Whenever Rajendra Giri noticed any slackness on the part of the besiegers he would make a lightening attack on their camp. As Ghulam Hussain Khan observed that 'Rajendra Giri used to set out with his armed followers and killed his enemies'.[94] Besides Madariya or Jalaliya Fakirs, the Bairagis, Gauriyas, Sikh Panthi and Dadu Panthi Nagas had similar fights with the Dasnami Nagas. Muhammed Mohsin Fani writing *Dabistan* in the middle of the seventeenth century describes that 'the Sannyasis being frequently engaged in war'. Similarly, Grant[95] referred to the assembly of the Sannyasis led by an old woman who defeated the army of Emperor Aurangzīb. While discussing the general character of these marauding groups of Sannyasis and Fakirs, Wilson,[96] referred to their 'use of arms . . . always travel with weapons . . . smear their bodies with ashes, allow their hair, beard and whiskers to grow and were projected braid of hair called the *jata*.' The Sannyasis, like the Bairagi Nagas used to carry arms and wandering search of employment in the armies of local power on condition that they were allowed to extort contributions from the common people. Since the Bairagis were not so well armed they were defeated by the Dasnamis in the religious fair at Hardwar in 1760. The Dadu Panthi Nagas were also frequently found in Marwar and Ajmer and the Raja of Jaipur used to entertain their armies of 10,000 soldiers. The same description is also found in the writings of William Irvine who mentioned the Dasnami's habit of lending their military services to the Raja of Jaipur, Nawabs of Awadh and also Raja of Bundelkhand. Their mercenary activities extended as far as to north-western provinces. A group of 1,400 fighting Nagas of Allahabad under the guidance of four able *mahants* assisted Mohan Singh, a usurper of Kumaon

---

vol. II, Shivlal Agarwala, Delhi, 1961 (2nd revd. edn.): 162-3.

94 Ghulam Hussain Khan, *Siyar-ul-Mutakherin: A Translation*, vol. III, James White, Calcutta, 1789: 298-9.

95 James Grant, *Cassell's Illustrated History of India*, vol. 1: Cassell Petter and Galpins, London, 1890: 159-60.

96 H.H. Wilson, *Sketch on the Religious Sects of the Hindus*, Bishop's College Press, Calcutta, 1846: 120.

on condition that they would be permitted to plunder Almora. As Atkinson[97] aptly remarked 'they entered Kumaon by the Kosi and under the pretence of being pilgrims on their way to Badrinath got as far as the confluence of Suwal and the Kosi before their real character was discovered'. This explains how the Dasnamis had been able to earn money which they used to invest either in trade or moneylending. The significance of their services as soldiers was that they interacted with the forces of regional powers. In most of the cases, the regional powers like the Nawabs of Awadh, the Marathas, Raja Balwant Singh of Benares and the Raja of Jaipur would recruit different types of soldiers among which the Dasnamis were one of them. The Dasnamis also joined with the Marathas and the Sikhs particularly after the defeat of Marathas in the third battle of Panipat (1761). A combined forces were like this '. . . the combined Hindu armies of Sikhs and Marathas . . . were joined by the Ram Kishen Mahant, Umrao Giri Gossain and other Sardars with their respective divisions'.[98] Their recruitment as soldiers went into full swing till the extension of East India Company's rule in Bengal presidency. T.D. Broughton wrote from the Maratha Camp at Doonee in 1809 that after the retirement of Anup Giri the Dasnami forces were headed by Kampta Giri, Ram Giri and Kanchan Giri who were said to be the disciples of Himmat Bahadur. They joined with the Maratha forces.

According to Pinch,[99] Rajendra Giri was said to have descended from a long line of Shaiva Gurus (Sadananda Giri, Anka Giri, Sotam Giri, Bhim Giri, Santosh Giri, Manohar Giri, Chandan Giri, Narayan Giri and Sanatan Giri). It is said that in 1745 Rajendra Giri seized the pargana of Moth (east of Jhansi) in Bundelkhand and came into possession of 114 villages there.[100]

[97] *The Himalayan Gazetteer* or *The Himalayan Districts of the North-Western Provinces*, vol. II, part 1, North-Western Provinces Government Press, Allahabad, 1884: 602-4.

[98] *Calendar of Persian Correspondence*, 1914: 5

[99] Pinch, 'Who was Himmat Bahadur? op. cit.

[100] A.L. Srivastava, *Shuja-ud-Daullah,* vol. I, Shivlal Agarwala, Delhi, 1961 (2nd revd. edn.): 163.

When Safdar Jang got involved in a war with the Afghan Chief Ahmad Khan Bangash of Farrukhabad in 1750, Rajendra Giri saved him from a humiliating defeat by risking his own life. Rajendra Giri, as commander of the troops of the army of Safdar Jang, was ordered to plunder the *jagirs* of the Turani nobles of Delhi and the Doab situated on the confluence of the rivers Ganga and Jamuna. This act of violence blocked the grain supply to Delhi and sharply raised food prices in the capital. On the evening of 14/15 June 1758, this reckless chief met his end at the battle of Talkotra. There remains some controversy regarding the death of Rajendra Giri among Persian chroniclers. The death defying commander of Safdar Jang's army sacrificed his life for the cause of his master.[101] Rajendra Giri's tragic death so shocked the *wazir* that the latter never went to any battle thereafter.

After Rajendra Giri's death, Umrao Giri and Anup Giri, popularly known as the Gossain brothers, *chelas* and successors of Rajendra Giri aligned themselves with the Awadh government and became close associates of Nawab Shuja-ud-Daullah (1754-64). Even, Shuja-ud-Daullah, the Nawab of Awadh, partly employed 10,000 Gossain mercenaries under the leadership of Anup Giri against the Marathas from 1757 to 1759. In the Maratha-Rohilla contest (1757-9), Shuja also employed 10,000 soldiers under the Gossain brothers. The Maratha danger was averted by the military leadership of Anup Giri and Umrao Giri. Anup Giri was the chief architect of the Awadhi army that reached its peak in the 1750s and 1760s. He established his sway as chieftain in Bundelkhand from the second half of the eighteenth century and became gradually involved in regional power politics. In 1755, following the destruction of a Hindu temple by the Nawab of Awadh, Balwant Singh, the Raja of Benares, broke into a revolt. The Naga Sannyasis under Anand Giri stood by the side of the Nawab and secured the surrender of the fort of Chunar in terms honourable to both the parties. As in the pre-British period, the Nawab of Awadh also employed Anup Giri to collect the

[101] Ibid.: 225.

annual tribute from Raja Hindupati of Mahoba in Bundelkhand in 1762. The contest took place at Tindwari in Banda district in 1762 and the Sannyasis fought bravely. The fighting quality of the Sannyasis led the Nawab of Awadh to secure the services of 5,000-6,000 Naga followers under Anup Giri in the battle of Panchapahari (3 May 1764) and Buxar (23 October 1764) against the British.[102] But with the defeat of Shuja-ud-Daullah, Anup Giri used the excuse of long overdue payment and left the Nawab's service to join Jawahir Singh Jat of Bharatpur. Eventually, he joined the Maratha camp. But when the Nawab of Awadh reorganized the army and the finance of his kingdom, Anup Giri re-entered the Nawab's service.[103] In early 1770 the depredation of the Marathas in the middle Ganga-Jamuna Doab and their capture of Etawah threatened the safety of Awadh, leading Nawab Shuja-ud-Daullah to post the Sannyasis at the frontier outpost of Kanpur to watch the Maratha activities.[104] From 1772 to 1774 they not only suppressed court rivalry but also succeeded in capturing Rohilkhand for Awadh.[105] The success in Rohilkhand led Asaf-ud-Daullah to appoint Anup Giri as the leader of an army in 1775 for the conquest of Bundelkhand, while Singha Giri reached Jhansi from Ghulsarai to assist Anup Giri in his campaign against Bundelkhand. Simultaneously, Mirch Giri was sent by the Nawab to Etawah against the Rohillas.[106]

On behalf of the Jat Raja the Sannyasis participated in the Jat-

[102] A. Broome, *History of the Rise and Progress of the Bengal Army*, Smith, Elder & Co., Corn Hill, London, 1850: 175; Ghulam Hussein Khan, *Siyar-ul-Mutakherin,* vol. I, James White, Calcutta, 1789: 298-9; Williams, op. cit.: 46.

[103] Srivastava, *Shuja-ud-Daullah*, vol. I: 48.

[104] R.B. Barnette, *North India Between Empires, Awadh, the Mughals and the British, 1720-1801*, University of California Press, Berkeley, 1960; *CPC*, Imperial Record Department, Calcutta, 1907, vol. I; Select, 3 August 1770.

[105] Hari Charan Das, op. cit.: 507; Sardesai, op. cit.: 280.

[106] Secret, 24 April 1775, no. 9; Sardesai, ibid.

Rohilla contest over the possession of Delhi in the year 1764.[107] When the Jat Raja failed to advance towards the Rohillas, the Sannyasis crossed the Jamuna and launched attacks upon the Rohillas.[108] Jawahir Singh was so pleased by the valour of the Sannyasis that he honoured Umrao Giri by lifting him to the *howdah* of his own elephant.[109] The defeat of the Jats at the hands of the Marathas led to a breach of understanding between Jawahir Singh and the Sannyasis. Retrenchment of the Awadh armed forces led to the dismissal of the Sannyasis from the Awadh service in 1775.[110] Such reversal of fortune led the Sannyasis to join the service of Mirza Najaf Khan, the Regent of Delhi, who allowed them the right to live by plunder.[111] The regional powers perhaps encouraged the Sannyasis' practice of plundering even though it was unlawful in the eyes of the East India Company's government.[112] The peasants evidently and greatly suffered from the extortion of the Sannyasis.[113] Anup Giri, acting on behalf of Mirza Najaf Khan, also marched against Phup Singh, a local ruler, when he made himself the master of Mursan and Sasni and of Rohilkhand in 1777.[114] The Sannyasis also besieged the fort of Lachmangarh in March 1788.

The martial valour of the Sannyasis led Mahadji Sindhia to employ them as soldiers against the British, Mughal and Rajput

[107] Hari Gir and Prithwi Gir, op. cit.: 68.

[108] Sarkar, *Fall of the Mughal Empire*, vol. I: 330-2.

[109] Sarkar, *Dasnami*: 167.

[110] Jadunath Sarkar, 'French Mercenaries in the Jat Campaign of 1775-1776', *Bengal Past and Present*, January-June, Calcutta Historical Society, Calcutta, 1936: 230-5; Kalikaranjan Kanungo, *History of the Jats: A Contribution to the History of Northern India*, vol. I, M.C. Sarkar, Calcutta, 1925: 189-90; Sardesai, op. cit.: 64; Jadunath Sarkar, *Persian Records of Maratha History, Parasnis Collection; Delhi Affairs (1761-1788)*, Director of Archives, Govt. of Bombay, Bombay, 1953: 10.

[111] Sarkar, 1936: 230-5.

[112] Bhattacharyya, 2012.

[113] *The Asiatic Journal and Monthly Register*, 1817.

[114] Sarkar, 1971; *Ibratnama*: 291; Secret, 3 November 1777, no. 17.

in the battle of Lalsot, Patan and Merta.[115] Anup Giri was so powerful that he himself made an alliance with Ali Bahadur, an illegitimate son of Peshwa Baji Rao, in the latter's attempt to conquer Bundelkhand. But the Maratha government's plan to turn Bundelkhand into a base of operation threatening to violate the Treaty of Bassein (1802) led the British to dispatch a force there. In these circumstances an apprehensive Anup Giri left the Maratha camp and joined the British to assist them in the conquest of Bundelkhand.[116] The British justification for an alliance with Anup Giri was strategic. The British believed that this alliance could prevent the Maratha armies from using that region as a staging ground in subsequent wars. One cannot agree with Pinch[117] that Anup Giri's alliance with the British was a defensive strategy on the part of the Sannyasis to avoid suppression by the British as had happened in Bengal a few decades earlier. Jodhpur's Raja Vijay Singh (1752-63) launched an expedition against Jai Apa Sindhia of Marwar in 1754. He enrolled 10,000 Sannyasis in nine regiments, each under a separate flag. The Sannyasis had been driven by the Marathas from Karauli.[118] It appears that the Sannyasis under Mahant Gulab Puri helped Vijay Singh and his successor Bhim Singh in securing his ancestral *jagir* of Nagore.[119] When Abu Shelukar, the agent of Nana Phadnis, ruthlessly collected tribute in Baroda, the Sannyasis, on behalf of Govind Rao Gaikwad, the Gaikwad of Baroda, started a campaign against Abu Shelukar, and ultimately defeated him in July 1800.[120]

In eastern India the Sannyasis also rendered important military service to local chiefs and princes. In his revolt against the Ahom

[115] Orr, op. cit.: 78-9.

[116] Padmakar, *Himmat Bahadur Virudabali*: 26-42; F.S. Growse, *Mathura, A District Memoir*, New Order Book, Ahmedabad, 1978: 308; W.W. Pogson, *History of the Boondelas*, B.R. Publishing, Delhi, 1974 (rpt.): 120-6.

[117] Pinch, 2006.

[118] Orr, 1940; Sarkar, *Dasnami*: 263-8.

[119] Sarkar, *Dasnami*: 264-6.

[120] Ibid.: 270.

Government in 1787, Assam's Krishna Narayan, the prince of Darang, employed a large group of Sannyasis recruited from Benares.[121] We learn from official sources that a Sannyasi leader, Jungle Giri, was employed by a chief of Assam to plunder Bhutan in 1793-4.[122] In Orissa also, the Sannyasis were employed by local zamindars such as Jasoda Nandan of Jellasore (Jalleswar), who sent Shogal Giri on a plundering expedition.[123] In Bengal the Sannyasis, though small in number, established political relations with the local zamindars in the pre-British period. But their armed service did not assume as much importance in Bengal as in other parts of India.

In Bengal, Mymensingh was a major stronghold of the Sannyasis. In the pre-British days Ramanath Lahiri, *izaradar* of Mymensingh, employed Gokul Giri and Dhirpurna Giri for the protection of his zamindari.[124] Haji Mustafa, a trusted lieutenant of Nawab Alivardi Khan, was accompanied by a large group of Sannyasis in his adventurous attempt to reach Muslipatnam through a large part of western Bengal and Pachet.[125] In Cooch Behar the Sannyasis were recruited by the zamindar of Rangamati, near Goalpara, as irregular troops long before the beginning of British rule.[126] They were even permitted by a former king of Cooch Behar to reside there.[127] Although the Maharaja of Cooch Behar had treated the Sannyasis quite well in return for

[121] S.K. Bhuyian, *Anglo-Assamese Relation (1771-1826)*, Deptt. of Historical and Antiquarian Studies, Gauhati, 1949: 258, 268, 377-8.

[122] Judicial (Criminal) (hereafter refer to JCR) 14.

[123] Committee of Revenue (hereafter refer to COR), 2 July 1781, no. 10.

[124] D.H.A. Kolff, '"Sannyasi" Trader-Soldiers', *Indian Economic and Social History Review*, vol. VIII, 1971: 35-43.

[125] William Irvine, 'The Bangash Nawabs of Farrukhabad: A Chronicle 1713-1857', *Journal of the Asiatic Society of Bengal*, no.1, pt. 1, Asiatic Society, Calcutta, 1962: 163-70.

[126] Committee of Circuit, Dinajpur, 21 January 1773.

[127] Revenue Department, Governor-General in Council (hereafter refer to RDG), 27 June 1787.

their services to him, Warren Hastings induced the Maharaja to dismiss the Sannyasis from his service to save money. But when the struggle for supremacy between Harendra Narayan of Cooch Behar and his *wazir*, Khagendra Narayan, broke out in 1787, the Sannyasis under Ganesh Giri were re-employed in large numbers by the *wazir* and they helped him in his abortive attempt to install himself as the Raja of Cooch Behar.[128] The armed Sannyasis, namely Bissen Giri, Gulab Giri, Subhangshu Giri, and others looted all the belongings of Maharaja Harendra Narayan and *Rajmata* (queen mother) Kamateswari and forced them to walk 6 *koss* (one to two miles) to Balarampore and confined them in the house of the *wazir*, Khagendra Narayan. The Sannyasis subjected the Maharaja and *Rajmata* to various hardships, including threats of murder and thus compelled them to sign several documents and blank papers.[129] The Sannyasis were regarded by the East India Company as ruinous and 'unlawful' and also identified them as enemies of the government.[130] The British notion of sovereignty and the rule of law is clearly reflected in their measures against the Sannyasis. Darpa Dev of Bhutan, in his ruthless exactions in and around Cooch Behar, Dinajpur, Assam and the territories adjoining the Gurkha country employed the Sannyasis as soldiers.[131]

In spite of his detailed study of the armed ascetics of northern India, Pinch has not been able to demonstrate how or why religious groups such as the Dasnamis or the Gossains entered military service. Such gaps in explanation were also found in the writings of Sir Jadunath Sarkar and W.G. Orr. These

[128] Surendranath Sen, *Prachin Bangla Patra Sangkalan* (in Bengali), Calcutta University, Calcutta, 1942: Introduction: 13-17.

[129] Sen: 23-7; W.K. Firminger, ed., *The Fifth Report on the Affairs of the East India Company*, Higginbotham & Co., Madras, 1928: 188-9; *Cooch Behar Select Records* (1869), vol. 1: 109-37.

[130] Ananda Bhattacharyya, 'Sannyasi and Fakir Uprising in North Bengal', *Vishwa Bharati Quarterly,* vol. 13, nos. 3 & 4 (2004-5): 112-30.

[131] Committee of Circuit, Rajmahal, 15 February 1773.

authors may have had difficulty in accessing the hagiographic literature in the Dasnami Akharas or supporting Persian or Marathi documents. Since these documents are now available to researchers this introduction aims to fill this lacuna by using rare documents and oral testimonies left behind by the disciples or the *mahants* of the different *maths* and *akharas*. The Dasnami Sannyasis first entered into military service at the beginning of the Turko-Afghan period because they were good fighters and not only to protect themselves in those violent days but also to preserve their material possession, particularly, *maths, akharas* and wealth. This was how they were naturally attracted to armed activities. This fact encouraged the regional powers to enlist their armed service in their own interest. The *Gosavi Vatyacha Sampradaya* frequently refers to the use of arms of the Dasnami Sannyasis and their services on behalf of Ghiyasuddin Balban, Alauddin Khilji and later on by the Lodis.[132] They even enjoyed a large degree of freedom from state interference in the observance of their traditional rites and customs. Their fighting propensities on behalf of the regional powers were not checked by the ruling powers during the period. They were encouraged by the Mughal government to recruit large number of armed members for their order. In this context, the attitude of Akbar, the Mughal emperor should be noted. Farquhar's comment finds support in the oral testimony given by the Mahant Gulab Giri of Mahanirvani Akhara at Daraganj, Allahabad, to the author during his interview in 1989. The martial valour of the Sannyasis during the Mughal period was also reflected in the Hindi pamphlets published from there. The alliance with Dasnami Naga Sannyasis or Gossains was useful for the regional powers. Their alliance with Himmat Bahadur was dictated by political and organizational factors. Anup Giri or Himmat Bahadur possessed remarkable skill in secret negotiations or intrigue. His followers, the Gossains, maintained highly skilled foot soldiers and horsemen who were ready to fight in battles, particularly guerrilla warfare. Their brave, militant, and

[132] Hari Gir and Prithwi Gir, op. cit.: 312-14; *Tarikh*, folio: 76-7b.

self-sacrificing nature in the battlefields was based on the *guru-chela* relationship and *akhara*-based organization that imparted a militant ideology and training.[133] Atal and Avahan *akharas* of different places of Uttar Pradesh produced many self-sacrificing heroes of the battlefields; a fact noted by Sir Jadunath in his other useful work.[134]

In fact the *guru-chela* relationship forged ties in the form of monastic loyalty, which formed a military chain of command among the *chelas*. Because of their military activities the Sannyasi leaders had to maintain armed groups under their own banners without reference to the rulers concerned. The purpose of the *akharas* was to uphold the ideas of Hinduism as well as to defend the faith from Muslim inroads. Due to recurring conflicts with the Fakirs since the medieval period,[135] the Sannyasis belonging to different orders ignored their theological differences and turned to their military leaders, who in the role of *mahants* of respective *akharas* could best provide effective protection. According to Surajit Sinha, the Naga Sannyasis gradually trained themselves as fighters and fought on behalf of such princely states as Kutch, Jodhpur, Indore, Gwalior and several others in western India against the Islamic invasion.[136] They were even believed to have fought in the battle of Jnanavapi at Benares against the Mughals in 1664 in an attempt to save Benares from destruction by Aurangzīb's forces.[137] The view of Jadunath Sarkar or Ghurye is also supported by *akhara* records left by Mahant Lakshman Giri of Mahanirvani Akhara.[138] In *samvat* 1721 (AD 1664) they (the

[133] Bhattacharyya, 2012.

[134] Sarkar, *Fall.* He was one of the pioneering historians who dealt with the history of the Dasnami Naga Sannyasis on the basis of the *akhara* records.

[135] Surajit Sinha and B.N. Saraswati, *Ascetics of Kashi*, N.K. Bose Memorial Foundation, Varanasi, 1978: 98-9.

[136] Ibid.: 101-4.

[137] Sarkar, *Dasnami*: 87-8.

[138] Ghurye, op. cit.: 105. See also *Shree Panch Dasanam Mahanirvani Akhra ka Sriti Patra (1929)* (in Hindi), January: 5-9.

Dasnamis) won the fight with the sultan and gained great glory. From sunrise to sunset the battle raged and the Dasnamis proved themselves heroes; they preserved the honour of Viswanath's seat. They defeated Mirza Ali, Turang Khan and Abdul Ali. Citing this pamphlet it may be said that 'in the time of the Delhi Badshahs, there used to be three thousand men in it. It used to be equipped with canon and *zamburaks* (i.e. long matchlocks mounted on the back of camels)'. The accuracy of Sarkar's claim cannot be challenged. Similarly, the *akharas* situated in Jodhpur during the Mughal period helped the Jodhpur Rajputs to repel the attacks of Muslims from Baluchistan and Kabul. The *akharas* turned into warehouses of weapons and the Sannyasis became well-organized experts in the field of warfare. Atal Akhara and Avan Akhara produced many heroes and fighters for the defence of the Hindu religion.[139] Even the Sannyasis who used to move from central India into the plains of Bengal kept a large armed force in their respective *akharas*. In Bengal temporary *akharas* came into existence during the early British rule, which became storehouses of weapons. Domer Giri, a noted Sannyasi moneylender was reported to have enrolled a large number of armed followers at his *akhara* in Mymensingh.[140]

The organized power of the Sannyasis owed much to the great authority of the *mahant*. The *mahant* or *guru* could expel with impunity or inflict condign punishment on any disciple who was found guilty.[141] Grierson has given a descriptive account of succession to the *mahantship* of Bodh Gaya Math. When a *mahant* dies, all his disciples nominate five Gossains of their own *math* as arbitrators to select a worthy and fit successor to the *gaddi* out of their own body; and all the disciples abide by the decision of the *panchayat* constituted. The *mahants* were in-charge of the *math* exchequer with a view to advancing money to

[139] Sarkar, *Dasnami*: 109-12.

[140] Board of Revenue (hereafter refer to BOR), 15 June 1789; RDG, 8 July 1789, nos. 21-2.

[141] Steale, op. cit.: 437.

his capable disciples for the purpose of trade. Even the selection of incumbents for the *gaddi* was done by the *mahant* who generally took the initiative when he could feel the imminence of his death. Generally, the most senior *chela* succeeded him while others, according to the dates of their initiation, could aspire for the *mahantship*. Thus, it can be summed up in this way that there was an inter-dependent relationship between the Sannyasis and the regional powers of India. The Sannyasis due to rendering their services were patronized by the regional powers in this way that the Dasnami Sannyasis were not only favoured but were given privileges, a large tract of rent-free land and also to keep armed forces under their banner. These types of privileges were curtailed after the assumption of British power in Bengal that culminated into a rebellion.

DASNAMIS IN WORLDLY AFFAIRS

Not only did the Sannyasis excel as soldiers, some of them also rose to high positions in the military and civil affairs of the Indian rulers. In the field of military administration, the Sannyasis were employed as *qiladar* (in-charge of fort), *faujdar* (in-charge of army), *thanadar* (in-charge of police station) and commander of armed groups while in civil administration they were employed as *amil* (in-charge of revenue), *izaradar* (in-charge of large tract of land), spies, revenue and tribute collectors and also diplomats.

Our earliest evidence of the Sannyasis' role in military administration in the pre-British days relates to Jhansi, a place situated between United Provinces and Central Provinces. Rajendra Giri was the *qiladar* of Jhansi[142] before entering service in the government of Awadh. Being the *qiladar,* he not only built a fort there, but also defeated Naro Shankar, the Maratha *subadar*, with the assistance of Ganga Puri, another Sannyasi. This victory enabled him to acquire a large number of villages in the vicinity. After entering the service of the Awadh government, Rajendra

[142] Srivastava, *Shiraj-ud-Daulah*, op. cit.: 162.

Giri held the post of *faujdar* in Saharanpur in 1752. Even the Nawab of Awadh sent him as the *faujdar* to capture Etawah that helped him take over the charge of the Doab. The achievement of Rajendra Giri as a *faujdar* was two-fold. First, the post of *faujdar* was normally enjoyed by the ruling family of Mughal lineage.[143] Second, it was Rajendra Giri who extracted revenue from the regional aristocrats without any discrimination, whereas his predecessors had failed to control those disloyal aristocrats. Hence, a court historian lamented 'the Afghans, Gujars and the Sayyids of Barha, who had never obeyed any faujdar before, were totally ruined'.[144] In Saharanpur Rajendra Giri impartially collected revenue from the Muslim zamindars of Etawah and Kora Jahanabad, who had long enjoyed preferential treatment in the past.[145]

As *subadar* (chief of the province) of the Bhonsle (house/family) of Nagpur, Manohar Giri was in-charge of the fort of Singhgarh in Nagpur and Ranjit Giri was appointed *qiladar* of Jatigarh near Agra.[146] Because of their military activities the Sannyasi leaders had to maintain armed groups under their own banners indcpcndent of their patrons. Their command over arms and followers turned them into semi-independent chiefs, enabling them to establish their authority in the Doab (the lands between two rivers, viz., Ganga and Jamuna). Because of his disagreement with the other Maratha leaders, Mahadji Sindhia employed Anup Giri and his brother to capture the *thana* (police station) of Firuzabad (not very far from Agra) and to raid Dobhai Kothar Mahal.[147]

In Bengal, the Sannasyais' role in military administration was not so significant. It appears that Hari Giri and Domer Giri were entrusted by the local zamindar with the duty of *thanadars* in the

[143] Sarkar, *Dasnami*, 136; *Tarikh:* 37-8.

[144] *Tarikh*: 46-7.

[145] *Tarikh*; *CPC* (1953): 255.

[146] Hari Gir and Prithwi Gir, op. cit.: 83; *CPC*, 1953: 255.

[147] Secret Committee Proceedings (hereafter referred to as Secret), 9 May 1786, no. 7; Sarkar, 1941: 142.

Jafarshahi Pargana (locality) of Mymensingh district (presently in Bangladesh) by the order of the zamindar.[148] Besides, Manick Giri as the *thanadar* of Bussarapore in Rajshahi detained some salt boats transporting their goods from Calcutta to some neighbouring places and back.[149]

The Sannyasis' role as revenue collectors was not as important as their role as soldiers. Anup Giri, as an army commander in the expeditions of the Regent of Delhi against Jaipur, recovered from Jaipur a tribute of Rs. 75,000 in 1779 when the Jaipur Raja failed to pay the stipulated amount to the representative of the Mughal emperor. Mirza Najaf was so pleased that he handsomely rewarded Anup Giri.[150] In Mymensingh, Chandan Giri was employed as an *izaradar* and Jairam Giri was an *amil* of Cuttah in Midnapur under whose leadership a large army was maintained.[151] Similarly, Doan Giri as the *tahsildar* (in-charge of cash) of Patashpur in Midnapur entertained a large number of Nagas as *barkandazes* (armed men) and horsemen under their authority.[152]

There is some evidence of the employment of Sannyasis as spies. They were employed by Durlabhram, the deputy governor of Orissa, for the purposes of espionage and also communication with different regions. Durlabhram depended on the Sannyasis to such an extent that he came to be controlled by them in various ways.[153] According to *Seir-ul-Mutakherin*, the Sannyasis in the service of Durlabhram were actually spies of Raghuji Bhonsle planted with Durlabhram.[154] Consequently, when a conspiracy was hatched by some leading aristocrats at the instigation of

[148] Preparer of Reports, 2 May 1789.

[149] Rangpur District Records, Bangladesh National Archives, Dhaka, Bangladesh (hereafter referred to as RDR), vol. 239: 283-4.

[150] Sarkar, 1941: 6-11.

[151] BOR, 3 August 1786, no. 11; RDR 239: 245.

[152] COR, 6 April 1786, no. 3.

[153] S.C. Mukhopadhyay, *The Career of Rajah Durlabhram Mahindra (Rai Durlabh), Diwan of Bengal, 1710-1770*, C. Mukherjee, Varanasi, 1974: 15-17.

[154] Ghulam Hussein Khan, *Seir-ul-Mutakherin*: 512.

Raghuji Bhonsle against Durlabhram, the Sannyasis persuaded Durlabhram to come to terms with Raghuji Bhonsle.

There is at least one exceptional case on record in which even the British employed a Sannyasi, Puran Giri, in diplomatic negotiations. In 1774 Hastings sent Puran Giri to accompany George Bogle on his celebrated 1773 mission to Tibet.[155] Bogle was greatly helped by Puran Giri who was highly competent to act both as interpreter and guide to the English mission on account of his knowledge of Tibetan and other languages and his experience of travelling in the Himalayan region. When Bogle was held up in Bhutan by message from the Panchen Lama asking him to go back, it was Puran Giri who first entered Tibet and persuaded the Lama to allow Bogle to visit his country.[156] In fact, the Gossain enjoyed the full confidence of the Tibetan authorities and respect of the Tibetan people. In the hope of opening up more distant regions of British trade and influence, Bogle was to undertake a visit to Peking in 1779. Puran Giri was sent to join the Lama's party in China. In this way he became a close associate of the Panchen Lama in China and was introduced by him to the emperor. Hence, when Hastings dispatched the mission of Samuel Turner to Tibet in the early part of 1783, Puran Giri was called upon to render the same services as before to the English mission.[157] He acted as Turner's guide and interpreter. Further, in 1785 Hastings selected Puran Giri as the English representative in Tibet through Bhutan. He reached Tashilhumpo on 8 May 1785 and had an interview with the Panchen Lama.[158]

Even Shuja-ud-Daullah of Awadh employed Anup Giri

[155] S. Turner, *An Account of an Embassy to the Court of the Teshoo Lama in Tibbet*, W. Balmer & Co., London, 1800: 419-31; *CPC*, 1907-69: 642-3; Bysack, 1890.

[156] S.C. Sircar, 'A Note on Puran Gir Gosain', *Bengal Past and Present*, vol. XLIII, Calcutta Historical Society, Calcutta, 1930: 45-58.

[157] RDG, 7 April 1786.

[158] C.R. Markham, *Narratives of the Mission of George Bogle to Tibet*, Trubner & Co., London, 1879: ixxii, 73-297.

on a diplomatic mission to negotiate an alliance with Mahadji Sindhia against the Rohillas.[159] The Bhonsle Raja of Nagpur appointed Uday Puri to settle the *chauth* and other administrative matters between the government of Orissa and the Company's government.[160] Uday Puri's second task was to establish friendship between the Bhonsle Raja and the Company's government. Puran Puri was appointed by the Raja of Benares to assist the Governor-General, Hastings, in administrative work.[161] Ajib Giri was deputed by Raja Ran Bahadur of Nepal in 1782 to place certain points before the Governor-General for a peaceful solution to a number of disputes.[162]

The Sannyasis became so powerful that sometimes they came to play a vital role in Mughal Court politics. It appears that following the death of Mirza Najaf Khan a scramble for power ensued among various factions.[163] The Sannyasis under Anup Giri took Afrasiyab Khan's side in the struggle for the regency and began to formulate the new Regent's policies. So, when Afrasiyab failed to meet the financial obligation to the Mughal emperor, Shah Alam, the latter's attempt to dismiss him from power was prevented by Anup Giri's personal influences. The Sannyasis then proposed a counter-alliance with Mahadji Sindhia to reduce the strength of Muhammad Beg Hamdani and Mirza Muhammad Shafi, who were opponents of Afrasiyab Khan.[164] Since Hamdani and Shafi were arch enemies of Sindhia, the Sannyasis murdered Shafi in 1783[165] and created disturbances in the environs of Kama (a place adjacent to Jaipur), the residential pargana of Hamdani (an aristocrat). But their plans failed due to the sudden and

[159] Select Committee Proceedings, 10 January 1772; Sarkar, *Fall of the Mughal Empire*, vol. III: 125.

[160] *CPC*, 1907: 63, 77-8.

[161] Jonathan Duncan, 'An Account of Two Fakeers with Their Portraits', *The Asiatic Researches*, vol. V, Asiatic Society, Calcutta, 1797: 23-44.

[162] *CPC*: 379.

[163] Sarkar, *Fall of the Mughal Empire*: 214.

[164] *Ibratnamah*.

[165] Sarkar, *Fall of the Mughal Empire*: 215.

unexpected murder of Afrasiyab Khan. With a view to control the Mughal empire as a de facto guardian, Anup Giri made Afrasiyab's infant son *mir bakshi* (commander of the army). The situation gave an opportunity to Anup Giri to attack Hamdani and to confiscate his property.[166] In this way the Sannyasis became virtual dictators in the Delhi Court.[167] This semi-independent attitude placed the Dasnamis in such a position that the conflict with the East India Company became inevitable.

PATRONAGE AND REWARD

Thus we see that in the pre-British and British period, there was no conflict between the Sannyasis and the Indian powers except Bengal. In fact, their relations were marked by mutual support and co-operation. For example, Prithviraj Chauhan favourably treated them by renovating their *akharas* in different parts of India.[168] The Sannyasis enjoyed a privileged position and were rewarded with lands, *jagirs*, pensions and high titles. The Mughal emperor generously favoured religious men, including the Sannyasis with *madad-i-maash* (rent-free lands) in different parts of India where they also acted as revenue farmers and moneylenders.[169] A Marathi source refers to the assignment of rent-free tenure in Khandesh sanctioned by the Emperor Alamgir II to Kaushal Giri.[170] In Allahabad the rise of *lakhiraj* (rent-free) tenures granted to religious groups, including the Sannyasis was so extensive that it might have helped the imperial authority in creating a class that was expected to be sympathetic towards the imperial interests.[171]

[166] K.D. Bhargava, ed., *Browne Correspondence*, National Archives of India, New Delhi, 1960: 220.

[167] Persian Letter Received 1784 (NAI): 88.

[168] Hari Gir and Prithwi Gir: 111.

[169] Muzaffar Alam, 'Some Aspects of the Changes in the Position of the Madad-i-Maash Holders in Oudh, 1676-1722', *Proceedings of the Indian History Congress*, Jadavpur, 1974.

[170] Hari Gir and Prithwi Gir, op. cit.: 261.

[171] S.N. Sinha, *Mid-Gangetic Region in the 18th Century: Some Obser-*

It seems that 55 *bighas* of land in the village of Cundrah in the pargana Afferowmah in Allahabad were given to the Sannyasis.[172] Similarly, in the year 1711, Hriday Sal and Jugut Raj, sons of the Prince Chattrasal of Bundelkhand granted rent-free tenures to Mohun Giri for the services rendered by the Sannyasis.[173] Rajendra Giri was given Moth as *jagir* by the Marathas where he built a fort for himself and made it his residence. Gradually, he acquired possession of a large number of villages in the vicinity. Even the Marathas, Nawabs of Awadh and Raja of Benares conferred on Rajendra Giri, Anup Giri and others a large number of rent-free properties. It is to be noted here that Mirza Najaf Khan, the Regent of Delhi and the Maratha rulers, granted such lands to the Sannyasis as were actually enjoyed by the members of ruling Mughal families and *jagirdars* (the holder of a *jagir*, i.e. hereditary assignment of land).[174] Similarly, as the representatives of Afrasiyab Khan and chief adviser of Sindhia, Anup Giri secured new *jagirs*. In gratitude for their participation in Bhim Singh's expedition against Jalor, the Sannyasis were given the village Lambhahala in Metta Parganas.[175] They gradually amassed wealth and used to lend money to the local Rajas and Ranas of that area at a compound rate of interest which varied between 24 and 72 per cent. The Dasnamis in that area used to collect contributions in the name of religion and 'continued to exhaust the resources of the people in outer Saraj tract of Kullu'. They were mostly found in Nadaun and Jwalamukhi. They monopolized trade in opium,

---

vations of Joseph Tiffenthaler, Shanti Prakashan, New Delhi, 1976: 11.

[172] Deposition of Subjeet Bharati: Correspondence and Proceedings of the Resident at Benares (hereafter referred to as CPRB), 30 July 1789: 469-72.

[173] Court case between the Collector of Bundelkhand and Illachee Geer: T.A.V. Row and T.S.K. Row, eds., *The Indian Decisions* (Old Series), Madras Government Press, Madras, 1925, vol. VI: 735.

[174] Henry Yule and A.C. Burnell, *Hobson-Jobson: A Glossary of Colloquial Anglo-Indian Words and Phrases etc.,* Rupa & Co., Calcutta, 1990: 446-7; Secret, 13 June 1776, no. 3.

[175] RDG, 1 December 1790, no. 28; COR, 28 July 1785, no. 38.

charas, wool and cloth. Their transactions extended to the Deccan. Most of the Kangra Gossains belonged to Giri suborder.[176]

Although it is not definitely known what sort of role the Sannyasis played in the civil and military administration of Bihar, there is some evidence that a considerable amount of rent-free land and monetary pensions were sanctioned by the zamindars of Mymensingh, Rajshahi and Cooch Behar in the pre-*diwani* period (before AD 1765). The Sannyasi leaders, in lieu of their services, were permitted by the Nawabs of Awadh to maintain the rank of 4,000 *zat* and 3,000 *sawar* under their personal command.[177] The status and prestige enjoyed by the Sannyasis amply show how greatly the regional powers valued their services. Thus, it is not difficult to understand how the Sannyasis were favoured by the regional powers. This favouritism was also marked in them performing religious activities, including their long-distance pilgrimage with armed group of followers in Bengal and outside. There is no denying the fact that their free movement was no doubt a root cause of conflict with the East India Company.

FREE MOVEMENT

Since the Sannyasis were a very privileged community, they naturally enjoyed a large degree of freedom from interference either by the Mughal emperors or by regional powers in observance of their traditional rites and customs. The Mughal government allowed them to recruit armed followers for their order and did not interfere with the armed Sannyasis.[178] During the period of Aurangzīb and also during the breakup of the Mughal rule the Sannyasis were permitted by the regional chiefs to travel with armed followers to levy contributions from the common

[176] Holland Rose, *Religious History of Islam*, Amar Prakashan, New Delhi, 1991: 304.

[177] Select, October 1768; Secret, 6 July 1776, no. 4; Davies, op. cit.

[178] Ghurye, op. cit.: 64-6; Farquhar, op. cit.

people.[179] They also imposed a military levy upon the citizens of Delhi leading to the confinement of some Muslim merchants.

This semi-independent conduct of the Sannyasis drew the attention of British observers such as James Forbes,[180] Grant Duff[181] and T.D. Broughton.[182] Even Sannyasis attached to the army of Safdar Jang were advised by the latter to plunder the *jagirs* of the Turani and Sayyid nobles residing in Delhi. Similarly, the Sannyasis in the early colonial period were also permitted to plunder by the Regent of Delhi. This practice of carrying arms and collecting contributions from the zamindars and common people of Bengal were major causes of the Sannyasis' armed clashes with the zamindars, peasantry and the East India Company. It appears that the peasants had become targets of the Sannyasis when they failed to meet their demands. This is inconsistent with the supposition that peasants backed the Sannyasis in their conflict with the English. This theory has been fondly nurtured by some Marxist historians.[183] The Sannyasis were also frequently involved in conspiracies and intrigues hatched by the regional powers. After 1786 an armed uprising led by the Sannyasis against Mahadji Sindhia in the Doab was suppressed, the Sannyasis were asked only to mend their ways. Mahadji dissuaded his generals from taking any stern steps against the Sannyasis. Similarly, the Sannyasis' participation in the coup of Jehangir Khan, *qiladar* of Aligarh,

[179] 'Sobah Singh's Remonstrance to Aurangzeb': *The Asiatic Journal and Annual Register*, vol. IV, July 1817, London: 21-2.

[180] *Oriental Memoirs*, White Cochrane and Co., London, 1813, vol. I: 68.

[181] *A History of the Marathas, 1789-1858*, vol. II, Longman, Brown and Green, London, 1864: 7.

[182] *Letters from a Maratha Camp during the year 1809*, K.P. Bagchi & Co., Calcutta, 1977, rpt.: 33-49.

[183] Suprakash Roy, *Bharater Krishok Vidroho O Ganatantric Sangram* (in Bengali), DNBA, Calcutta, 1966; Suranjan Chatterjee, 'New Reflections on the Sannyasi, Fakir and Peasant War', *Economic and Political Weekly*, January 1984, PE: 2-15; Atis Dasgupta, *The Fakirs and Sannyasi Uprisings*, K.P. Bagchi, Calcutta, 1992.

against the Mughal emperor was ignored by the emperor. Since the Indian regional powers did not have the British notion of 'state' and 'sovereignty' they did not consider the Sannyasis armed rising as an 'offence' and threat to the government. This explains why the Mughal government, Mahadji Sindhia, and Nawab Shuja-ud-Daullah of Awadh paid no attention to the British request for the expulsion of the Sannyasis from their respective territories, whereas, the British considered the Sannyasis' conspiracy against the Maharaja of Cooch Behar in 1787 an offence and regarded them as enemies. Various other practices of the Sannyasis were tolerated by the Mughals and other Indian rulers. The Mughals tolerated the practice of Nagas going naked in public but the British did not. Ghurye has shown how the procession of the naked Sannyasis taking their sacred bath at the time of the Kumbha was tolerated by the Indian powers.[184] The usual clashes over the question of precedence in bathing ceremonies such as the Kumbha Mela were often ignored by the regional powers.[185] The Sannyasis' semi-independent and authoritative attitude in the management of the fairs was also tolerated by the regional powers in the later period. But the Sannyasis were permitted to carry on their activities excepting the carrying of arms.

ECONOMIC ACTIVITIES

Some features of the Sannyasis trading activities are notable. The pre-colonial Indian powers neither imposed any restriction on their trading activities nor declared such activities as illegal. On the contrary, they recognized them as lawful merchants. Second, they carried on their trading activities along with their religious pilgrimage and mercenary occupations. Their well-knit organization enabled them to carry on their different types of activities successfully. Third, the Sannyasis primarily maintained trade relations with the upper strata of society successfully, which

[184] Ghurye: 98-9.

[185] Hardwicke cited in Sarkar, *Dasnami:* 100-1.

is amply proved by the costly and luxurious nature of their merchandise.

The Sannyasis were moneylenders who lent money to the Indian princes, local zamindars and peasants. Their operations were mostly confined to north India, the Deccan, Bihar and some parts of Bengal. Since the medieval period they lent money, and by the early eighteenth century the Indian powers were highly dependent on them. Loans ranged from 1.5 per cent interest to 36 per cent in the period. The Sannyasis transacted their moneylending operation through the *maths* situated in Benares and Mirzapur. Along with religious activities, the *maths* also served as customs houses. As B.S. Cohn[186] has shown the Sannyasis' centres of pilgrimage and *maths* could be viewed as branches of a far-flung commercial and banking network, which facilitated their transaction of money and goods. In the city of Benares alone, more than forty leading business houses of the Sannyasis were listed in the eighteenth century.[187]

In north India local powers such as the Maharajas, Ranas, zamindars and the people belonging to the Dasnami order mostly took loans from the Sannyasi merchants. Raja Fateh Bahadur Chand of Benares borrowed a large amount of Rs. 11,000 from the Sannyasi merchants Turant Giri and Sirdha Giri. Similarly, the local Ranas of Kangra Hills and Simla owed them a huge sum.[188] There was no uniform rate of interest; instead it varied between 24 and 72 per cent. In Benares and Mirzapur, Chanchal Puri, Sukhdev Puri, Pitambar Giri, Ram Giri, Badal Giri, and others were the principal moneylenders.[189] Thus, it proves that

[186] B.S. Cohn, 'The Role of Gossains in the Economy of Eighteenth and Nineteenth Century Upper India', *Indian Economic and Social History Review* 1, 4 (1964): 175-83.

[187] Moti Chandra, *Kashi Ka Itihas* (in Hindi), Hindi Grantha Ratnakar, Bombay, 1962: 444-5.

[188] H.A. Rose, *Lesser known Tribes of North-West India and Pakistan; Based on the Census Reports of 1883 and 1892*, Amar Prakashan, New Delhi, 1991 (rpt.): 303-4.

[189] CPRB: 19 May 1789.

the Sannyasis were very much active as traders in north India. Besides their transactions with outsiders, they also carried on their moneylending activities among themselves.

In Bengal most of the transactions were carried on with the zamindars, chaudhuries and peasants. Places such as Alepsingh, Mymensingh, Sherpur in Bagura, Pookareah in Rajshahi, Dacca, Mamudshahi, Rangpur and Cooch Behar were the major centres of the moneylending operations of the Sannyasi *mahajans*. Besides moneylending, a wide range of trade links helped the Sannyasis establish close contacts with various regions of India and even some Himalayan countries. Since north India occupied an important place in the world of commerce for a long period, the Sannyasis' trade activities centred on the major markets of Benares and Mirzapur. In this way, an interconnected economic organization developed on a pan-India level.

The gradual decline of Murshidabad as a silk-producing centre seems to be a major reason for the rise of Benares (centring round Mirzapur) as the country's most important commercial centre in the silk trade.[190] Second, the religious character of Benares was an additional factor in attracting people, including traders, from different parts of India to Benares and Mirzapur. The Sannyasis' *maths*, scattered throughout north India, also drew traders to Benares, Mirzapur and other places. Their centres of pilgrimage and banking networks facilitated the transmission of money and goods. The religious character and commercial resources naturally made Benares a prime centre of Sannyasi activities. Pilgrims to Benares were from such widely scattered regions as western India, Kashmir, Nepal and Tibet, the purpose being not just pilgrimage but also trade. Duties were collected from the merchants for the regular transmission of goods between Mirzapur and other interior parts of Hindustan. Jonathan Duncan settled with Raja Chait Singh of Benares how much these duties were to be and

[190] C.A. Bayly, *Rulers, Townsmen and Bazars: North Indian Society in the Age of Expansion, 1770-1870,* Oxford University Press, New Delhi, 1998 (rpt.): 104, 174.

wrote to the members of the Council of Fort William in October 1773 stating that this arrangement would 'be a benefit to the fair traders, and of course a general encouragement to the exportation of goods from Bengal'.[191]

The trade marts of Mirzapur and Benares were considered meeting places of the trading communities and the Sannyasi merchants. Merchants from Dacca, northern and western provinces assembled there for the sale of their commodities and goods from northern countries such as Nepal and Tibet.[192] In a letter to Hastings in 1776, F. Fowke commented upon the importance of Mirzapur to the merchants of India.[193] Thus, Benares, Mirzapur and Ghazipur controlled the intersection of the south-west and north-west routes. In such circumstances it was only natural for the Sannyasis living in different parts of India such as Nagpur, Poona, Bengal, and Gujarat, and even in the neighbouring countries of Nepal, Bhutan and Tibet, to develop a close connection with Benares and Mirzapur. According to a report by the Resident of Benares Kashi Bharati, Jubaraj Bharati and Bhaboot Bharati of Nagpur who were engaged in trading met their partners at Benares for the purchase of merchandise in the second half of the eighteenth century.[194] The cotton and silk piece-goods produced in Benares and also in Bengal were transported to Nagpur,[195] a fact noticed by Joseph Tieffenthaler, who commented upon

[191] Secret, 4 October 1773, nos. 2 and 15.

[192] Settlement Papers and Duncan Records, 24 August 1787; K.P. Mishra, *Benares in Transition (1738-1793): A Socio-Economic Study*, Munshiram Monoharlal, New Delhi, 1975: 100; William Buyers, *Recollections of Northern India with Observations on the Origin, Customs, and Moral sentiments of the Hindoos etc.*, John Snow, Paternoster Row; Glasgow, William Collins, London, 1848: 357-65.

[193] Secret, 3 October 1773.

[194] CPRB, 5 May 1788.

[195] A.F.M. Abdul Wali, 'Commercial and Social Intercourse between the Honourable East India Company and the Poona Court in the 18th Century', *Bengal Past and Present,* vol. XXXVI, Calcutta Historical Society, Calcutta, 1929: 78-98.

'the Sannyasis' trade with the mid-Gangetic region.[196] Trade with Mirzapur and Benares in silk brocades, muslin and other goods was chiefly in the hands of the Sannyasis.[197] The trading operations of the Sannyasis were so extensive that the silk trade of Commercooly in Rajshahi was conducted by the Sannyasi merchants of Gujarat.[198]

The geographical location of Benares also helped it to serve as a link in the commerce with Malda and other parts of Bengal. The commercial resources of Bengal attracted the Sannyasi traders of Benares and Mirzapur and a direct trading link was established connecting these places. It appears that large quantities of silk produced in Malda were sent to Mirzapur and Benares through the Sannyasi traders. Jonathan Duncan, Resident at Benares, reported that Beni Giri (the noted Sannyasi merchant of Benares who also held a large estate in Mymensingh) had trading connections with Malda.[199] Similarly, William Harwood wrote to the Members of the Committee of Circuit in 1773 informing them that a considerable quantity of Malda silk was purchased by the Sannyasis. The trading activity of the Sannyasis between Malda and Benares is also corroborated by other reports of a later period.[200] This trade link was so advantageous to the Sannyasis that Mahant Man Giri, Subal Giri and other Sannyasi merchants of Malda sent a petition to the Governor-General in 1794 for the abolition of police tax imposed on the traders in order to increase their trading capacities between Malda and Benares.[201] Further, the

[196] S.N. Sinha, *Mid-Gangetic Region in the 18th Century*, New Delhi, 1976: 20-1.

[197] R. Jenkins, *Report on the Territories of Rajah of Nagpore*, Antiquarian and Scientific Society of the Central Provinces, Nagpore, 1866: 92.

[198] Board of Trade (Commercial) (hereafter refer to BOT, 13 March 1789, no. 13.

[199] CPRB, 19 May 1791; Alexander Shakespeare, *Selections from the Duncan Records*, vol. II, Benares, 1873: 16-17.

[200] CCRP, 11 March 1773, 24 May 1773, CPRB, 24 May 1773 and 7 February 1791.

[201] JCR, 14 September 1794, no. 13; *CPC*, 1969: 147.

evidence of Sadananda Bandyopadhyaya, a silk broker, recorded in 1789, suggests that even the raw silk of Murshidabad was sent to Benares, Mirzapur and Nagpur. Gautam Bhadra has written of the trading connections between the Basra market in Mirzapur and Murshidabad in silk piece-goods and the role of Sannyasi merchants as a link between the two centres.[202] Mirzapur thus appears to have been a distribution centre of Murshidabad raw silk and silk piece-goods. Murshidabad raw silk and silk piece-goods were distributed through Mirzapur, as shown by records of the banker and trader Chanchal Puri who purchased that silk.[203] This connection between trading centres was quite close during the period of rebellion, and this was made possible because the British officially approved the trading activities of the Sannyasis.[204]

The Sannyasis had old trade links with Nepal, Tibet and Bhutan. They used to export gold, silver, Bengal cloth, raw silk, and import Tibetan products such as musk, tincal [*sic*], etc., via Nepal and Benares to different parts of Hindustan.[205] It appears from a representation submitted by Gyan Giri, a Sannyasi merchant of Benares, which the volume of trade with Nepal was carried on in white cloth, chintzes [*sic*], spices and emeralds.[206] James Logan's memorandum to Verelest (Governor of Bengal) also describes the commercial transactions of the Sannyasis between Patna and Kathmandu.[207] The Sannyasis also established trade links between Bengal and Tibet. In this context the role of Puran Giri in bringing minerals such as gold, gold dust and silver from Tibet deserves mention.[208] It was important because it was the

[202] Gautam Bhadra, 'Social Groups and Relations in the Town of Murshidabad', *The Indian Historical Review*, vol. II, no. 2 (January 1976), New Delhi: 165-78.

[203] CPRB, 11 November 1788.

[204] CCRP, 11 March 1773 and 22 March 1773.

[205] W. Kirkpatrick, *An Account of the Kingdom of Nepal*, New Delhi, 1975: 202-5; Turner, op. cit.: 370-1; Sircar, op. cit.: 154-65.

[206] CPRB, 9 September 1791.

[207] Sircar, 1939: 98-109.

[208] O'Malley and Chakraborty, op. cit.

first important mission sent by the East India Company to their neighbouring regions. As Gautam Bhadra has rightly observed, a trade connection developed between Tibet and the Bhot Bagan Monastery situated at Howrah in Bengal.[209] The Sannaysis' network of trade even included regions as far away as Bhutan.[210] The ulterior motive of the religious pilgrimage was to expand trade. Puran Puri and Bhagwan Puri travelled on one occasion as far as Russia for the expansion of their commercial activities.[211] There is no denying the fact that it was through trade and moneylending that the Sannyasis, residing in different parts of India, often met at common centres for the purpose of commercial necessities. The Sannyasis' existing trading network provided a great opportunity to the insurgent Sannyasis to build up an organized framework through which they could carry on their rebellious activities. Moreover, since the Sannyasi traders were heavily patronized by the Indian powers, they had the privilege of travelling as traders in large groups to different parts of Bengal and Bihar and they could thus carry on their activities as earlier. Thus, they could carry arms on their long-distance travels as lawful merchants, which is corroborated by the minutes of Hastings sent to the Board in 1773.[212]

CONCLUSION

The socio-religious entity commonly known as the Sannyasis emerged as a distinctive political agency during the transitional phases of eighteenth-century India. Before this period their relations with established political power structures such as the

[209] Gautam Bhadra, *Mughal Yuge Krishi Arthaniti O Krishak Bidroho* (in Bengali), Subarnarekha, Calcutta, 1983: 96.

[210] R.B. Singh, ed., *Fort William India House Correspondence* (*1786-1788*), and other contemporary papers relating there to vol. X, National Archives of India, Manager of Publications, Delhi, 1972: 213.

[211] Duncan: 23-44.

[212] Secret, 21 January 1773, no. 5.

centralized empire of the Mughals remains rather obscure. But it is during the period of political flux and loosening of central authorities in different parts of India that their mercenary character emerges in full view of other political powers of India, such as the East India Company, Nawabs of Awadh, the Marathas and the kingdom of Bengal. It is these powers that made full political use of their abilities as foot soldiers, and in some cases as diplomatic and military agents. It is noteworthy that in the fluid and volatile political conditions of the eighteenth century, during which the concept of political sovereignty in many parts of the country was defined in a nebulous manner, the changing loyalty of the Sannyasis and their constantly shifting political locations had important relevance for states that were emerging, looking for a legitimacy and defining their own position vis-à-vis a central authority. On the other hand, when the ideology of the centralized monarchy was under constant threat and pressure, the activities of the Sannyasis, particularly their changing loyalties, was politically symptomatic of the times. Further research should seek to determine if they served as a catalytic agent in forging political identities or construction of regional or local power structures. From the evidence gathered so far it is clear that they were a much sought-after military and commercial force. One needs to further examine the point whether the disbanding of centralized standing armies and the devolution of centralized military command structure had something to do with patronage to such mercenary social groups.

The biggest advantage that the Sannyasis had was the existence of a supra-regional network cutting across the boundaries of regional kingdoms and principalities, interlinked with one another through the *maths* and *akharas* and commanding enough resources to sustain continuous movement across frontiers. This network virtually paralleled the network of administration of the Mughals and the regional states. While the *akharas* were nurseries for young men aspiring to join mercenary militant groups, the *maths* were commercial warehouses cum religious/ideological indoctrinating schools. Within this supra-regional network spread across Bengal and northern India, the Sannyasis acted as conduits of economic transaction, lending money and trading. In Bengal they have been found as moneylenders in various districts. They have also been mentioned as traders coming from north India through various routes into Murshidabad and Malda. Here, they acted chiefly as traders in mulberry and also other textiles. The trading activities of the Sannyasis continued up to the second half of the nineteenth century not only outside Bengal but also some parts of Bengal.

APPENDIX 1

DASNAMI ASCETICS ACCORDING TO THE SANKARACHARYA

Headquarters	*Order*	*Jurisdiction*
Sringeri, Mysore	1. Saraswati	Andhra, Dravida
	2. Bharati	Kerala, Karnataka, etc.
	3. Puri	
Sarada, Dwarka	4. Tirtha	Sindhu, Sauvira
	5. Ashrama	Saurashtra, Maharashtra, etc.
Joshi, Garhwal	6. Giri	Kuru, Kashmir, Panchal
	7. Parvata	Kamboja, etc.
	8. Sagara	
Govardhan, Puri	9. Aranya	Anga, Vanga, Kalinga,
	10. Vana	Utkal, etc.

Source: Kaviraj Gopinath, *Bharatiya Sadhanar Dhara* (in Bengali), Sanskrit College, Calcutta, 1965: 168.

BIBLIOGRAPHY

Primary Sources

Allahabad Regional Archives, Allahabad

(a) Correspondence and Proceedings of the Resident at Benares (1787-95).
(b) Settlement Papers, Duncan Records (1776-95).

Bangladesh National Archives, Dhaka, Bangladesh

Rangpur District Records (1770-1800)

National Archives of India, New Delhi

(a) Select Committee Proceedings (1761-72).
(b) Secret Committee Proceedings (1772-89).
(c) Home (Public) Proceedings (1773-90).
(d) Persian Letter Received (1784-6).
(e) Foreign (Misc.), vol. 41 A.

Uttar Pradesh State Archives, Lucknow

(a) Board of Revenue at Fort William (1803-6).

Supreme Court Records, Calcutta High Court

(a) Court Cases (1786-90).

West Bengal State Archives, Calcutta

(a) Board of Revenue (1786-1800).
(b) Board of Trade (Commercial) 1789.
(c) Committee of Revenue (1781-6).
(d) Controlling Council of Revenue at Patna (1771-3).
(e) Judicial (Criminal) 1793-6.
(f) Revenue Department, Governor-General in Council (1773-9).
(g) Committee of Circuit, Rajmehal, 15 February 1773.
(h) Committee of Circuit, Dinajpur, 21 January 1773.
(i) Preparer of Reports, 2 May 1789.

Unpublished Manuscript

Persian and Marathi Sources

(a) *Tarikh-i-Ahmadshahi* (translated into English by Jadunath Sarkar, 1937).
(b) *Readings in History of the Hindustan, 1732-1774*, Marathi Sources, Sitamau, 1941, unpublished.

(c) *Reading in Maratha History (1751-1781)*, translated from Marathi to English by Jadunath Sarkar, n.p., 1941.
(d) Khairuddin Muhammad Allahabadi, *Ibratnama* manuscript.

Akhara Records

Shree Panch Dasanam Mahanirvani Akhra ka Smriti Patra (in Hindi), January 1929: 5-9.

Secondary Sources (English, Bengali, Marathi, Urdu, Persian and Hindi)

Abu'l Fazl, *Ain-i-Akbari*, vol. II, translated by H. Blochmann in 1927 and vol. III by H.S. Jarret, in 1949 with corrections by Jadunath Sarkar, Asiatic Society, Calcutta.

Ahmad, Nizamuddin, *Tabakat-i-Akbari*, tr. Elliot and Dowson, *The History of India as Told by its Own Historians*, vol. V, S. Gupta, Delhi, 1990.

Alam, Muzaffar, 'Some Aspects of the Changes in the Position of the Madad-i-Maash Holders in Oudh, 1676-1722', *Proceedings of the Indian History Congress*, Jadavpur, 1974.

Atkinson, E.T., ed., *Statistical, Descriptive and Historical Account of the North-Western Provinces of India*, vol. 1, Government Press, Lucknow, 1874.

———, *The Himalayan Districts of the North-Western Provinces*, vol. II, part 1, North-Western Provinces Government Press, Allahabad, 1884.

Baines, J.A., *Imperial Census of 1881: Operation and Results in the Residency of Bombay including Sind*, vol. I, Bombay Central Press, Bombay, 1892.

Barbosa, Duarte, *A Description of the Coasts of East Africa and Malabar in the Beginning of the Sixteenth Century*, notes and preface by Henry E.J. Stanley, Hakluyt Society, London, 1866.

Barnett, R.B., *North India Between Empires, Awadh, the Mughals, and the British, 1720-1801*, California University Press, Berkeley, 1960.

Basu, Haridas, *Dhakar Katha* (in Bengali), Haridas Vasu, Koltabazar, Dacca, 1331 BS/AD 1924.

Bayly, C.A., *Rulers, Townsmen and Bazars: North Indian Society in the Age of British Expansion, 1770-1870*, Oxford University Press, New Delhi, 1998 (rpt.).

Bhadra, Gautam, 'Social Groups and Relations in the Town of Murshidabad', *The Indian Historical Review*, January, vol. II, no. 2 (1976), New Delhi.

———, *Mughal Yuge Krishi Arthaniti O Krishak Bidroho* (in Bengali), Subarnarekha, Calcutta, 1983: 96.

Bhargava, K.D., ed., *Browne Correspondence*, National Archives of India, New Delhi, 1960.

Bhattacharyya, Ananda, 'Sannyasi and Fakir Uprising in North Bengal', *Vishwa Bharati Quarterly*, vol. 13, nos. 3 & 4 (2004-5).

———, 'Reconsidering Sannyasi Rebellion', *Social Scientist*, vol. 40, nos. 3-4, March-April 2012.

———, *Sannyasi and Fakir Rebellion: Jamini Mohan Ghosh Revisited*, Manohar, New Delhi, 2013.

———, 'The Peripatetic Sannyasis: A Challenge to Peasant Stability and Colonial Rule?' *Indian Historical Review*, vol. 41.1.

———, *Dasnami Sannyasis in Worldly and Soldierly Activities*, New Delhi, Kunal Books, 2014.

———, 'Dasnami Sannyasis: Polity and Economy', *Studies in History*, vol. 30, no. 2, August 2014.

Bhattacharya, Durgaprasad and Bibhabati Bhattacharya, eds., *Census of India, 1961: Report on* the *Population Estimates of India (1820-1830)*, Office of the Registrar General, India, New Delhi, 1963.

Bhuyian, S.K., *Anglo-Assamese Relation (1771-1826*), Deptt. of Historical and Antiquarian Studies, Gauhati, 1949.

Broughton, T.D., *Letters from the Maratha Camp*, John Murray, London, 1813.

———, *Letters from a Maratha Camp during the Year 1809*, K.P. Bagchi & Co., Calcutta, 1977 (rpt.).

Buchanan-Hamilton, Francis, *An Account of the District of Sahabad in 1812-13*, Bihar and Orissa Research Society, Patna, 1934.

———, *An Account of the District of Purnea in 1809-1810* (edited from the Buchanan MSS in the India Office Library, Bihar and Orissa Research Society, Patna, 1928.

Buyers, William, *Recollections of Northern India with Observations on the Hindoos and Remarks on the Country and Principal Places on the Ganges etc.*, John Snow, Paternoster Row, Glasgow, W. Collins, London, 1848.

Bysack, Gour Das, 'Notes on a Buddhist Monastery at Bhot Bagan in Howrah', *Journal of the Asiatic Society of Bengal*, Asiatic Society, Calcutta, 1890.

Calendar of Persian Correspondence (11 vols), Office of the Supdt. Govt. Printing, Calcutta, 1907-69.

Calendar of Records of the Secret Committee at Fort William, Bengal Secretariat Press, Calcutta, 1915.

Chandra, A.N., *The Sannyasi Rebellion*, Aruna Prakashani, Calcutta, 1977.

Chandra, Moti, *Kashi Ka Itihas* (in Hindi), Hindi Grantha Ratnakar, Bombay, 1962.

Chatterjee, Suranjan, 'New Reflections on the Sannyasi, Fakir and Peasant War', *Economic and Political Weekly*, January 1984.

Cohn, B.S., 'The Role of Gossains in the Economy of Eighteenth and Nineteenth Century Upper India', *Indian Economic and Social History Review* 1, 4 (1964).

Constable, A., ed., *Travels in the Mogul Empire, 1656-1668*; a revised and improved, based upon Irving Brock's tr., S. Chand, Delhi, 1968.

Cooch Behar Select Records (1869), vol. 1, Cooch Behar Government Press, Cooch Behar, 1869.

Crooke, William, *The Tribes and Castes of the North-West India*, vol. II, Amar Prakashan, Delhi, 1974 (rpt.).

Dani, A.H., *Dacca: A Record of its Changing Fortunes*, Mrs. S.S. Dani, Dacca, 1956.

Das, Haricharan, *Chahar Gulzar Shujai* (in Persian), Newal Kishore Press, Lucknow, n.d.

Dasgupta, Atis, *The Fakirs and Sannyasi Uprisings*, K.P. Bagchi, Calcutta, 1992.

Dasgupta, Bhagwan, 'The Foundation of the British Rule in Bundelkhand', *Proceedings of the Indian History Congress, Kurukshetra*, Peoples Publishing House, New Delhi, 1982.

Davies, C.C., *Warren Hastings and Oudh*: Oxford University Press, Oxford, 1939.

Della Valle, Pietro, *The Pilgrim: The Travels of Pietro Della Valle*, abridged edition, tr. G. Bull Hutchinson, London, 1990.

Drew, W.W., ed., *Census of Bombay and its Feudatories*, vol. VIII, part II, *Imperial Tables*, Bombay General Press, Bombay, 1892.

Duff, James Grant, *History of the Marathas*, vol. I, Amar Prakashan, New Delhi, 1971 (rpt.).

Duncan, Jonathan, 'An Account of Two Fakeers with Their Portraits', *The Asiatic Researches*, vol. V, Asiatic Society, Calcutta, 1797.

Elliot and Dowson, *The History of India as Told by its Own Historians*, vol. 3, S. Gupta, Delhi, 1990 (rpt.).

Farquhar, J.N., 'The Organisation of the Sannyasis of Vedanta', *Journal of the Royal Asiatic Society of Great Britain and Ireland*, Cambridge University Press, London, July 1925.

Firminger, W.K., ed., *The Fifth Report on the Affairs of the East India Company*, Higginbotham & Co., Madras, 1928.

Forbes, James, *Oriental Memoirs*, vol. I, White Cochrane and Co., London, 1813.

Franklin, William, *Military Memoirs of George Thomas*, John Stockdale, London, 1805.

Gazetteer of the Province of Oudh, vol. I: *North Western Provinces and Oudh*, Government Press, Allahabad, 1877.

Ghosh, Jamini Mohan, *Sannyasis in Mymensingh*, Pranballabh Sen, Dacca, 1923.

———, *Sannyasi and Fakirs Raiders in Bengal*, Bengal Secretariat Press, Calcutta, 1930.

Ghurye, G.S., *Indian Sadhus: A Sociological Survey*, 2nd edn., Popular Prakashan, Bombay, 1964.

Gir, Hari and Prithwi Gir, *Gosavi Vatyacha Sampradaya* (in Marathi), Baroda Press, Yeotmal, 1931.

Grant, James, *A History of the Marathas, 1789-1858*, vol. II, Longman, Brown and Green, London, 1864.

———, *Cassell's Illustrated History of India*, vol. I, Cassell Petter & Galphins, London, 1890.

Grierson, G.A., ed., *A Brief History of Bodh Gaya Math, District Gaya*, compiled by Anugrah Narayan Singh, Bengal Secretariat Press, Calcutta, 1863.

Guha, Ranajit, *A Rule of Property for Bengal: An Essays on the Idea of Permanent Settlement*, Orient Longman, New Delhi, 1982 (2nd revd. edn.).

———, *An Elementary Aspect of Peasant Insurgency in Colonial India*, Oxford University Press, New Delhi, 1992.

Hastings, J., ed., *Encyclopedia of Religion and Ethics*, vol. VI, New York University Press, New York, 1981.

Hess, Linda and Sukhdeva Sinha, *Bijak Kabir*, tr. Linda Hess and Sukhdeva Sinha, essay and notes by Linda Hess, Oxford University Press, New York, 2002.

Hunter, W.W., *A Statistical Account of Bengal*, vol. VII, John Murray, London, 1876.

Hutton, J.H., ed., *Census of India, 1931*, vol. 1, part 1, *Report*, Office of the Registrar General, New Delhi, 1932.

Ibbetson, Denzil, 1916, *Punjab Castes, Being a Report of the Chapter on*

'The Races, Castes and Tribes of the People', vol. II, Superintendent Government Printing, Lahore, 1916.

Irvine, William, 'The Bangash Nawabs of Farukhabad: A Chronicle 1713-1857', *Journal of the Asiatic Society of Bengal*, Calcutta, pt. 1, 1879.

Jenkins, R., *Report on the Territories of Rajah of Nagpore*, Antiquarian and Scientific Society of the Central Provinces, Nagpore, 1866.

Kanungo, Kalikaranjan, *History of the Jats: A Contribution to the History of Northern India*, vol. I, M.C. Sarkar, Calcutta, 1925.

Kaviraj, Gopinath, *Bharatiya Sadhanar Dhara* (in Bengali), Sanskrit College, Calcutta, 1965.

Khairuddin Mohammad Allahabadi, *Ibratnama* (unpublished Persian Manuscript).

Khan, Ghulam Hussain, *Siyar-ul-Mutakherin: A Translation*, vol. III, James White, Calcutta, 1789.

Kirkpatrick, W., *An Account of the Kingdom of Nepal*, Asian Publication Services, New Delhi, 1975.

Kitts, I.J., *Tribes and Castes of Bombay and Central Provinces*, Secretariat Press, Bombay, 1885.

Kolff, D.H.A., 'Sannyasi Trader–Soldiers', *Indian Economic and Social History Review*, vol. VIII, New Delhi, 1971.

Lorenzen, D.N., 'Warrior Ascetics in Indian History', *Journal of the American Oriental Society*, New Haven, Boston, vol. 98, 1978.

———, *Travels of Ludivico di Varthema (1503-1508)*, trans. and ed. John Winter Jones, notes and introduction by Geoge Perry Badger, Hakluyt Society, London, 1863.

Mallick, Shyamlal, *Charidham Bhraman* (in Bengali), Mahendra Library, Calcutta, 1331 BS.

Markham, C.R., *Narratives of the Mission of George Bogle to Tibet, etc.* Trubner & Co., London, 1879.

Mishra, K.P., *Benares in Transition (1738-1793): A Socio-Economic Study*, Munshiram Manoharlal, New Delhi, 1975.

Morinis, E., *Pilgrimage in the Hindu Tradition: A Case Study of West Bengal*, South Asian Studies Series, Oxford University Press, New Delhi, 1984.

Mukhopadhyay, S.C., *The Career of Rajah Durlabhram Mahindra (Rai-Durlab), Diwan of Bengal, 1710-1770*, C. Mukherjee, Varanasi, 1974.

Muntakhabut Tawarikh, vol. II, translated by W.H. Lowe, Cosmo Publication, New Delhi, 1990 (rpt.).

Naqvi, Ghulam Ali, *Imad-us-Sadat* (in Urdu), Newal Kishore Press, Lucknow, n.d.

'Narrative of a Journey to Srinagar', *Asiatic Annual Registrar* (VI), Baptist Mission Press, Serampore, 1799.

Neveill, H.R., *District Gazetteer of the United Provinces of Agra and Oudh, Moradabad,* Secretariat Press, Allahabad, 1903.

———, *District Gazetteer of the United Provinces of Agra and Oudh, Shaharanpur Gazetteer*, vol. II, Secretariat Press, Allahabad, 1909.

———, *Bulandshahr Gazetteer*, Secretariat Press, Allahabad, 1909.

O'Malley, L.S.S. and S.K. Chakraborty, *Bengal District Gazetteer, Howrah*, Bengal Secretariat Press, Calcutta, 1909.

Orr, W.G., 'Armed Religious Ascetics in Northern India', *Bulletin of the John Rylands Library*, XXIV, Manchester, 1940.

Padmakar, *Himmat Bahadur Virudabali* (in Hindi), ed. Lala Bhagavanadin, Varanasi Nagari Pracharani Sabha, Varanasi, 1908.

Pinch, William R., 'Who was Himmat Bahadur? Gosains, Rajputs and the British in Bundelkhand, 1800', *Indian Economic and Social History Review*, 35, 3, 1998.

———, *Warrior, Ascetics and Indian Empire*, South Asian Edition, Cambridge University Press, New Delhi, 2006.

Report on the Census of British India taken on the 17 February 1881, Office of the Registrar General India, New Delhi, 1883.

Rose, H.A., *Lesser Known Tribes of North-West India and Pakistan*; *Based on the Census Reports of 1883 and 1892*, Amar Prakashan, New Delhi, 1991 (rpt.).

Rose, Holland, *Religious History of Islam*, Amar Prakashan, Delhi, 1991.

Row, T.A.V. and T.S.K. Row, eds., *The Indian Decisions,* vol. VI (Old Series), Madras Government Press, Madras, 1925.

Roy, Suprakash, *Bharater Krishok Vidroho O Ganatantric Sangram* (in Bengali), DNBA, Calcutta, 1966.

Sardesai, G.S., ed., *Selections from the Peshwa Daftar*, Central Secretariat Press, Bombay, 1930-4.

———, *Historical Papers Relating to Mahadji Sindiā* (unpublished papers from Marathi to English), Alijah Darbar Press, Gwalior, 1937, with a Foreword by Jadunath Sarkar.

Sarkar, Jadunath, 'French Mercenaries in the Jat Campaign of 1775-1776', *Bengal Past and Present,* Calcutta Historical Society, Calcutta, January-June 1936.

———, 'Readings in History of Hindustan, 1732-1774', Marathi Sources, Sitamau, 1941 (unpublished).

———, ed., *English Records of Maratha History: Poona Residency Correspondence*, vol. I, Printed at Govt. Printing Press, Bombay, 1937.

———, *A History of the Dasnami Naga Sannyasis*, Panchayati Mahanirvani Akhara, Allahabad, n.d.

———, *Persian Records of Maratha History, Delhi Affairs (1761-1788), Parasnis Collection*, Bombay Printing Press, Bombay, 1953.

———, *Fall of the Mughal Empire*, vol. III, Orient Longman, Bombay, 1971 (rpt.).

Sen, Surendranath, *Prachin Bangla Patra Sangkalan*, Calcutta University, Calcutta, 1942.

Sengupta, Haripada and Murari Mohan Chattopadhyay, *Tarakeswarer Mohantalila* (in Bengali), 3 parts, 1923.

Shakespeare, Alexander, *Selections from the Duncan Records*, vol. II, Benares, 1873.

Shea, David and Anthony Troyer, eds., *The Dabistan or School of Manners*, translated from the original Persian, with notes and illustrations, Oriental Translation Fund of Great Britain and Ireland, Paris, 1843.

Sherring, M.A., *Hindu Tribes and Castes as Represented in Benares*, Trubner & Co., London, 1872.

Singh, R.B., ed., *Fort William India House Correspondence (1786-1788)*, vol. X, National Archives of India, New Delhi, 1972.

Sinha, Sukhadeva, ed., *Kabiradasa: Kabira-bijaka*, Oxford University Press, New York, 2002.

Sinha, Surajit and B.N. Saraswati, *Ascetics of Kashi*, N.K. Bose Memorial Foundation, Varanasi, 1978.

Sircar, S.C., 'A Note on Puran Gir Gossain', *Bengal Past and Present*, vol. XLIII, Calcutta Historical Society, Calcutta, 1932.

Sinha, S.N., *Mid-Gangetic Region in the 18th Century, Some Observations of Joseph Tiffenthaler*, Shanti Prakashan, New Delhi, 1976.

Sleeman, W.H., *Journey through the Kingdom of Awadh in 1849-50*, John Murray, London, n.d.

'Sobah Singh's Remonstrance to Aurangzeb', *The Asiatic Journal and Annual Register*, vol. IV, London, July 1817.

Srivastava, A.L., *Shuja-ud-Daullah*, vol. I, Shivlal Agarwala, Delhi, 1961.

———, *The First Two Nawabs of Oudh*, Upper India Publishing House, Lucknow, 1933.

Steale, Arthur, *The Law and Customs of the Hindu Castes,* W.H. Allen & Co., London, 1868.

Sudan, *Sujan Charita* (in Hindi), ed. Radhakrishnadas, Varanasi Nagari Pracharani Sabha, Varanasi, 1923 (2nd edn.).

Temple, R.C., ed., *Travels of Peter Mundy in Europe and Asia, 1608-1667,* vol. II: *Travels in Asia, 1603-1614,* Hakluyt Society, London, 1914.

Thiel-Horstmann, Monika, 'Soldiers of God: Soldiers of Fortune: A Chapter of Indian Religion and Military History (unpublished paper).

———, 'On the Dual Identity of Nagas', in D.L. Eck and F. Mallison, eds., *Devotion Divine: Bhakti Traditions from the Regions of India (Studies in Honour of Charlotte Vaudeville),* Groningen, 1991.

———, *Symbiotic Antimony: The Social Organisation of a North Indian Sect,* Australian National University, Canberra, 1986.

———, 'The Example in Dadupanthi Homletics', in *Tellings and Texts: Music, Literature and Performance in North India,* ed. Francesca Orsini and Katherine Butler Schofield, Open Book Publishers, Cambridge, 2015.

Turner, S., *An Account of an Embassy to the Court of the Teshoo Lama in Tibbet,* W. Balmer & Co., London, 1800 .

Wali, A.F.M. Abdul, 'Commercial and Social Intercourse between the Honourable East India Company and the Poona Court in the 18th Century', *Bengal Past and Present,* vol. XXXVI, Calcutta Historical Society, Calcutta, 1929.

Williams, John, *A Historical Account of the Rise and Progress of the Bengal Native Infantry from the Formation in 1757 to 1796,* John Murray, London, 1817.

Williams, J.C., ed., *The Report on the Census of Oudh,* vol. I, *General Report,* Oudh Government Press, Lucknow, 1869.

Wilson, H.H., *Sketch on the Religious Sects of the Hindus,* Bishop's College Press, Calcutta, 1846.

———, *Hindu Religions;* or *An Account of the Various Religious Sects of India,* The Society for the Resucitation of Indian Literature, Calcutta, 1899.

Van der Veer, Peter, *Gods on Earth: Management of Religious Experience and Identity in a North Indian Pilgrimage Centre,* Oxford University Press, Delhi, 1989.

Yule, Henry and A.C. Burnell, *Hobson-Jobson: A Glossary of Colloquial Anglo-Indian Words and Phrases etc.,* Rupa & Co., Calcutta, 1990.

JADUNATH SARKAR

A History of the Dasnami Naga Sannyasis

Foreword

The Dashnami Sampradaya is perhaps the most powerful monastic order, which has played a great part in the history of India.

The cult of the Nagas, naked ascetics, has a pretero-historic ancestry. It must have been founded when Uttar Pradesh and Bihar were no more than swamps. The famous Mohenjo-daro seal depicts Pashupati sitting naked and being worshipped by animals. The Vedas refer to the longhaired ascetics. Lord Shiva sitting on Mount Kailash, almost naked and besmeared with ashes, is their appropriate guardian deity.

Monastic orders of such ascetics existed in India long before the dawn of history. The Greeks, when they came with Alexander, met the naked philosophers, the Gymnosophists. Buddha and Mahavir were in fact leaders of two Orders of monks who later spread their doctrines. The *Digambars,* the Nagas of the Jain persuasion, are still found. Most of the Nagas go without ceremonial occasions. Some of them, however, adhere to their vows of keeping no possessions.

Most of the Nagas belong to the Dashnami Sampradaya organised by Shankaracharya the oldest, the biggest and the most effective of our monastic Orders.

On initiation, the Dashnami, as the very name indicates, is given a name combined with one of the ten words: Giri, Puri, Bharati, Van, Aranya, Parvat, Sagar, Tirth, Ashram or Saraswati. The initiate has to make strict vows not to indulge in more then one meal a day; not to beg for food from more than seven houses; not to sleep any where but upon the ground; not to salute, not to praise, nor speak ill of anyone; not to bow to anyone but a sanyasi of a higher order; not to cover himself with a cloth, unless it were a *bhagwa* (brownish-red) colour.

Like other Orders, it has its learned sannyasis, who enjoy spiritual leadership; its yogis, who specialise in yogic practices; its *mahants*, who look after the temples, monasteries and *akharas* as well and its ordinary sadhus and lay members, called Darbari *Gosais*, who marry and follow normal avocations in various parts of the country, but are pledged to the glory of the Order.

The Dashnamis are divided into two sections: the *Shastradharis*, who specialise in sacred lore, and the *Astradharis*, who specialise in arms. The sannyasis, are ranged in four ranks: *Kutichak, Bahudak, Hansa* and *Parmahansa*—the last being the highest. The fighting wing is organised into *akharas*, and, in the past, played a historic role

Rajya Bhavan Lucknow,
Uttar Pradesh.

K.M. MUNSHI

Preface to the First Edition

The size of this book has been greatly reduced from what was originally planned, because of the necessity to reduce the cost of printing, and therefore many useful details have been unavoidably cut out. But it is the author's hope that even in its shortened form this book will give a general picture of the main course of the history of the Dasnami sect and their past service and present position in the life of the Indian nation. The chapters on Rajendra Giri and his disciples have been written by Professor Nirod Bhusan Roy M.A. (of the Santiniketan University). He has incorporated my *previous* writings on the subject (in my *Fall on the Mughal Empire*, 4 vols.) and also used my manuscript notes and summaries on that period. His final draft has been revised and passed by me before printing. I thank him for this collaboration, which has made it possible to complete the book without further delay.

As the author, I must thank Mahant Dattagir of the Nirvani Akhara, Allahabad, for the invaluable help which he has given me by the mass of original documents and authentic records placed by him in my hands. But for these materials a trustworthy history of the sect would have been impossible. For thirty years Mahant Dattagir has corresponded and travelled all over India, visiting *maths*, princely states, and notable individuals and exploring their records and taking transcripts of useful documents for this history. If there is any merit in this volume the reader's gratitude is due to this history-loving monk, Dattagirji.

Jadunath Sarkar

CHAPTER 1

Life of Shankarāchārya

The entire course of Hindu life and thought after the age of Buddhism has been dominated by the influence of two intellectual giants and made to flow in two nearly allied channels which were laid down in their teachings. Between them they have divided the empire of Hindu philosophy and religious organisation. Other leaders of thought, I admit, there have been among us; but they were men of lesser note; they have influenced smaller or local sections of the population only, and the philosophy that inspires their teaching has derived itself from one or other of these two originators of thought, sometimes in a modified, sometimes in a hostile form. Among the founders of Vaishnav theology, Nimbārka and Mādhwa Āchārya, Chaitanya and Vallabh Āchārya occupy the highest places and exert the widest influence; Chaitanya dominates the religious life of Bengal, Orissa and (partly) Assam, while Vallabha's sect prevails in Gujrat, Mewar and some other regions.

These two directors of Hindu religious thought as we know it to-day, are Shankarāchārya and Rāmānuja. Both combined saintly purity with Shastric learning and intellectual acumen of the highest degree; both have continued to be venerated by millions as two incarnations of the God-head. Of them Rāmānuja was later in point of time, and his influence has spread over a smaller circle of men and a more restricted empire than Shankar's. Moreover, the school of Rāmānuja is professedly a breakaway from that of Shankar, it carries his philosophy on to a new line and therefore implies the previous existence of the latter.

So much for Shankar's place in the history of the evolution of Indian philosophy. His influence on the daily life of the people has been equally great, and this marks him out from mere abstract philosophers, however, eminent such philosophers might be in thought.

Europe has long debated the question as to how Christianity could convert the Roman empire. A century and a quarter after Gibbon's famous analysis of the causes of this marvellous success, English scholars have come to the conclusion that the early Christian Church by imitating the administrative organisation of the Roman Empire, built up a system of work which no other religion had adopted and which made its conversion of the Roman world so easy and Speedy. The organisation of the Dasnāmi orders is the eternal monument to Shankarāchārya's disciples who completed the great Master's mission on earth, as will be described in Chapter 5 of this book.

Long before the birth of Shankar, monastic orders, or organised brotherhoods of religious devotees living together under the discipline of a superior authority and coordinating the efforts of different houses of the same sect, had been given to India by Buddha. He had valued his monks as instrument of his religion so highly that he had made the Monastic order called *Sangha* a member of the Buddhist Trinity, equal to Buddha and *Dharma:* "I seek refuge with the Buddha; I seek refuge with the *Dharma,* I seek refuge with the *Sangha,*" this is the cardinal prayer of the Buddhist in every land where that faith is still pure. And monastic regulations called *Vinaya,* are an essential part of the Buddhist scriptures. Solitary anchorites and religious ascetics living apart from the busy world and seeking their individual salvation had been known in India from the Vedic age, or probably even earlier, from the first dawning of conscience in the human race. But the Dasnāmi orders made Hindu monachism serve the good of the vast body of Hindu society, of which the only parallel was supplied by Mahayan Buddhism in its best days.

The Dasnāmi monks have held the twofold ideal of *astra* and *shastra* (sword and scripture), i.e. the cultivation of theology for the spiritual education of the people and the pursuit of arms for the defence of their religion against the attacks of brute force. In this respect they have anticipated the fighting monks of Christianity, who originated as late as the twelfth century;[1] while the *Nagas* or militant Sannyasis of India first appear in history several centuries earlier. Therefore, a study of these orders must start at its source, with the life and work of Shankarāchārya.

The extant biographies of Shankar were all composed several centuries after his death. Two of them hold a prominent place, namely (1) *Samkahepa-Shankara-jayah,* written in verse by Mādhavāchārya, and (2) *Shankara-Digvijay* by Ananta-Ānanda Giri. This second work is much later than Mādhav's book, though it has been wrongly ascribed by some to Shankar's personal disciple Ānanda-giri, the famous commentator. Both these works profess to derive their information from a now lost life of Shankar, which is traditionally supposed to have been written by a direct disciple of Shankar. Nearly 800 verses alleged to be quoted from this lost book, are given in the old commentary on Mādhava's work by Dhanpati Suri, and some more in Ananta-Ānanda-Giri's book. Thus, the modern historian of Shankar is left with only the legend of Shankar as developed by pious tradition, and he must try to judge of the narratives in the light of probability and the known facts about the Indian world in the supposed age of Shankar.

Leaving out the supernatural legends that have gathered round the name of Shankar in the course of several centuries, we shall trace the outline of his career as far as it is now possible to reconstruct it. There may be questions about the exact epoch of Shankar and the incidents of his life; but there can be no two opinions about his profound influence on Indian religion and philosophy in all subsequent ages. It is his synthetic monist philosophy (*Adwaita-vad*) which is of primary concern to mankind. Therefore, only a

[1] The monastic order of Knights Templers was founded in AD 1118 and that of the Teutonic Knights in AD 1190.

brief summary of his legendary life will precede our exposition of his philosophy and our description of the organisation of his church.

More than a thousand years ago, at the village of Keledi in the Kerala country (or Cochin) in the extreme south of the Indian Peninsula, near the bank of the Purnā River, there lived a Brāhman named Vidyādhirāj. He was devoted solely to learning and piety, as the entire village had been granted as a free gift (*agrahar*) to a Brāhman colony which settled round a temple to the god Shiva, built by an ancient king named Rajashekhar (who must not be confounded with the historical personage, the author of *Karpura manjari.* His scholarly son Shiva-guru and saintly daughter-in-law Sati, were devoted adorers of Shiva, and by the grace of that god they were blessed with a son of marvellous beauty and superhuman intellectual power. The boy, having lost his father in infancy, was sent at the age of five to a teacher's house, where in two years he mastered the entire cycle of Hindu learning that others normally take sixteen years to go through. Returning to his mother's lonely home, this infant prodigy set up as a teacher of the Shāstrās and drew crowds of pupils by his wonderful genius and scholarship. Even the local Raja besought his aid in correcting and improving his own three dramatic compositions in the Sanskrit language. At the age of eight, the boy-professor was inwardly seized with *vairagya* or the passion for renouncing the world and its joys, while his fond mother was scheming to marry him to a suitable bride and settle him at home. But home is not the place for a redeemer of mankind. Shankar persuaded his mother to set him free and work out his evident destiny. He took up the robe of Brahmachari or theological student and set out from home with a view to learning the rules and practices of monastic devotion from a master of spiritual knowledge (*Brahma-vidya*).

Going to Onkār-Māndhātā, a rocky island in the middle of the Narmadā River, Shankar entered himself as a disciple of the celebrated philosopher Govindapāda, who was popularly believed to be the ancient sage Patanjali himself, living a thousand years in a state of yogic trance in a cave nearby. The primeval sage awoke at the arrival of his destined disciple and heir to his philosophical mission. Here under his expert teaching, Shankar mastered the full theory and practice of *yoga.* At last the preceptor addressed him thus: "My son! I have nothing more to teach you, I know that you are Siva himself, come to earth in human shape for teaching the divine lore of Monism (*Adwaita Brahma-vidya*). . . . I have fitted you with knowledge for the task, and I now throw away the earthly body which I had preserved these thousand years solely for this object." Here Shankar was initiated as a Sannyasi by Govindapāda and clad in the red robe which is the outward mark of Hindu monks. Then after bidding Shankar to go to Benares, the religious centre of all the Hindus, as the best place for his propaganda. Govindapāda passed into the *Nirvana* of voluntarily suspended animation by yogic power (cf. *Kalidas*: *Yogen-ante tanu-tyajam*).

At Benares, Shankar's new exposition of the Shāstrās and his persuasive commentary on the *Brahma Sutra* (aphorisms of God-knowledge) and the supernatural genius displayed by such a youthful teacher, created the greatest astonishment among the circle of scholars and devotees who had assembled there from all parts of India. The pandits who presumed to challenge him to controversy, were quickly silenced by his wonderful scholarship, logical keenness, and gift of lucid exposition. At this holy city he made his first disciple, Sanandan, a Brāhman youth from the bank of the Kaveri in the Chola country (Eastern *Karnatak*), who had come there on a tour in search of a true teacher; he was instinctively drawn towards Shankar, and after having been tested for some days was found to be of the true stuff, and was initiated by Shankar as a monk. He became the great Master's first apostle under the name of Padmapāda. This disciple lived to be his right-hand man in theological writing and propaganda work.

A charming story is told in Mādhav's poetical life (Canto VI, Stanzas 25-51), One day Shankar, on his way to the holy river at Benares, met a man of the lowest caste (*Antyaja*) and shouted to him, "Be off; dont pollute me with your touch". The seeming sweeper replied, "You consider me as separate from yourself, and yet you profess to be a Monist and to hold that the Divine Soul animates all creation and that the material world is a mere illusion without any real existence; You thus admit that there is a material distinction between a pure and an impure man." The argument was unanswerable. Shankar was dumbfounded and humbled himself before the stranger, who then revealed himself as the God Shiva in disguise and vanished after pronouncing this blessing, "You will triumphantly esablish the Monist view of the godhead (*Adwaita-vad*) in the world".

And at Benares, too, Shankar had another very interesting encounter (Mādhav, Canto VII, Stanzas 1-57). One day, he is said to have been accosted by an old Brāhman looking like a simpleton. It was really Vyās, the composer of the sacred Vedas and the epic *Mahābhārat*, who had come to test him. The course of their controversy is of extreme interest, but it can be fully appreciated only by readers who have a thorough knowledge of Sanskrit grammar and philosophy. At last the highly gratified sage Vyās revealed himself as his trueself and left after pronouncing this blessing:

"My child: Fate gave you eight years of life; you have earned eight more by your genius (*Sudhiya*). And by the grace of Shiva you will enjoy sixteen additional years of life, while your commentary (*Bhashya*) of my (*Brahma Sutra*) will live as long as the sun, the moon and the stars shall endure. During these sixteen years, with your words which are ever vigilant in uprooting the sprouts of pride in the champions of false faith (Dualism), you will make the opponents of Monism give up their belief in the distinct existence of the Creator and Creation (*Bheda Vidya*)".

Thereafter, Shankar was seized with a longing to meet Kumārila Bhatta, the first great Hindu scholar who had raised his head against the dominant Buddhistic philosophy and tried to restore the supremacy of the Vedic religion. He was a Brāhman of the

Chola Country[2] and the paternal uncle of the famous Buddhist philosopher Dharma-Kirti.

Shankar met the aged Kumārila at Allahabad. That venerable scholar was then on the point of death. But he was so impressed by reading Shankar's commentary on the *Brahma Sutra* that he blessed the young scholar and predicted that Shankar would establish Vedantic monotheism (*Adwaita*) for more extensively and triumphantly than he himself had succeeded in doing (Mādhav, Vll. 62-end).

Then, as directed by Kumārila with his last breath, Shankar went to Mahishmati on the Narmadā, in order to meet Mandan Mishra, whom Kumārila held to be his best pupil and almost his second self. Mandan was the highest expert practitioner of the Vedic sacrifices and other rituals in that age. He was blessed with a wife named Saraswati (*alias* Ubhay Bhārati) who even surpassed him in learning and was popularly held to be the Goddess of Learning (Saraswati) incarnate. She alone was fitted to act as judge in the ensuing theological controversy between her husband and Shankar.

The story goes that when our shaven-headed youthful mendicant from the Kerala country, was rudely turned out by the porters at the gate of Mandan's palatial residence, he displayed his supernatural yogic powers and effected an entrance into the hall by vaulting over its wall, to the surprise and anger of the aristocratic Mandan Then ensued a word-combat between the two philosophers which is the delight of all who can understand Sanskrit. The play on the double meaning of words and the logical thrust and parry of their rival tongues, which had been sharpened by the constant practice of grammatical and philosophical disputation, in the course of this short preliminary skirmish

[2] Kumārila's south-Indian origin has been disputed with admirable arguments by Ramaswami and a Bengali scholar. (See the *Bharatvarsha*, Bengali Magazine, for Jyaishtha 1347.)

between the two, have been given in Mādhava's biography, Canto VIII. It is unique in Sanskrit literature, but defies translation into English without spoiling its full effect.

Then followed a regular intellectual duel. For 18 days in succession the two debated before the lady Saraswati seated in the judge's seat. At last Mandan admitted himself beaten by the superior learning of Shankar, became his disciple and agreed to write a Vārtika on Shankar's famous Bhashya of the *Brahma Sutra*. This work was destined to establish Vedantic monism against Budhism and other hostile creeds in the Indian world of scholarship. Mandan renounced the world and turned sannyasi; his wife gave up her earthly body because a Sanyasi cannot be accompanied by a wife. Such is the legend.

After his long drawn-out victory over Mandan Mishra, Shankar set out on the conquest of the then known world of scholarship. This is the famous *Digvijaya* or world-empire of the intellect, in the course of which he defeated the champions of Buddhism, Jainism, Tantricism and every other religion that refused to accept Monism. The details fill many pages in his extant biographies (Canto XIV).

Then, at the end of a long tour of pilgrimage (Cantos XI and XII), after visits to Srishailam (an all but inaccessible hilltop in the heart of the Nala Mālāi forest of the Kurnool district), Gokarna on the West Coast, and other famous shrines, Shankar settled for a time at the forest-village of Shringa-Giri (Sringeri) in the Western Chalukya empire. At a Brāhman village named Sriveli, he gained as his disciple, an infant prodigy thenceforth known as Hastāmalak Āchārya. In the pure, lovely and solitary environment of nature which he found at Sringeri, Shankar founded his first monastery, on the bank of the Tungabhadra River, around which a colony of his lay admirers and followers soon sprang up. The Raja of the country and his officers gave every help, thatched cottages for residence were built by the hundred for pilgrims and devotees, so that the place grew into a hermitage or *tapovan* of Rishis. Among the permanent structures the first to be built was a temple to the Goddess of learning (*Sarada*). This typified the combination of theological learning with daily devotional rites, which is the cardinal point of Shankar's creed and the subject of his constant charge to his disciple.[3]

Shankar passed many years at Sringeri, composing books and teaching his followers. This was the most fertile period of his brain and the literary products of this period have remained as his permanent legacy for the instruction and consolation of seekers after truth.

He had previously enlisted among his disciples three men destined to be leaders after him: Padmapād, Sureshwar and Hastamalak, and now at Sringeri he secured another genius, Trotak Āchārya, formerly called Giri.

These four with other disciples formed a great school of learning and wrote many Sanskrit works popularising Shankar's teaching in a clear charming style. Sringeri thus became a living fountain of God-knowledge and Hindu scholarship.

From Sringeri Shankar paid a visit to his native village in order to attend his mother in her last illness, perform her funeral, and dispose of her property. The king of the Kerala country highly honoured him and by his advice turned to the improvement of the condition of his kingdom and people in many ways. Then followed another four of intellectual conquest or *digvijaya,* this time southwards to Cape Comorin Mādhav, Canto XV). In the course of it, every sect that he met with at last came over to his conception of religion and worship. At Conjeveram he established temples which became in time a centre of Hindu learning famous throughout the continent. At Jagannāth Puri he extinguished the predominance of Buddhism and founded the Govardhan Math as the second or eastern centre of his church, the other two being the Sāradā Math of Dwārka in the west (Kathiawad) and the Joshi Math of Kedārnāth in the north (Himalayas).

[3] There is a different legend too, which states that she was allowed to go to Sringeri and pass the rest of her life in the hermitage there.

No part of India and 'Greater India' from Balkh to Cambodia was, so runs the tradition, left unvisited by Shankar, and everywhere he reformed the people's religion, established his own faith, and founded schools of learning. At the Sārda-pith in Kasmir, situated at the confluence of the Krishna Gangā and the Madhumati, embosomed among seven snow-clad hills, the assembled Pandits representing all the schools of Indian thought conferred on him the title of Omniscient (*Sarvajna*), and the Goddess Saraswati acclaimed the justice of this award (Mādhav, Canto XVI). At last, travelling to Badri-Kedārnāth in the Central Himalayas, he cast off his mortal body there at the age of thirty-two (Mādhav, Canto XVI, St. 93-end).

The Math at Sringeri is situated in the midst of a tract of land about 8 miles long by 6 miles wide, which was given as a rent-free endowment (*jagir*) to the head of the Shiva Monastery, by Harihara, the first Emperor of Vijayanagar, in 1346, according to an inscription preserved at the Math. The inscription mentions among the donors, Harihara's four brothers Kampanna, Bukanna, Narappa and Mudappa and his son-in-law Ballappa Dannayaka and the latter's son Savanna. It is now included in the Koppa Taluq of the Mysore kingdom. The river Tunga runs through it from the south-west to the north-east.

The village of Sringeri stands on the left bank of the Tunga, about 15 miles south-west of the *qasba* of Koppa, in 13° 25' North latitude and 75° 19' East longitude. The name Sringeri is a corruption of Sringa giri or *Rishya Sringa-giri,* the place where Vibhāndaka Rishi performed penance and where *Rishya Sringa,* a character celebrated in Valmiki's *Ramayan* was born. Shankar Āchārya settled here as directed by the image of Sāradāmmā or Saraswati; which he had brought from Kashmir. There are 120 temples in this sacred village.

Sringeri consists of a long street, with a loop on one side, encircling a small hill called Sringagiri, on which stands a temple of Mallikarjuna. At the head of the street is the Math of the Jagatguru, within which stands the temple of Sāradāmmā, whose image is said to be of pure gold. At the side of the Math is the temple of Vidyā Shankara, an ornamental building of the Chalukyan style, on a raised terrace. Round the outer wall are sculptured image of various gods. At an angle on the right of the front entrance is a statue of Vyās, wearing a conical cap, the sacred thread and a *dhoti,* his right hand is raised in the *abhaya* posture. He is imparting instruction to Shankar Āchārya, whose statue is at right angles to him. Shankar has a palmyra leaf book in his left hand. Towards Vidyāranya-pura on the bank of the Tunga, is a small temple with an image of Shankar Āchārya seated as an ascetic (*yati*) (*Mysore Gazetteer,* II. 407-9).

CHAPTER 2

The Date of Shankarāchārya

For nearly a hundred years now, the extact time of Shankar-āchārya has been a point of dispute among scholars, and the range of difference of opinion as to the year of his birth has varied from 44 BC (held by Swāmi Prajnānanda Saraswati, a highly erudite modern Bengali Dean and monk) to AD 788 (held by Prof. K.B. Pathak, and accepted after him by Max Müller and almost all the other modern scholars). In between the two, a very learned and widely travelled Bengali scholar named Rajendra Nath Ghose who later became a Dasnāmi monk under the name of Swāmi Chidghananda, has suggested the year AD 686 and he has refuted at great length and with wide critical learning and convincing arguments, the theory of Swāmi Prajnananda. All other proposed dates, including K.T. Telang's conjectural "end of the sixth century AD", may be dismissed without consideration, because modern Indology has advanced so far since Telang wrote that we are on surer ground as to Shankar's times and can now confine his career within a short time range with almost absolute certainty. Our difficulty is due to two facts: (1) No life of Shankar-āchārya has been preserved that was not written at least six centuries later than his death, and (2) No authentic old historical record has been preserved in Shankara's first great monastery, the Sringeri Math.

Taking the first point, the earliest biographies of Shankar are two Sanskrit works, (a) the *Shankar-Jaya* of Mādhavāchārya, (b) the *Shankar Dig-Vijaya* of Ānandagiri. Scholars are now agreed that this Mādhav was not the same person as the famous

Vidyānanya, who is credited with having helped in the foundation of the Vijayanagar empire in the fourteenth century AD, but a later and more obscure scholar. They are also of opinion that the other biographer Ānandagiri, who calls himself in his own work 'Anant-Ānand-giri' was not the famous commentator Ānanda-giri who was a personal disciple of Shankar, but some Brāhman who flourished in the fifteenth century. All other lives of Shankar are still more modern.

What authentic old records did these two earliest biographers of Shankar use in compiling their books? None at all; they merely put the current popular traditions down in writing, and we know how historical error by the hundred creep into a narrative which has been handed down from mouth without writing, for more than six centuries. Mādhav states that his *Samkshepa Shankar Jaya* is based on materials compiled from an earlier work—"Verily I am collecting here the substance of the old *Shankar Jaya*". But he nowhere quotes from this old source, nor does he tell us who wrote that biography and when. In a commentary on Mādhav's biography written by Dhanpati Suri, nearly 800 verses alleged to have come from the old and now lost *Shankar Vijaya,* are quoted, and some more in Ananta-Ānanda Giri's book, but they do not give us much historical information, nor is their genuineness beyond doubt.

Secondly, the succession list of the gurus at Sringeri Math from Shankar downwards, is now shown to visitors, was compiled about 1875, by the then Mohant Narasingha Bhārati VIII. R.N. Ghose when visiting Sringeri during the Mohantship of the next pontiff, Shiv-abhinav Nrishingha (AD 1818-1912), was told by the latter, "At the request of modern archaeologists, my guru constructed' this list, in which Shankar Āchārya's birth date is given as 14 Vikram Samvat and his immediate successor Sureshwar is stated to have lived as the head of the monastary for eight hundred years, dying in AD 757. You may take it as true or false as you like" (Bengali V. D. vol. 1, p. 98 n).

Now, in this succession list no other *mahant* is given a supernatural life of eight centuries, but all (except one) of eighty-five years or much less, like normal human beings. This credibly long life of Sureshwar has been explained away by some modern writers by the theory that Sureshwar died after a normal life of seventy or eighty years, but that the names of all his successors till the year AD 757 have been lost through the perishing of the old records, so that the next *mahant* who came to the office in AD 755 has been wrongly described as Sureshwar's immediate successor. This very defence condemns the entire list of names before AD 757 as untrustworthy. No paper earlier than the nineteenth century has been preserved on the Sringeri Math, and the name list can be accepted as correct at the best from the thirteenth century downwards, but not earlier than that period.

R.N. Ghose has suggested a plausible theory, that Shankar's alleged birth date, year 30 of the Vikram era, means, not the 30th year of the famous Vikram Samvat beginning in 57 BC and named after Vikramaditya of Ujjain, but the 30th year of the reign of Vikramānka I, of the western Chalukya dynasty (which would make the year equivalent to AD 700).

A copper-plate shown at Sringeri, ascribing a pre-christian antiquity to Shankar Āchārya has been similarly rejected by scholars as a modern fabrication, on epigraphic, linguistic and historical grounds. The mere fact that something is found inscribed in the Sanskrit or Kanarese language on a copper-plate does, not, in itself, make it a genuine document or even prove that it was produced at the time alleged in the inscription. A genuine inscription of King Harsha tells us that forged copper plates (*Kutashasana*) were known in his time (seventh century).

We are thus left to the internal evidence of Shankar's writings and to dated authentic references to him, in determining his age. Happily modern researches in Tibet, China and Cambodia, besides India, have helped to throw reliable sidelights on him, which will be now discussed here.

According to the two earliest lives of Shankar, he met Kumārila Bhatta, an old man and his senior. Now, we know from other sources that Kumārila was certainly alive about AD 650, and came after Bhartrihari, whose verses are quoted in Kumārila's *Tantra-vartika.*

Secondly, the same authorities say that young Shankar was initiated by Govinda Yati, whose guru was Gaudapāda. This Gaudapāda's *Bhashya* is known to have been translated into Chinese about AD 570-600.

Thirdly, one of these two writers of tradition (Mādhav) speaks of the famous Sanskrit authors, Bana Bhatta, Mayura and Dandin as having lived in the age of Shankar, and we know that Bāna Bhatta lived in the first half of the AD seventh century.

Leaving traditions aside as of doubtful value, we must now examine Shankar's own writings and see what light they throw on his age. In his commentary on the *Brahma Sutra* Shankar quotes the *Alambana Pariksha* of Dignāga (who lived AD 550-600). Shankar's own disciples Sureshwar and Ānand Giri quote Dharma-kirti, a famous Buddhistic scholar, who lived between 640 and 660, because Itsing mentions him as a recent celebrity, while Yuan Chwang who had left India earlier in 39, does not mention his name. Secondly, Shankar in his *Bhashya* mentions a king named Purna Varmā, and there was such a king in Magadh between AD 590 and 630. Shankara was unknown even by name or fame to Yuan Chwang and Itsing who travelled in India between 629 and 682 and who have mentioned all the great Buddhistic scholars and their Hindu opponents then living or dead sometime before.

So much for the internal evidence. Beside this, a date between AD 688 and 788 for the birth of Shankar Āchārya is exactly in agreement with the known history of Buddhism in India and the course of the changes in the religious thought of this land, Kern, writing on the authority of the erudite historians Tārānāth and Wassalief, states, "It is in the sixth and seventh centuries that Buddhist scholasticism had its palmy days. . . . On the whole Buddhism was still flourishing when Yuan Chwang visited India (AD 630-43). The decline dates, roughly speaking, from AD 750, Kumārila and Shankar live in the traditions of the Buddhists as the most formidable enemies to their creed, as the two great dialecticians whose activity caused the ruin of Buddhism in India" (*Manual of Indian Buddhism* 130-1).

Finally, when we make a comparative study of the style and words of Shankar's writings side by side with the works of other Sanskrit poets and prose writers of known dates, it becomes indisputably clear that Shankar wrote after Kālidās and Bhartrihari, but before the growth of the wordy logic and worthless conventional poetry which characterised the Sanskrit literature produced in the tenth century and later. Hence, Shankar's place in the eighth or ninth century AD exactly fits in with the known course of the development of the Sanskrit language and literature in India.

In the above discussion on the age of Shankar, use has been made of the following authorities mainly: In English (1) Mahamahopadhyay V.S. Shastri in *I.H. Quarterly*, vol. VI, p. 169 and vol. IX, p. 979. In Sanskrit, (2) P.G. Ranade's Introduction to the Ānandashram (Poona) edition of the Mādhav's *Shankar Digvijay* (3rd edn., 19: 2 (3) Gurunath Venkatesh Kittur's *Shri Shankar Vijay Churnika* (Nirnay Sagar Press, Bombay, 1898). In Marathi, (4) Gosavi Prithvigir Harigiri's *Gosavi Tyacha Sampradaya,* vol. I (1926), pp. 216-28. In Bengali the most valuable and detailed source is (5) Swāmi Prajnānand Saraswati's *Vedanta Darshaner Itihas,* vol. I. as edited and criticised by Rajendra Nath Ghose (1925), vol. I, pp. 90-146, (6) R.N. Ghosh's *Shankar O Rāmānuja.*

Previous to these Mr. C.N. Krishnaswami Aiyar's *Shankar Āchārya: His Life and Teachings* (4th edn., Madras), had summarized the views of scholars. All earlier and now more or lees obsolete writings on this question, have been left out of account.

Most fortunately for our inquiry, there exists the record of a man who had personally studied under Shankar Āchārya and who caused this fact to be stated in a stone inscription carved in his life-time, in a certain year between AD 878 and 887. This inscription has been discovered by the French and given to the world by the famous scholar G. Coedes in his *Inscriptions du*

Cambodge, vol. I, 1937), pp. 37 ff. Dr. R.C. Majumdar has made it known to us in an article in the *Indian Review,* 1940. On a pillar of the temple known as Prasat Kandol Dom in Cambodia (Indo-China) there is an inscription in Sanskrit verses recording that an image of Shiva entitled Bhadreshwar, was installed by a Pandit named Shiva Soma, who was the Guru of King Indra-Verman of Kamboja, between AD 878 and 887. Among the verses describing the scholarship and piety of this Shiva Soma there is one (verse no. 39) which tells us that "He learnt the Shāstras from Bhagavān named Shankar himself, whose lotus-like feet were rubbed by the heads, of scholars coming to him like rows of bees."[1]

This proves that Shankar-Āchārya was living and teaching in the first half of the ninth century, and that scholars from all parts of the Hindu world were drawn to him by the fame of his scholarship and sanctity.

This date is supported by the *Jagat-guru Paramparastotra,* still read at the Sringeri Math, which says that Shankar was born in Kaliyuga era 3889-710 Shalivāhan Shaka AD 788.

1 Combodian Sanskrit inscription —
येनाधीतानि शस्त्राणि भगबच्छंकरा ह्वयात।

CHAPTER 3

Shankarāchārya's Teachings

The greatness of Shankarāchārya is best expressed in the following sentences by Sister Nivedita of the Rāmakrishna Vivekānand Order: Western people can hardly imagine a personality like that of Shankar Āchārya. In the course of a few years to have nominated the founders of no less than ten great religious orders, of which four have fully retained their prestige to the present day, to have acquired such a mass of Sanskrit learning as to create a distinct philosophy and impress himself on the Scholarly imagination of India, is a pre-eminence that twelve hundred years have not sufficed to shake; to have written poems whose grandeur makes them unmistakable, even to foreign and unlearned ears, and at the same time to have lived with his disciples in all the radiant love and simple pathos of the saints, this is the greatness that we must appreciate but cannot understand.

We contemplate with wonder and delight the devotion of Francis of Assissi, the intellect of Abelard, the virile force and freedom of Martin Luther, and the political efficiency of Ignatius Loyola; but who could imagine all these united in one person?"

Shankar's philosophy is known as *Adwaita-vad* or the Theory of Monism. Briefly speaking he held that matter or the created universe is a mere illusion, as it has no existence apart from the creative Mind (*Atman* or Brahma), who is the sole Reality. This Universal Soul dwells in every individual man, other creatures and material objects; hence the recognition of one's own separate personality or individual existence, feelings and interests (in

Sanskrit, *ahamkar*) is a supreme folly, and the highest sage or saint is the man who, by constant meditation and righteous conduct, has attained to the truth that he is noway different from other created beings, but stands as the personation of the Universal Soul which dwells within all of us (*Aham Brahma, Aham Shiva*).

Detailed expositions of Shankar's system will be found in every book on Indian philosophy, and this volume is not the proper place for repeating the same. But in order to prove that Shankar's doctrine was not a dreamy pantheism, I give some quotations from his own writings (translated by me) which will show that he insisted on as high a standard of right conduct or holy living as any revealed religion of the world. The objective method followed by me will bring the subject home to even the most unphilosophic common reader.

TRANSLATION

"Who is thy wife and who thy son? This world is a very strange place. Brother, just ponder on the question, 'Whose thou art and whence hast thou come?' Boast not of your wealth, followers, or youth; in a twinkle or the eye. Time snatches them all away.[1]

Cast off this unreal universe and quickly enter into the Supreme Brahma through knowledge. Tremulous as a drop of water on a lotus-leaf, is human life; it is only the society of good men, however momentary, that can enable us to be ferried over the ocean of existence.

Day follows night, eveniug follows morning, autumn and spring seasons follow each other in regular succession. Time plays, Life oozes out, and yet man will not abandon his windy hopes.

[1] Many centuries later an English poet unconsciously copied this, when wrote—

The boast' of heraldry, the pomp of power,
And all that beauty, all that wealth e'er gave,
Awaits alike the inevitable hour,
The paths of glory lead but to the grave. (Gray).

His limbs are falling off, his head is grey, his mouth is toothless, the stick in his hand is shaking; and yet he will not give up his bag of vain desires.

Dost thou wish to attain to Vishnu-hood promptly? Then be the same to all; make no distinction, as of love and hate, in thy attitude to friend and foe, sons, and friends; Vishnu is present in thee, in me and in all other men. Why then do you vainly lose patience with me in anger? Behold the Soul of all others as present within thee: everywhere give up the notion of the difference of individual personality. Recognise the soul within you, realise who thou art, by conquering lust and anger, greed and delusion. Fools who have not attained to self-knowledge will rot deep down in hell (*Moha-mudgar*).

Who is a captive? He who is devoted to earthly things.

What is liberation? The conquest of desire for earthly things.

What is the darkest hell? Your own body.

What is heaven? The total removal of passions.

Who is the happy man? He who is absorbed in religious meditation.

Who is wakeful? The man whose conscience can distinguish between good and evil.

Who are your enemies? Your five organs of the senses; but conquer your passions, and your very senses will be your friends.

What is highest of ornaments? A moral character.

What is the holiest place of all pilgrimage? Your own mind when pure.

What things are abominable? Women and gold.

What should we constantly hear? The counsel of our religious preceptors and the teachings of the scriptures

How can we attain to God? Through association with the good, charity, right judgement and contentment (*Mani Ratna Mala*).

Verily, blessed are the monks with loin-bands (*kaupin*) for all their clothing.

Blessed indeed are the *kaupin*-clad, whose bed is the root of trees, whose hands are not employed in gathering food, and who fling away Fortune like a tattered old quilt.

They, they along are blessed, who find enternal solace in the natural delight of their hearts, all of whose passions are controlled and pacified, and who revel day and night in divine communion.

Truly they alone can be called blessed who constantly chant the name of Brahma (The Universal soul), who reflect, "I am Brahma", and who wander in the four quarter, living on food given as alms (*kaupina-panchak*).

"Who art thou, child? and whose son? with-her art thou going? What's thy name, and whence hast thou come? Tell me clearly."

"I am not man or deity or aerial spirit I am neither Brāhman, Kshatriya, Vaishya or Shudra by caste; I am not a celebate student, householder, forest-dweller nor homeless mendicant by my stage of life. I am the self-conscious Soul. . . . It am the eternally perceptive soul . . . boundless and free from all distinctive attributes such as the sky is, and the cause of the activitv of the mind and the senses".

I am that eternally-intelligent soul which is inherent in all objects, though no object can touch him; I am ever pure and clear as the sky. As pure crystals take the colour of the object in which they are set, so different minds imagine the diversity of personality (instead of preceiving the unchangeable oneness of all, who are inspired by the same *Atma*) [*Hastamalak*].

I am not body nor any organ of the senses; I am not consciousness of individuality, nor life, nor intellect. Away from wife and son, land and wealth, I am the Eternal Witness merged in the individual soul, I am Shiva.

As a fool mistakes a rope for a snake, so do mankind mistake the All-pervasive Soul for a creature. . . . He who is truly enlightened in God-knowledge gets rid of this illusion; he realises "I am not a creature, I am Shiva (the Universal Soul)".

This world is no other than my own self. The countless things we see outside ourselves are a mere illusion of the mind (and possessed of no real existence) like the images which a mirror produce by reflection. All things manifest themselves in me, the one (*Adwaita*). Therefore I am *Shiva*.

I am not a body; how then can I have birth or death? I am not life; how then can I have hunger or thirst? I am not heart; how then can I feel grief or stupor? I am not active; how then can I be subject to bondage or liberation? (*Atma-shatak*).

I am companion-less, beyond doubt; I manifest myself as *Sat-chit* and *Ananda*. I am that changeless I (i.e. Brahma).

I am eternally pure and detached. I am formless, imperishable; I manifest myself as the Perfect Bliss (*Bhumanānda*). I am that absolute I (i.e. Brahma).

I am pure Consciousness, I am the self-revelling

Soul, I am the one indivisible bliss, I reveal myself by myself alone, I am made up solely of consciousness (*chit*), I am the Supreme Soul (*Atma*), the ever-constant I.

No name have I, nor form; in Consciousness (*chit*) am I known, I am the changeless imperishable I, manifested in bliss.

I am beyond growth, beyond action, I am the soul of all and eternal, the deathless I (*Brahma Namavali Mala*). The pitcher is made out of clay; therefore a pitcher has no existence independent of clay, the term 'pitcher' being merely a technical name. Brahma is the sole Existence (*Sat*), therefore all that is created by Brahma is existent (*Sat*), because creation has no real existence apart from the Creator (*Brahma*).

He who denies this truth has a mind engrossed in error, and talks like a man in a dream (*Kavaloham*).

Study the Vedas constantly, practise the rites laid down therein, and thus realise within your soul the Divine Presence. Cast off all desires for pleasure, wash off your sins, trace out the transitoriness of earthly joys, pursue self-knowledge, and quickly issue forth from your own 'house' ('House' here is interpreted to mean the body, and 'to quit the house' means to realise the difference between the body and the indwelling soul).

Live in the society of holy men; direct your undeviating devotion (*bhakti*) to God; set your self to cultivate peace of mind, the spirit, of Self-sacrifice, self-control, abstinence. Venerate the truly learned, daily pray that you may, attain to Brahma in one syllable (*Om*), and enter into the spirit of Vedantic teaching.

Live blissfully in a lonely place, set your heart finally on the Supreme Brahma. So look at the world that you can realise the truth that the subtle all-pervasive Supreme Soul is diffused through the universe,—and dwell in the essence of Brahma (*Sadhana-Panchak*).

SHANKAR AND OTHER PHILOSOPHERS

"Kumārila vindicated the ancient Vedic rites. . . . Following the *Mimansa* school, he ascribed the universe to a divine act of creation, and assumed an all-powerful God as the cause of the existence, continuation and dissolution of the world. The doctrine of this personal deity, the one existent and universal soul without a second, or *Advaita*,—embodies the philosophical argument against the Buddhists . . . Shankar Āchārya moulded the later Mimānsa or Vedanta philosophy into its final form and popularised it as a national religion, and since then every new Hindu sect has had to start with a personal God.

"Shankarāchārya taught that there was one sole and Supreme God, distinct both from any member of the old Brahma Trinity and from the modern Hindu pantheon. The ruler of the Universe is to be worshipped not by sacrifices but, my meditation and in spirit and in truth. But Shankar realized that such a faith is for the few. To those who could not rise to so high a conception of the Godhead, he allowed the practice of any rites prescribed by the Veda, or by later orthodox Hindu teachers, to what so ever form of the Godhead they might be addressed. But Shiva-worship claims Shankarāchārya as its apostle in a special sense. It represents the popular side of his teaching, and the piety of his followers has elevated Shankar into an incarnation of Shiva himself.

"In strong contract with the pomp of Vaishnava temples is the simplicity and solemnity of the worship of Shiva. . . . The worship of Rudra and Shiva has continued from the time of the Vedic seers to be the cult of the Brāhmans. It was adapted by Shankarāchārya and his successors to popular worship . . . .

Shankarāchārya's teaching gave an impulse to it throughout India, and in the hands of his followers and apostolic successors Shiva-worship became one of the two chief religions of India. As at once Destroyer and Reproducer, Shiva represented profound philosophical doctrines, and was early recognised as the first god or Adidev of the Brāhmans. To them he was the symbol of death as merely a change of life. . . . He thus became alike the deity of the highest and of the lowest castes.

"The moral code of the Shaiva school declares it to be a grievous thing to tell a lie, to eat fish, onion, garlic and similar forbidden articles as food, and to commit theft, adultery and offences against society. Followers are also enjoined to give up pride, anger and ambition. . . . Every living soul being identical with Brahma, the destruction of animal life is strictly prohibited. So long as a man has not acquired the highest knowledge or *Brahmajnan*, he is bound to observe the ritual prescribed in the Vedas. It is only to obtain a correct notion of the impersonal Brahma that the worship of a deity endued with some tangible form is recommended (Campbell's *Bombay Gazetteer*, vol. II, part I, pp. 533-42).

The philosophy of Shankar will be still more clearly understood by the general public from the following illustration of its difference from the systems of two other eminent saints:

"The doctrine of the Rāmānujis is called *Vishisht-Advaita*, that is unity with attributes or non-duality with a difference. Under this doctrine Brahma or Vishnu is a personal God (*Paramatma*) related to the individual soul *chit* and nature *achit* as the spirit is to the body, the individual souls being distinct among themselves and from God. The Rāmānujis worship Vishnu as Nārāyan.

"The Rāmānandi or Rāmāvāt sect was founded by Rāmānanda a follower of Rāmānuj, owing to a difference on the single point, privacy in preparing and taking food, on which Rāmānuja laid great stress. He inculcated the worship of Vishnu as Rām with Sīta and Lakshman. . . . Their brow-mark is like the Rāmānujis and made of *gopichandan* clay. . . . Marriage is allowed among a division of the Rāmānandi Sadhus called *Sanjogi*, but forbidden to the division called '*Naga*' or naked. Their chief moral tenets are mercy, charity, and a virtuous life.

"The famous Vallabhāchari sect . . . (holds) the philosophical doctrine called *Shuddh-Advaita* of Shankarāchārya and Vishisht-Advaita of Rāmānuj. It teaches that God, though eternal is ended with a celestial form, and all visible phenomena emanate from Him at His will. The individual human soul (*Jiv-atma*) is believed to be a part from the supreme soul (*Param-atma*), separate in form but identical in essence. . . . In this new creed the element of love for the Deity predominates, and final bliss is held to consist in this love for the Deity in *Go-loka* . . . and obtainable only by offering worship to Krishna with loving devotion as a woman would towards her beloved."

THE SYSTEM OF SHANKAR AND RĀMĀNUJA CONTRASTED

1. Acording to Shankar, God alone is real, and the Universe is an illusion, that is, it appears before the eye but has no existence; the individual creature is not different from Brahma, and by means of salvation is converted into Brahma, there being then no distinction between the two.

Rāmānuja, on the other hand, holds that God, the Universe and the individual creature are all real, the latter two being only the body (or outward manifestation) of Brahma; the Universe and the individual after attaining to salvation are not turned into Brahma but dwell within Him.

2. According to Shankar, the Universe is the fruit of the illusion (*maya*) of the Creator, and creatures come into existence out of connection with this illusion.

3. In Shankar's philosophy salvation comes from knowledge of the One Brahma; in Rāmānuja's system, salvation proceeds from the grace of God and therefore knowledge of God is merely a limb of worship, and not the be-all and end-all of it as in Shankar's theory.

4. Shankar holds the Supreme God to be one, without

duality, without individual differentiation and without attribute, Rāmānuja declares Brahma to be one, non-dual, but particularised and possessed of attributes (*Sa-vishesh-gun*).

5. Shankar declares Brahma, Vishnu, Shiva and Shakti (the female Energy or counterpart of Shiva) as different aspects of Brahma caused by connection with illusion, and that all the above deites eqully deserve to be adored according to the worshipper's stage of spiritual development (*Adhikar-Bheda*). But Rāmānuja declares Vishnu as the sole object of adoration.

6. Shankar holds that the objects of our delusion are incapable of description, and they are born of ignorance while we are under a delusion.

Rāmānuja holds that the object of our illusion have existence; for example, we mistake an oyster-shell for silver because the oyster-shell really has some little particle (or attribute) of silver; or, in other words, there is no such thing as absolute illusion, it is merely a convenient application of the term.

7. With Shankar, creation is Brahma in its essence; hence God manifests Himself as *Sat*, *Chit* and *Anand*; the Ignorance and the work of Ignorance in a creature merely represent the shadow of Brahma in the creature's mind.

But Rāmānānda distinguishes the Brahma made up of *Chit* from creation, and he holds that even after a creature's salvation this separateness will not be abolished, because even then the individual soul will not be endowed with the power of creation like the Universal soul.

8. In Shankar's opinion, delusion, self-consciousness and ignorance (*maya, avidya, ajnan*) are identical and based on Brahma, Rāmānuja makes a distinction here namely the *maya* and *avidya* are expressions of the Creator's power, but ignorance (*ajnan*) appertains to the creature and entangles him.

9. Shankar admits liberation of the soul (*mukti*) to be possible even while a creature retains his body; but according to Rāmānuja, liberation is impossible while the soul inhabits the body.

10. According to Shankar, true liberation is *nirvan* (i.e. complete absorption of the individual soul in the Universal soul

or Brahma); it does not mean attainment of 'Vishnu's heaven (*Vaikunth*) or Shiva's heaven (*Kaliash*) which are mere spheres of bliss (*Swarga*). But with Rāmānuja supreme salvation consists in arrival at *Vaikunth*, and salvation in the form of *nirvan* is an impossibility, and the very conception of it is an idea of self-extinction

11. Shankar holds that the Vedanta leads to an attributeless (impersonal) Brahma who can be known only in terms of negation (i.e. stating what he is not, or how he is unlike all created things known to us). But Rāmānuja maintains that the Vedānta teaches a Brahma who is to be worshipped through his attributes.

12. A man may be said to have mastered the Vedanta according to Shankar, if he has achieved four kinds of devotion (*sadhan*); according to Rāmānuja, seven kinds of *sadhan*.

According to Shankar, the Vedanta can be mastered by a man if he has studied the Vedas and the Upanishads and performed the four Sadhans, even though he has abstained from all Vedic ritual. But Rāmānuja insists on the necessity of performing Vedic ritual (*kriyakaram*) plus at least six *sadhans*, before a man can be said to have mastered the Vedanta. In Shankar's philosophy *Sannyas* (monastic ordination) is an indispensable condition, in Rāmānuja's it is ritual; and each omits this first condition of the other. But the rest of Ramanuja's system is included in Shankar's.

With Shankar the highest spiritual master is the sannyasi, while men belonging to other orders (such as house-holders & c.) can reach only lesser kinds of spiritual advancement; but Rāmānuja holds that all orders of society can be first rate masters of spirituality

13. Shankar's theory of creation: Creation has sprung from illusion (*maya*) characterised by the three attributes *Sattya*, *Rajas* and *Tamas*, these are really not attributes, but a sort of rope binding Brahma. The fruit of Illusion, when attached to Brahma, is the universe. This Illusion is known variously as *avidya*, *ajan*, *prakriti avykta* & c. From *avidya* (i.e. belief in the seprate existance of myself as an individual inhabiting my body) has originated the sky, from the sky wind, from wind fire, from fire water, from water

the earth. The combind *Sattya* essence of these five elements has formed the mind (of man) which contains, cognition, intelligence, heart and preception of individuality.

14. Shankar teaches that salvation comes from cognition or knowledge that the individual (myself) is identical with Brahma; worship and ritual merely purify the heart, so that some masters are above the need of worship and ritual in their progress towards salvation.

Rāmānuja holds that salvation can come only from devotion (*bhakti*) in religious worship and throwing one's self on the grace of God as a supplaint (*prapatti*); both knowledge and worship are necessary, because God-knowledge is a limb of worship.

15. According to Shankar, when an individual attains to 'living liberation' (*jivan mukti*) he retains his body, but when he gains supreme salvation he discards his body. But according to Rāmānuja, after final salvation a man retains his atomic body (*sukshma sharir*) in which he (i.e. his soul) enjoys life in *Vaikunth*.

16. Both Shankar and Rāmānuja regard knowledge as self-revealing and self-evident; both of them regard the Vedas as the ultimate reason (*praman*).

CHAPTER 4

The Ten Orders or Dasnamis

The mission of Shankarāchārya has endured and will endure as long as Hinduism as a philosophy of life survives on earth, through the books that he wrote and the monastic orders that trace their origin to him. But it is highly improbable that he himself actually organised these orders. His life was too short, and that short span was too much filled with touring, disputation, lecturing and writing to allow him time to attend to the thousand and one administrative details and daily problems of a new and growing religious community. It would be more correct to hold that Shankar was the inspirer rather than the actual builder of the Dasnami orders. This latter work is ascribed by learned Dasnamis to Sureshwar-āchārya, the third in pontifical succession to Shankarāchārya at the Sringeri abbey.

What Shankar and his disciples did was to combine the scattered atoms of individual asceticism known in India from the Vedic age or even before, and place them together under regular discipline and the control of a central authority. This was no easy task, and its importance for the good of the community needs to be here explained.

Sannyas or the practice of renouncing the active world and becoming a homeless wandering religious mendicant, is as old as the dawn of God-consciousness in the soul of the primitive man. Even in the earliest Veda we meet with 'the longhaired ascetic or Muni dressed in rags of a reddish colour', to whom the Sun in the sky is likened (*Rigveda,* viii, 17, 59; x. 130). As Indo-Aryan society advanced, such wandering asceticism was recognised as the regular fourth or last stage (*Ashram*) in the life of a true Brahma. The sixth Book of Manu's law code is entirely devoted to the rules for the guidance of the ascetic life. "Old men, after having paid their debts to the gods and to the dead (ancestors), abandoned secular life and (embraced Sannyās) in order to reach holiness before dying". (Poussin).

But at first for many centuries the result of this natural impulse was the growth of indisciplined individualism. As A.S. Geden writes:

"Mysticism in India has shunned companionship . . . A second respect in which historically Indian monasticism in general has been distinguished from Buddhist or Christian, is the dificiency of co-ordination or of a central control. The ideal of the Indian ascetic or monk is not, and never has been, a fixed residence and occupation, but rather freedom to wander at pleasure, to visit various sacred places and shrines, and to dispose his manner of life and time independently."

This absence of system and discipline required to be reformed and the reform first came with the Jaina and the Buddha. As the great French scholar De La Vallee Poussion observes:

"From about the eighth to the sixth century BC, a number of religious leaders gave a regular form to the wandering ascetic life. The best of them had a high moral standard and a high intellectual standpoint. They preached a path to salvation and contrived to adapt to this lofty aim the penetential and ecstatic practices. They were great organisers and also great men; while the brotherhoods which they had established were living, robust organisms, they themselves became the gods of new religions.

"The task of the religious leaders was in short (1) to group ascetics under a certain rule of life, and (2) to give a spiritual meaning to the ascetic, mystical and orgiastic practices" (i.e., *tapas* and *yoga*. In the monastic orders founded by them, "while a mendicant, who was hitherto his own master, has to become a member of an organised body, to undergo a novitiate, to submit himself to the authority of a fixed rule or of the elders, he is expected to become at the same time, a philosopher . . . for spiritual progress."

Here De La Vallee. Poussin is speaking of Mahavir and Buddha, But my readers will at once perceive that his words apply exactly to Shankar also, and fittingly describe his character and position in the phrases . . . "They had a high moral standard and a high intellectual standpoint" . . . "They were great organizers and also great men" ... "they became the gods of new religions".

The ten branches of the Adwaita school of Shaivaism which Shankarāchārya organized (or as others hold, revived) are known as the Dasanama or 'Ten Names', from the ten words which form the suffixes to the names taken by the monks of these orders after their initiation (*diksha*). These words are—*Giri* (hill), *Puri* (city), *Bharti* (learning), *Ban* (wood). *Aranya* (forest), *Parbat* (mountain), *Sagar* (ocean), *Tirtha* (temple), *Ashram* (hermitage), and Saraswati (perfect knowledge).

Tradition is not agreed as to the names of the four direct disciples of Shankar whom he placed as the first heads of his four great monasteries at the four strategic points of India, namely.

(i) South—The Sringeri Math, under Prithvidhar Āchārya, (popularly known as Hasta-malak). To this the Puri, Bharti and Saraswati branches are attached.

(ii) East—The Govardhan Math at Jagannath Puri, placed in charge of Padmapad Āchārya (originally called Sanāndan). The Ban and Aranya orders are attached to this centre.

(iii) North—The Joshi Math at Badri-Kedarnath in the Himalayas, under Trotak-āchārya originally named (Giri). To this the Giri, Parbat and Sagar orders are attached.

(iv) West—The Sarada Math at Dwarka, placed in charge of Swarup-āchārya.
The Tirtha and Ashram branches are assigned to this Math.

We may here clearly mark out the character and Jurisdiction of these four great centres.

(i) Sringeri: Jurisdiction—Andhra, Dravid, Karnatak and Keral countries. *Yajurveda* followed. Novices affix the title of Chaitanya to their names. Motto, *Aham Brahmasmi* or "I am the Supreme soul". Branches attached, *Puri, Bharti* and *Saraswati* (these titles being added to the name conferred on the fully initiated Goswamis). Bhuribar section. Holy Shrine (*Kshetra*) Rameshwar.

(ii) Govardhan—Anga, Banga, Kalinga, Magadh, Utkal and Barbar. *Rigveda* followed. Novices affix the title—Prakash to their names. Motto *Prajnanam Brahma* or "The Divine is perfect knowledge". Branches attached, —*Ban* and *Aranya* (these titles being taken by the Goswamis at ordination) *Bhog-bar* section. Holy shrine (*Kshetra*) Jagannath Puri.

(iii) Joshi (or Jyotir): Jurisdiction—Kuru, Pānchāl i.e. Delhi, Punjab, Kashmir, Kamboj or Tibet &c. *Atharvaveda* followed. Novices take the title of *Ananda.* Motto *Ayamatma Brahma* or "This soul is the Divine being". Branches attached, —Giri, Parbat and Sagar. Ānand-bar section. Holy shrine, Badrikashram. (This Math has now been again placed under a Dasnāmi Gosain, the present head being named Swāmi Brāhmanand Saraswati.) The servitors of the Srisimha Badari have long been Smārta Brāhmans of the Tenjore district, under the Natu Chetti Math of Gayā.

(iv) Sarada: Jurisdiction—Sindhu, Sauvira, Saurashtra, and Maharashtra, i.e. Western India and Kathiawad, including Sindh. *Samaveda* followed. Novices are given the title of *Swarup.* Motto, *Tattwam-asi* or "Thou are He". Branches attached, *Tirtha* and *Ashram. Kutibar* section, Holy shrine, Dwarka.

The four great *maths* of the Dasnāmi orders have, in the course of centuries, come to adopt certain definite rules of affiliation and organisation. A sannyasi must first of all enrol himself in a *marhi,* which word may be roughly translated as a "recruiting or initiating centre". A *math* can take members belonging to one *marhi* only, but all the 52 *marhis* or any smaller number of them can become members of an *akhara.*

There are 52 *marhis,* which were originally thus distributed:

under the Giris, 27, under the Puris, 16,̇ under the Bharatis, 4 under the Bans, 4 under the Lāmās one.

Of the ten names, the *Tirthas, Ashramas* and *Saraswatis* and half of the *Bharatis* are called *Dandis,* while the remaining six and a half groups are entitled to call themselves *Gosains.*

There is some difference as to the exact names of the *marhis,* and the list given below is the one admitted by the Nirvāni *Akharas.*

List of 53 Marhis

A. *Giri,* Anandbar section, Meghnathpanthi:
1. Ramdatti. 2. Durganathi 3. Ridhinathi. 4. Brāhmanathi. (Lesser) 5. Patambarnathi. 6. Balabhadranathi 7. Lesser Jnannathi. 8. Greater Jnannathi. 9. Aghornathi. 10. Sanjnathi. 11. Bbavanathi. 12. Jagjivannathi, 13. Greater Brāhmanathi.

B. *Giri,* Aparnathpanthi:
1. Onkari. 2. Paramanandi. 3. Bodla. 4. Yati. 5. Nagendranathi. 6. Sagarnathi. 7. Bodhnathi 8. Kumasnathi. 9. Shahjhnati. 10. Parsanathi. 11. Marnathi. 12. Vishwambharnathi. 13. Taranathi. 14. Rudranathi.

C. *Puri,* Bhurbar section:
1. Bhagwanpuri. 2. Bhagwant Puri. 3. Ganga Daryab 4. Lahar Daryab. 5. Puranpuri. 6. Jarbharat Puri. 7. Sahajpuri. 8. Mani Meghnadpuri. 9. Bodha Ajodhyapuri. 10. Jnannath. 11. Arjun Puri. 12. Nilkanth Puri. 13. Hameman Puri. 14. Vaikunthi. 15. Multani. 16. Mathura Puri. (Some add) 17. Keval Puri. 18. Dasnāmi Tilak Narad Puri.

D. *Ban:*
1. Shyamsundar Ban. 2. Ramchandra Ban. 3. Shankbadhari Ban. 4. Balabhadra Ban.

E. *Bharati:*
1. Narsingh Bharati. 2. Man Mukund Bharati. 3. Vishwambhar Bharati. 4. Padmanav Bharati.

F. *Lama Marhi.*

Stages of Spiritual Advance among the Dasnāmi Monks

So much for the names of the ten orders. But within each order the monks are graded according to their spiritual progress or sanctity of character into four classes, namely *Kutichak, Bahudak, Hansa* and *Paramhansa.* The first two of these classes bear the title or *Tri-dandis*[1] (i.e. holding there rods) to symbolise their vow of controlling speech thought and action, while a *Hansa* or a *Paramhansa* is called an *Ekdandi* or *Dandi* (carrying one staff only).

A *Kutichak* (also called *Kavichar*) is an ascetic who has renounced the world and lives in a hut in the forest, engaged in religious contemplation and worship. He does not travel nor beg alms, but lives on the alms given to him unasked by the passers-by.

A *Bahudak* is a wandering religious mendicant, who collects alms in kind (never in cash) and must not stay for more than three days in one place.

The *Hansas* are ascetics versed in the Vedanta philosophy and pursue the aim of attaining to full knowledge of the Supreme Being in the *Brahma-lok.* Remaining in one places they live on charity and devote themselves faithfully to the Yoga practices.

The *Paramhansa* represents the highest stage of spiritual evolution. He is a man who has attained to perfect beatitude and merged himself in the Supreme Soul, and thus become a perfect master of spiritual knowledge and the highest religious teacher to mankind.

A *Kutichak* is, according to philologists, so called because he lives in a *Kutt* or hut (Sanskrit *Kutir*), a *Bahudak* because he drinks the water of many places (*Bahudaka*) in the course of his vow of wandering life. A *Hansa* is a swan floating in the holy lake of Mānas, the seat of Brahma, who has thus become a master of God—knowledge by the direct communion of the individual soul (*Jiv-atma*) with the Divine soul (*Param-atma*). After attaining to

[1] Tridandis are found only among the Ramanujis, while the Shiva *Dasnāmis* have *Dandis* only.

the supreme truth the *Hansa* and *Paramhansa* have risen above the need of worshipping idols (which is necessary at the lower stages of a man's spiritual evolution); but some of them worship the *Devi* or the Great Mother of the Universe.

Naturally the Dandi Sannyasis enjoy the highest esteem among the Hindus, as these ascetics are believed to have been spiritually elevated from humanity into the rank of the God Nārāyan himself.

There is further classification—or more correctly a cross-division, of the Sannyasis according to their various observances or customs. These are: (1) *Bhog-bar,* i.e. those who are indifferent to all earthly things (*bhoga* means enjoyment except what is absolutely necessary for life, (2) *Kit-bar,* or those who attempt to eat only a small quantity of food, (3) *Anand-bar,* or those who abstain from begging and merely live on freely given alms (4) *Bhuri-bar*, or those who live in forest produce and herbs only.

CHAPTER 5

Rules and Practices of Dasnami Monks

Qualifications of a Monk

People who seek initiation (*Diksha*) as monks, are moved by one of these two motives, namely, (1) disgust with the life of a house-holder, owing to misfortune or sorrow, and (2) a deliberate choice of the devotee's life as a means of the highest spiritual improvement, Vyāsa writes: "Any man, in any of the three earlier stages of life, whether a *Brahmachari* (student) a householder (*Grihastha*) or a forest dweller (*Vanaprastha*), if he withdraws his heart from all earthly desires, should take refuge in the state of a wandering monk (*Parivrajak*)".

Again, the *Saura Purana* says:

"When your mind becomes detached from all things, then only should you take to Sannyas (Monachism), otherwise you will be a sinner."

Also, the *Atri Samhita* declares:

"A man will not be released from sorrow and the chains of birth and death, so long as he does not gladly embrace the sign of Vishnu (i.e. the begging friar's rod)."

Another Sanskrit work declares the following classes of men as eternally unworthy of being made sannyasis—licentious, wrathful, boastful, greedy, deluded, overcome by illusions (*maya*), fond of company, devoted to luxury, subject to passion, or always sickly.

Castes Entitled to Become Sannyasis

On this point there is some ambiguity among the writers of ancient Smriti books, and this has led to much controversy and differences of opinion. All are agreed that Brāhman are entitled to enter this fourth stage of earthly life. But some later writers restrict this option to the Brāhmans, while others extent it to all the three twice-born castes, by using the word *'dwija'* which includes Kshatriyas and Vaishyas in addition to Brāhmans. In a work named '*Traivarik-Sannyas-sar*' Kailash Parvat quotes from *Yajnavalka Smriti* and *Brahma Baivarta Puran* verses to prove that the first three castes are undoubtedly entitled to receive initiation as Sannyasis. An example is quoted from the *Kurma Puran,* 12th Chapter) which tells us that a Kshatriya prince named Sushil, the grandson of Prithu, was given sannyas by a saint Swetashatar Muni, and then taught divine knowledge. On the other hand, Gopalanand Paramhans, in his *Sannyas-grahan Paddhati* (p. 5) asserts that none but Brāhmans have this right, and quotes various verses to prove that Kshatriyas and Vaishyas are specially excluded.

But in modern times we see that all the three higher castes are being made sannyasis by the holy heads of monasteries, and the members are placed above caste and beyond caste after their full initiation.

The Ceremonies and Hymns of Initiation as a Sannyasi

When a person has made up his mind to enter the monastic order (Sannyas Ashram) he signifies his intention to the head of an institution of sannyasis, and after being examined and granted permission as a worthy person, he grows through many ceremonies, which are described fully below, on the authority of the *Sannnyass-Grahan Paddhait* of Paramhansa Gopalanand (Benares, 1998 Vikram Samvat) and the *Yatidharma Sangraha* of Visheshwar Saraswati (Anand Ashram Press, AD 1909).

First of all, he purifies his body by undergoing four prescribed austerities (*Krichchhan*).

Next he must go through the act of *sankalpa* or determination.

On the following day, he should bathe, offer his Sandhya prayers and the day's worship of Vishnu, and then go to some river or other sheet of water and perform the *shradha* (funeral obsequies) of all his ancestors. He should methodically offer oblations (*tarpan* to, the eight gods connected with the funeral ceremony, chant the necessary vedic hymns and perform the gift (*dana*) and other duties of the occasion.

These funeral rites may extend over seven or eight days, after which he must have his beard, moustaches and head shaved off, keeping only the scalp lock (Shikha).

Next he must give away all his earthly possessions except a lioncloth (*kopin*), a staff (*danda*) and a waterpot (*kamandal*) with ceremonies and Mantras appropriate to such an occasion.

The sacrifice (*yajna*) performed at this time is called the *Prajapati-auhti.* Having kindled the holy fire (*homagni*), the novice sits down before it, keeping faggots (*samidh*); ghee (*ajya*) and milk pudding (*charu*) ready to obtain.

After this preparation the sannyasi cooks the milk pudding (Charu) in the domestic fire, divides the ghee and performs the *Viraja-hom* or purificatory sacrifice by chanting the sixteen verses of the *Purush Sukta* (*Rigved*, X. 90), and pouring out libation of ghee at the end of every verse.

The Purusha Sukta, or Hymn in the Creative Spirit

1. *Purusha* (the Universal soul, animating all creation) has a thousand heads, a thousand eyes, a thousand feet. He encircles the Earth in all directions and spreads beyond it for ten fingers'.... breadth.

2. Verily, *Purusha* is all this existing world, and all that was and all that will be. He is also the giver of immortality, because he has passed beyond His spirit-form and assured the shape of the Visible Universe for the nourishment of all creatures.

3. The Universe of all the ages—past, present and future—is

the manifestation of His glory. He is greater than all these: all Beings are but one-fourth of Him; His other three-fourths abide immortal as self-revealed.

4. This three-quarter of *Purusha* dwells majestically on high, above our material Universe. His remaining fourth-part enters again and again into this world of illusion, and thus assuming diverse forms in spirit all animate and inanimate Creation.

5. From that primeval Purusha has sprung this vast Universal Body (Virat), and from this Body has issued the Male Spirit (or the Creative agent), who brought into existence the gods and man, and thereafter the earth and animals.

6. When the gods performed the sacrifice with Purusha (imagined) as their oblation (*ghrita*)—at that sacrifice spring served as the butter, summer, as the faggots and autumn as the meat.

7. They immolated upon the sacred grass, as their victim, that Purusha who was born at the dawn of Creation. The gods headed by Prajapati and the Rishis performed their sacrifice, while they regarded the Purusha as the sacrificial animal.

8. That sacrifice in which the Purusha (Universal soul) was immolated, produced the mixture of curds and butter (*prishad-ajya*). That sacrifice also produced those animals, both wild and domesticated, over whom the wind (Vayu) is the deity.

9. From that sacrifice at which the Universal soul was immolated, sprang the Rik and *Samaveda, Gayatri* and other *mantras,* and the *Yajurveda.*

10. From that sacrifice were born horses and whatever animals have two rows of teeth, and cows and goats and sheep.

11. When the gods thus sacrificed the Purusha, into what different parts did they divide him? What was his mouth called, what his arms, what his thighs and what his feet?

12. His mouth became the Brahma, his arms the Rajanya, his thighs the Vaishya, and from his feet came the Shudra.

13. The moon was born from his mind, the sun from his eye, Indra and Agni from his mouth, and Vayu from his breath Prana).

14. From his navel came the firmament, from his head the heaven (*dyuloka*), from his feet the earth, from his ear the quarters of space (*dik*). Thus did the gods imagine the world.

15. At that sacrifice the seven metres were contemplated as the enclosures, the 21 substances as the logs of fuel. And the gods who celebrated the sacrifice, bound the Purusha to the stake as the victim.

16. By means of sacrifice did the gods worship Him who is also the sacrifice in Himself. Therefore, those were the first duties (Dharmam). That heaven where the ancient gods (Sadhyas) dwell, is also attained by the great-souled ones of the present age, who worship the *Virat Purusha* .

THE PURIFICATORY SACRIFICE
(*Viraja Hom*)

Pouring out *ghee* into the fire with a wooden ladle, the sannyasi should chant the following *mantras*:

Om: May the wind in all parts of myself—such as life (Pran), feeling (akuti), intestines, throat, navel and all other limbs—be purified: I am a stainless, sinless light; this *ghee* is poured into the fire for my good. I bow to the wind within myself.

May my speech, mind, eyes, ear, tongue, smell intellect and intentions be purified: I am a stainless, sinless light; this ghee is poured *&c.* (as in verse no. 1 above).

May my skin, flesh, blood, fat, marrow, nerves and bones be purified: I am &c. (as in verse no. 1 above).

May my head, feet, leg, sides, back, belly, thighs be purified: I am &c. (as in verse no. 1 above)

May the Divine Spirit (Devi) purify me. I am etc. (as in verse no. 1 above).

May earth, water, light, air, and sky purify me. I am &c. (as in verse no. 1 above).

May sound, touch, colour, taste and smell purify me. I am etc. (as in verse no. 1 above).

May my mind, speech, form and action be purified.

May the Divine Light purify me from unexpressed thought and self-cognition (*ahamkar*).

May my Atma, Antar-atma and Paramatma be purified.

I pour this libation of *ghee* to hunger and thirst, to true knowledge (Vividya; and the precepts of the *Rigveda*, the *Yajurveda*, the *Samaveda* and the *Atharveda*. And so on.

Having thus offered oblations of faggots, *ghee* and milk pudding to each of these separately at the end of each of the above verses (*mantra*) of the Viraja Hom, he should pour *ghee* in the name of and make his bow to Fire, Prajapati, Atma, Antaratma, Paramatma, Jnanatma. This will be followed by hom with the sixteen verses of the *Purusha Sukta* each chanted separately.

Next he should pray with the Vedic and Upanishadic verses, such as:

Om: The Absolute Brahma (or Cause) is Universal (or Perfect), the Brahma with attributes (or Active Brahma) also is Universal. From the Universal comes the Universal. When we have abstracted the fulness of the Perfect (or Universal), the Perfect (or Universal) Brahma indeed is left behind in our hearts (*Vrihadaranyak Upnishad*, 5-1-1).

After performing these *yajnas,* he renounces his children and friends, saying 'Listen, all ye: By the grace of my teacher I am eager to go beyond wordly life (Sansar). I have given up my attachment to all. I have renounced my love for son, wealth and followers. You too should give up your attachment to me, and not obstruct my embracing of sannyas. Taking water in the scooped palms of his hands, he should chant the full Vedic hymn, beginning with *'Ashup Shishanah'* and at the end of it pour the water on the ground as an offering to all the gods.

Next he should go to a sheet of water or river, perform his bath and Sandhya and take the vow that he would embrace the sannyasi mode of life (Ashram) which removes man's numberless sorrows and enables him to attain to the highest bliss and the supreme perfection of manhood. After making oblations of water, he should recite the prayers for fearlessness and then call upon the Sun and the Moon, Wind and Fire, Earth and Sky, Heart and Mind, Day and Night, the Morning Twilight and the Evening Twilight—as well as all the gods, to be witnessed to his resolution of becoming a sannyasi. Going down into the water up to his navel, he should recite the *Gayatri* verse—Om: Bhur Bhuvah, Swah, and certain other prayers, and make an oblation.

Standing thus in the tank or river, he should take some water out of it in the palm of his hand, and recite the *Praisha Mantra*,—"Om: Earth, I have become a Sannyasi. Om: Heaven I have become a Sannyasi. Om: Hell, I have become a Sannyasi." This is to be repeated thrice, with voice modulated to three pitches. After throwing into the water a full oblation of water taken into both his hands joined together, while facing the east and saying, "May all creatures be free from fear from me."

The next ceremony is that of discarding his sacred thread, and cutting off the tuft of hair on the crown of his head (*shikha*).

The last stage of the initiation

After the new sannyasi has come out of the water, cast off his clothes and taken five or seven steps with uplifted face, as naked as at his birth, his preceptor (Āchārya), after prostrating himself before him, would induce him to wear a loin-cloth (*kopin*) for decency before ordinary men, and give him a staff (*danda*) to guard against horned cattle, snakes &c. and a waterpot (*kamandalu*).

A dying Sannyasi is made to sit in an erect posture, with a wooden frame placed under his arms to prevent his falling back. The corpse along with the frame is buried in this posture in a *Samadhi* or grave dug in the ground, some *bhang* (cannabis sativus) and a hollowed gourd or water-flask being placed by its side. The dead faces the East or North-East. After this, salt and spices are thrown into the grave to hasten putrefaction. On a day between the 13th and 40th after death, or even within six months or a year, his disciple feeds a number of Brāhmans and sadhu. This is called '*bhandara*'. Over the graves of very holy men or rich *mahants,* temples or tombs are erected, and in these lamps are kept lighted and daily worship is offered.

A holy places on the banks of the Ganges, such as Hardwar, Benares, and Prayag, the dead bodies of rich sannyasis, especially Mahants and Mandaleshwars, are placed in stone coffing, called '*Tankas*' covered with a stone lid, which is tightly fastened down, and then thrown into the sacred river. In the case of poorer monks, their corpses have two stones tied to the head and legs, and then buried in the water. Many examples of burial in stone or masonry tombs are to be found in Both Gaya and other inland *maths.* It may be here pointed out that the Bengali Vaishnav monks of Chaitanya's sect always bury their dead in a hole in the ground, in a sitting posture, though this sect originated many centuries after the Dasnāmis,

The sannyasis worship Shiva in the ordinary way and Shakti (or Shiva's female consort) with a special secret ritual called *Marga* or path of Salvation. As Shiva himself wears a rosary of *Rudraksha* seeds, every sannyasi does the same. A *Rudraksha* seed with only one line of depressions (*ek-mukhi*) is considered to have the greatest sanctity and mystic power, and is often sold at incredible prices; the next lower degree of sanctity is possessed by a seed with *eleven-mukhs.*

The Nagas and Tapaswis smear their whole body with ashes (regarded as the Bibhuti of Shiva the yogi), other sannyasis only mark the *tri-pundarik* (three lines) with ashes on their forehad, and similar lines on eleven other places of the body— the whole being known as *dwadash bibhuti.*

The marks of an ideal sannyasi are—an earthen pot (for drinking water); the roots of trees (for food), coarse cloth, total solitude, equanimity towards all.

कपालं वृक्षमूलानि कुचैलम् असहायता
समताचैव सर्वस्मिन् एतद् मुक्तस्य लक्षणम।

Rules to be observed by a sannyasi in his personal conduct (1) When he goes out begging, he should wear one cloth round the waist above the knees and below the navel, and another over the shoulders, (2) He shall eat only one meal in 24 hours, (3) He shall live outside inhabited quarters, (4) He shall beg from seven, and not more than seven houses, except in the case of a Kutichak excepted, (5) He shall sleep on the ground,' (7) He shall not salute any one nor praise or speak ill of anybody, (8) He shall bow only to sannyasis of a higher order or of longer standing than himself, (9) He may not cover himself with cloth except one of the reddish colour (Gaurik).[1]

Succession to Headship

Many *maths* have their own special customs or rules of succession, but the majority of these monasteries have not. In their case the general practice is for the reigning *mahant* to nominate a disciple (*chela*) orally or by written will. On the 13th day after a *mahant's* death, his *bhandara* is held, at which a dinner is given to the inmates of the neighbouring *maths*. Then his *karbhari* announces the contents of his will. The assembled monks have the right of setting aside the nominee of the dead abbot if they deem him unworthy; in that case they then and there appoint another *chela* of the deceased to the vacant *gaddi*. In case the late *mahant* has left no instructions for the succession, nor any *chela*, the succession will fall to his own *chela's chela*, or to his *Gurubhai* or his *Gurubhai's chela*, in that order of preference. If none of these categories is available, the assembled monks can take up a *dwija* lad, cut off his scalp-lock (*shikha*) on the tomb of the late *mahant* and appoint him his successor.

Administration

All the *maths* of a district taken together form a single unit, called Mandal; the head of one of these *maths* is elected as the local president (*mahant* of the Mandal) by all the monks of the district.

[1] H.K. Kaul in Ceusus Report of the Punjab.

He is paid Rs. 1/4/ by every *math* in his circle at every ceremony held in it. He appoints his minister (*karbhari*) and provost (*kotwal*). As judge he holds the trial of offending monks in that district and issues orders regarding fine, expulsion &c.

Spread of Learning

The chief work of the *Math-dharis* being the propagation of religion among the people, great attention is paid to the education of the monks in the knowledge of Sanskrit and theology. The head or Mandaleshwar, whom we may compare to the Dean of an English Cathedral, or rather the President of a mediaeval Catholic University, must be a master of grammar, logic, astronomy, the Vedas and Philosophy (Vedanta). He is called a *Paramahansa,* and tours the country at the head of a hundred to two hundred *sadhus,* whom he teaches theology and the method of preaching *adwaita* (monist) philosophy. There are large Sanskrit colleges of this sect at Hrishikesh, Hardwar, Allahabad, Benares and some other cities. When the Mandaleshwar is out on tour, his best desciple conducts the teaching in the *math* during his absence.

It would be a mistake to suppose that the two sections of the Dasnāmis, namely the fighters and the theologians (*Astradharis* and *Shastradharis*) are kept separate in watertight compartments as regards their functions. A good deal of valuable teaching in scriptures is also done by the *akharas.* For examples, the Nirvani Akhara has established schools, at Allahabad (the Nirvan Veda Vidyalaya), Hardwar (Kankhal Pathshala) &c.

CHAPTER 6

The Akharas and their Constitution

Past History of the Akharas

Unfortunately we possess no contemporary record of the origin and history of the different Akharas before the line of Gosain Rajendra Giri, who became famous in the affairs of the Delhi Empire about 1750. Since that time we have detailed and correct accounts of the doings of the fighting monks (Nagas).

A Hindi manuscript has been found in the possession of the hereditary bard (*bhat*) of the Nirvani Akhara, which professes to give the dates of the foundation of the different Akharas and some of the battles which they fought with the name of the horses. This book merely gives the story as preserved by tradition from mouth to mouth among this family of bards; and the present manuscript (*pothi*) judging by its paper, handwriting, and colour of ink, cannot be more than fifty years old. Moreover, it represents the tradition current among the bards of only one Akhara, namely the Nirvani, and therefore it can be argued that if any other Akhara had poets of their own, they might have told a different tale. Subject to the above warning and making full allowances for the natural distortion of history in passing from mouth to mouth for many hundred years, I give the following summary of the account found in this *pothi*.

I. *Ahvān Akhara*

Mirich Giri, Dinānāth Giri, Ratan Giri Nāgā, Chaturi Giri Nāgā, Dalpat Giri Janghāri, Bhavaharan Puri, Uday Puri, Ganesh Puri.

Jharheshwari Mankaran Puri, Damri, Chandan Ban, Triloki Onkar Ban, Patakeshwari Ratan Ban Mauni, Maunse Jogdhāri.

Hirā Bharāti, Siddha Gudarbāl Bhārāti planted the banner. Ganpat Bharati blew the trumpet. Hardwar Bharati built the Akhara in vs 603, Jyaishtha dark 9th, Friday (if the figure for one thousand has been omitted before the year,—as used to be done in old writings. Such as Portuguese official records, then the year would be 1603 vs—AD 1547).

II. *Atal Akhara*

Bankhand Bhārati, Sāgar Bharti *Jahari,* Shiv Charan Bharati *Jangdhari* (or Jogdhari) Ajodhya Puri, Atal Nirvān, Dutta Puri, Tribhuban Puri *Urdhbahu, Chhote* Ranjit Puri, Sarvan Giri *Aloni* (abstained from salt), Dayal Giri *Mauni,* Mahesh Giri Nakhi (with long nails), Beni Mahesh Giri Bankhandi, Himachal Ban, Pratit Ban *Pauhari*, built the Akhara. Vikram Samvat 703 in the Gondwana country (*dharti*), *margashirsha* bright 4th Sunday (if the year was vs 1704, it would be AD 1646).

Mahesh Giri and Manohar Giri (*Abadhut*) released Shaikh Singh from captivity. Rājendra Giri the hero. Pratap Giri, in the country (*dharti*) of Narwar, took Ramraj Singh prisoner. Rameshwar Puri beat the war-drum. Umrao Giri gained victory in the battle, and forced Maur Bundela Ram Singh and Jawahir Singh to turn their backs Sanja (?) Bharati took Shova Singh Bundela prisoner. Jangdhari Puri and Dip Ban took the life of Bhola Singh Bundela.

Ratdevji *Bhat* sang of these heroic exploits Kanchan Hazāri received as reward a pearl necklace of 30 (beads?) and three camels for carrying the flag.

III. *Nirvani Akhara*

Rup Giri Siddha, Uttam Giri Siddha, Ram Swarup Giri Siddha, Shankar Puri *Mauni, Digambar* Bhawani Puri *Aloni Urdhbahu,* Dev *Mauni, Digambar* Onkar Bharati Tapeshwari, Purnanda

Bharati Agnihotri, in the plain of Garh Kunda,[1] in the country of Jhārkhand, lifted up the banner of religion, in the courtyard of the Siddheshwar temple(?), and planted their umbrella on the umbrella of Kal Bhairav Ganesh.

Joganand Chandan Puri *Naga,* Zorawar Puri *Naga,* Ram Narsingh *Mauni,* Narayan Bhopat Giri *Jangdhari,* Gautam Ban Singhasani, Amar Bharati, Nakkhi Giri, Narayan Giri, Sundar Giri, Anand Giri, Khusal Giri, Basant Giri, Rup Giri.

Vikram Samvat 805 Agrahayan bright 10th, Thursday, Akhara Shova Shital Nirvan, Ṣant, Mahant united and set up the flag. The Nirvan Akhara was built by Shuva-Karan (if the Vikram year was 1805, it would be AD 1749).

The Nirvani Akhara gained a victory in battle over Bhavanand, Sur-Suranand and Kamalanand Vairagis in Samvat 1310 (AD 136) in the Chauk of Hardwar, Chaib Giri Maharaj, Lachmi Giri Maharaj, Abhaynath Bharati *Mauni,* Jivan Puri *Jangdhari,* Vishal Puri Maharaj, Bankhandi Bharati Maharaj, Sahaj Ban Agnihotri, Bahadur Giri Maharaj, Dhyan Giri Maharaj, Parashuram Giri who held the sword; Indra Giri, Mauj Giri Maharaj (held) the mace (*gadka*).

At Hardwar *kshetra* they blew conches and planted their flags and standards. They destroyed the Rama *Dal.* Ram Bharati blew the trumpet. The Maratha troops after going to the Akhara, unfurled the victorious banner called *Bhagwa.* The Nirvani Akhara gained the credit of heroic valour. Khushal Bhat composed the song in honour of the fighting.

BATTLE OF THE JNAN BAPI

At Benares *kshetra,* near the Jnan Bapi temple, Raman Giri, Lakshman *Mauni*, Desh Giri Nakkhi fought Raja Haridas Kesari, Narendra Das, and Hari Maharaj *Maha-matuni* Lakshman

[1] Kunda, in the old Palamau Kingdom of Chota Nagpur. Situated 24°.13' North Latitude. 84°.45' East Longitude. The fort of Kunda was conquered by Aurangzeb's governor of Bihar in May 1661.

Mauni, Gopal *Mauni*, Bansha Gopal Muni (g), Har Sidh Mauni . . . Sarada *Mauni* and Balbhadra *Mauni* did heroic deeds. Ghanashyam Puri planted the Rup Bhagwa banner. Dharam Puri Harihet—Jangsar (?) played the naubat music. Bishwambhar Bharati held the sword, Lalit Bhagwan Puri held the peacock fan. Jogindra received honour. Narayan Ban's family was holder of the mace. This victory increased the glory of Kashi.

At the Kashi *kshetra* in Samvat 1721 (AD 1664) they won, the victory in a fight with the Sultan (? Aurangzīb) and gained great glory. From sunrise to sunset the battle raged and the Dasnamis proved themselves heroes; they preserved the honour of Viswanath's seat. They defeated the Muslims Mirza Ali and Turang Khan? and Abdul Ali.

Shuja-ud-daula, was about to be defeated by Najib Khan Pathan. . . . But Shiva gave help and thus saved the honour of the Dasnami.

IV. Anand *Akhara*

In Vikram Samvat 912 (AD 856), Jyaishtha bright 5th Sunday, in the country of Berar, — Kantha Giri Maharaj, Harihar Giri Maharaj, Rameshwar Giri Maharaj, *Khalsa,* Patan Giri Maharaj *Sawai-both,* Devdat Bharati *Chautal,* Harihar Bharati *Siddha,* and seven others? Shivashyam Puri Khemandal, Patar-Gopal *Dharbibhuti,* Hem Ban *Kevri,* Sarvan Puri *Falari,* Gangeshwar Bharati *Surati* built the Anand Akhara.

V. Niranjani *Akhara*

Atri *Mauui Siddha,* Sarajunath Purushottam Giri, Hari Shankar Giri *Jaugdhari,* Shripada Giri, *Paohari*, Batuk Giri *Naga,* Jagannath Giri *Digambar,* Jaykaran Giri *Bhandari,* Ranchhor Bharati, Jagjivan Bharati *Patambari* (clad in treebark), Arjun Bharati *Dankeshwari* (beat the big drum), Guman Bharati, Jagannath Puri *Falahari* Swabhav Puri, Kailash Puri, *Tuktukia,* Kharag Narayan Puri, Bakhtawar Puri *Urdhababu,* Uchit Puri *Naga Udambari,*

Khem Ban Agnihotri, Uday Ban Fateh Ban Udambari, Bhim Ban *Kotwal*—built the Akhara in the Kachh country, place Mandavi, in vs 960, Kartik dark 6th Monday (AD 904 or 1904).

VI. Juna *Akhara* (originally named *Bhairav*)

In vs 1202, Kartik bright 10th, Tuesday, this *akhara* was built at Badri Karan-Prayag in the Uttarkhand country by Mokham Giri, Sundar Giri *Mauni Digambar,* Dalpat Giri *Naga,* Lakshman Giri *Pratapi,* Raghunath Puri *Kotwal,* Dev Bharati, Raghunath Ban, Daya Ban *Thareshwari,* Parag Bharati *Bhandari,* Maha Bharati, Nilkanth Bhārati Dhwajaband (in charge of the flag), Shankar Puri *Avadhut,* Beni Puri *Avadhut, Mauni* Devan Puri, Vaikuntha Puri.

Mahant Lakshman Giri, the head of the Maha Nirvani Akhara, at Allahabad, wrote a Hindi account, of the akharas, on 5 January 1929, which has been printed. Important extracts from it are translated below:

"The Atal Akhara is the oldest of the seven akharas. In the time of the Delhi Badshahs, there used to be three hundred thousand men in it. It used to be equipped with canon and zamburaks (i.e. long matchlocks mounted on the back of camels). The Atal Akhara has produced many heroes and fighters for the defence of the Hindu religion. It used to reside mostly in the Jodhpur State. When Muslims from Kabul and Baluchistan invaded Jodhpur and levied tribute from the Rajah, the force of the Atal Sannyasis arrived there, defeated the Muslims, took away their arms and made them swear on the *Quran* that they would never again invade Marwar. The Rajah in gratitude granted Nagor *taluqa* to the Gosains, whose Nagor *berhe* still holds it."

"The Abahan Akhara produced many great heroes who were honoured by the Delhi Badshah and the Lucknow Nawab, such as Anup Giri and Umrao Giri."

HISTORY OF THE DASNĀMI MONKS

Mandaleshwars

In British India at the beginning of the nineteenth century, the attacks on Hinduism by the missionaries of other religions and by the spread of modern thought and English civilisation, set our thoughtful leaders to organise a movement for meeting this challenge to our faith. A new line was opened for the activities of the Dasnami Sannyasis to meet the needs of the age. It was found necessary to send forth highly intellectual champions of Hinduism who would be able to meet the attacks on our religion by Christian missionaries and Indian free thinkers on more than equal terms and who would train up pupils in advanced Shastric learning for the purpose of acting as missionaries of our religion and removing the ignorance of the mass of the Hindu population. The Hindus must no longer stand aloof and silently see their religion attacked by other sects without making a proper defence with the help of learning and philosophy. So long as the two older divisions of *Astradharis* and *Shastradharis* lived each within its' own monasteries, or toured the country without acting as teachers and missionaries of Hinduism to the outer public, they could not undertake this new work.

It was now decided to set up centres of Sanskrit learning and religious teaching under the greatest scholars of this sect and prepare bands of competent monks for religious propaganda among the public. This was the best way of meeting the champions of other religions in controversy.

Holy men who were equally famous for saintly character and Shastric knowledge, were chosen as teachers. In former ages they were called *Paramhansas,* but since about AD 1800 they have been called *Mandaleshwars.* This title is conferred only by the Dasnāmis in one of their seven *akharas*, or in the particular *math* of a lately deceased *mahant,* when his successor is judged to be an intellectual giant. After his election, *tika* is applied to the new *mandaleshwar's* forehead, a certain number of rupees is paid as *nazar,* and a long scarf (*chadar*) is waved over his head and presented to him, by the other members of his own *akhara* or *math.*

One *akhara* may be so fortunate as to possess three or four such intellectual giants, and only the most learned among them is chosen for preeminence and installed as the *achārya* of that *akhara.* His position is roughly equivalent to that of the Dean of a mediaeval Christian Cathedral combined with some of the functions of the head of a self-contained College of Theology.

Several of these *Mandaleshwars* have gone out of the parent *akhara* and established new *maths* of their own, which act as independent colleges, and their work is continued in these places after their death, by some equally eminent Sanskrit scholar and holy man elected from among the Dasnāmi monks.

The highly beneficial expansion of the work of the Dasnāmi sect will be best illustrated by some personal examples.

A. *Nirvani Akhara:* The order of succession of *Mandaleshwars* is—(1) Swāmi Sukdev Giriji, who lived and taught in Nichi Bagh, near the Company's Garden at Benares. (2) Swami Dhani Giriji, (3) Swāmi Govindanandji, who built the house in the Terhe Nim quarter in AD 1900. It is known as the Nirvani Govind Math, (4) Swami Jain Puriji, (5) Swami Krishnanand Giri, who is the present Āchārya of the Nirvani Akhara.

B. *Juna Akhara:* The line of succession of Mandaleshwars is—(1) Kutastha Swāmi, (2) Swāmi Phanindra Yati, called the "Yati Mandaleshwar", (3) Swāmi Paramatmanand, who built the house of the *math,* (4) Swāmi Swarupanand, (5) Swāmi Paramanand.

C. *Niranjani Akhara:* Line of succession of Mandaleshwar: (1) Swāmi Ram Giriji, (2) Swāmi Sachchidanand Yati, (3) Ramanandji, (4) Swāmi Nai Giriji.

Apart from these regular *akharas* there are some independent *maths* under their respective *Mandaleshwars*, e.g.,

D. *Hrishikesh Kailash Math:* Order of succession—(1) Swāmi Ram Puri, (2) Swāmi Dhanraj Giriji, (3) Swāmi Janardan Giri, and when he left, his place was filled by Swāmi Ram Giri, (4) Swāmi Govindanandaji, (5) Swāmi Vishnu Devanand.

E. Swāmi Vidyanand, a Naga monk of the Nirvani Akhara, (who, however, was not the Āchārya of that *akhara*), was a powerful preacher and founded the Gita Mandir at Ahmadabad, Baroda and other cities, and established the Gita Dharma Press at Benares with its own magazine.

F. Another Swāmi Krishnanand (also of the Nirvani Akhara) built the *math* at Amritsar.

G. Swāmi Bhagavatanand of Ghanta Kothi (Kankhal) is a very learned teacher, and has a *math* at Benares (Jalpadevi). He joins the Nirvani Nagas at the Kumbh bath and dinners.

(Most of these teaching *maths* are called *Ashrams* or hermitages for teachers and disciples, guru-shishya, as celebrated in the *Ramayan* and the poems of Kalidas.)

Development of Theological Colleges within the Akharas

At the beginning of the twentieth century, the leaders of the Nirvani Akhara at their sea-bath at Ganga-sagar, assembled at shrine of their tutelary saint, Kapil Muni, and came to a resolution for establishing schools for teaching the Sanskrit language and the Hindu scriptures (the Vedas, Vedangas &c.) throughout the country, so as to give to Brāhman lads and *math-dhari* disciples a suffciently high education and thus supply a band of competent preachers of the Hindu dharma. Accordingly, in AD 1911, the Maha Nirvan Veda Vidyalaya was opened at Hardwar. But after some years it was found to be more fruitful to transfer this college to Allahabad, which was done in February 1916. The college is now directly under the supervision of the Maha Nirvani Akhara in Daraganj, Allahabad.

It teaches for all the five Sanskrit grades—namely Entrance First, Intermediate, Shastri and Āchārya degree examinations, and in each class the subjects taught are Grammar, Logic, Vedant, Literature, Scripture &c., following the curriculum of the Benares Government Sanskrit College.

The Governing Body of this College consists of President—Swāmi Jayendra Puri, Mandaleshwar, Benares. Vice-President—

Mahant Balak Puri, Nirvani Allahabad Akhara. Secretary—M. Mahadev Giri, Nirvani Allahabad Akhara.

The title of *Āchārya* is of the highest dignity, and it is conferred on that one of the five or six *Mandaleshwars* living at the time who is recognised as the most learned man among them.

RIGHT OF BATHING AT KUMBH

Every twelfth year, when the planet Jupiter (*Vrihaspati*) enters the sign of Aquarius (*Kumbh*), the event is considered most sacred and Hindus believe that they can wash away their sins by bathing in some sacred river, especially the Ganges, or the Godavari (called the Dakshini Ganga) in Southern India. The occasion is called the *Kumbh Jog.* In addition to it, every year, the day when the Sun enters the sign of Capricornus (*Makar*) on the new moon of the month of Magh (in January), is celebrated by purifying baths and religious ceremonies all over India; it is called *Makar Sankranti,* three months later than this, i.e. in April, comes the *Mesh Sakranti,* or the day when the sun enters the sign of Aries (*Mesh*), which is celebrated similarly, especially at the confluence of the Ganges and the Jamuna at Allahabad. These two *Sankrantis* become doubly auspicious every twelfth year when Jupiter happens to be in Aquarius (*Kumbh*) on the Makar and Mesh *Sankranti* new moons, and then they are called the Makar *Kumbh* and Mesh *Kumbh* respectively. Extraordinarily large crowds of Hindus assembled at Hardwar and Allahabad on these *Kumbh* bath days (e.g. 20 lakhs at Hardwar in 1796 according to Capt. Hardwicke).

The Kumbh *melas* are held at four different places at a stated time for each, namely:

(1) The *Makar* Kumbh bath at Allahabad, when the Sun enters Capricornus (*Makar*), Jupiter being then in Aquarius (*Kumbh*).

(2) The *Mesh* Kumbh bath at Hardwar, when Jupiter enter Aquarius, the Sun being in Aries (*Mesh*).

(3) The *Singh* Kumbh bath at Trimbak on the Godavari, when the Sun enters Leo (*Singh*).

(4) The Kumbh at Ujjain in the Gwalior State.

The question of precedence in bathing on these occasions formerly led to bloody fights. But the British Government, after inquiring into the old time-honoured practice, have laid down the following rules, which are strictly enforced by the Magistrate—First the Naga Gosains (i.e. *akharas*) will bathe, then the Vaishnav Bairagi Sadhus, next the Udasi Nanak Panthi Sikhs, and lastly the Nirmala Sadhu Sikhs.

Among the *akharas* the following orders is observed and enforced: At Hardwar *first* the Niranjani Akhara accompanied by the Juna, Abahan and Ananda Akharas; *second* the Nirvani, accompanied by the Atal.

At Allahabad, *first* the Nirvani accompanied by the Atal Akhara, and then come the other four *akharas.* The first ceremonial bath is taken on the *Makar Sankranti,* the second on *Magh Amavasya* (new moon), the third on *Vasant Panchami.*

On this occasion, on the sand bank at the confluence of the Ganges and the Jumna, the Nirvani Akhara from their camp and plant two flags 52 cubits high, under which the holy *Chandi* is constantly read. While the flags are standing, every comer is supplied with free food. After the three baths mentioned above, a *hom* (fire sacrifice) is held, accompanied by *Chandi* reading and the feeding of sadhus, learned scholars (*mandaleshwars*) and ordinary Brāhmans; which costs Rs. 525.

On each of the above holy days (*parv*) this *akhara* gives away in charity one horse, 5¼ maunds of boiled rice and peas (*khichri*) and Rs. 525 in cash or as the price of other things.

Each mela costs the Nirvani Akhara at least Rs. 30,000. At the end of it, these monks move off to Benares.

The first English account of the *Kumbh* that we have was written in 1796 when Hardwar was in the possession of the Marathas. On 8 April 1796, an English officer named Captain Thomas Hardwicke, accompanied by Dr. Hunter paid a visit to

Hardwar during the mela held on that date which was the *Mesh Sankranti.*

"But every 12th year, when Jupiter is in Aquarius, at the time of the Sun's entering Aries, the concourse of people is greatly augmented. The present is one of those periods, and the multitude collected here on this occasion may, I think, with moderation, be computed at two million of souls.

"The Gosains . . . are the first here in point of numbers and power . . . in the early part of the fair, this sect of *faqirs* erected the standard of superiority, and proclaimed themselves regulators of the police. . . . They published an edict, prohibiting all other tribes from entering the place with their swords or arms of any other description. . . . The Vairagis, who were the next powerful sect, gave up the point, and next followed their example. Thus the Gosains paraded with their swords and shields, while every other tribe carried only bamboos through the fair.

"The ruling power was consequently held by the priests of the Gosains, distinguished by the appellation of *Mahants,* and during the continuance of the fair, the police was under their authority, and all duties levied and collected by them, . . . no part is remitted to the Maratha State. These *mahants* meet in council daily; hear and decide upon all complaints brought before them, either against individuals or of a nature tending to disturb the tranquillity, and the well management of this immense multitude.

"The Gosains maintained an uncontested authority, till the arrival of about 12,000 or 14,000 Sikh horsemen, with their families &c., who encamped on the plains about Jalalpur. . . . The three chiefs of the Sikh force were Raja Sahib Singh of Patiala, and Rai Singh and Sher Singh of Buria.

"On the morning of the 10th of April (which day concluded the *mela*), about 8 o'clock in the morning the Sikhs . . . assembled in force and proceeded to the different watering places, where they attacked with swords, spears, and fire-arms, every tribe of faqirs that came in their way. These people being all on foot and few if any having fire-arms, the contest was unequal; and the Sikhs who were all mounted, drove the Sannyasis, Vairagis, Gosains, Nagas

&c., before them with irresistible fury . . . and having slaughtered a great number pursued the remainder.

"Accounts agree that the faqirs lost about 5,000 men killed, among whom was one of their mahants named Manpuri and they had many wounded: of the Sikhs about 20 were killed" (*Asiatic Researches,* vol. VI).

A graphic description of the *Makar Sankranti mela* at Allahabad in 1840 is given by a Protestant missionary who visited it and spent ten days in preaching Christianity there. He writes:

"The *sankrant* . . : from which the mela began, occurred on the 20th January 1840. Previous to that time people began to encamp in large numbers on the beach. Several sects of religious mendicants, began at an early period, to fit up quarters for themselves. Among these were two sects of *Nagas,* who came only once in six years. One of these sects is called *Nirvani* and the other *Niranjani.* . . . They are divided into two sects, rather for the sake of convenience in their begging perigrinations than from any difference of (doctrinal) opinion among them members of the former sect told us, that they at present number in their fraternity about 5,000 persons, and of the latter that they number about 2,000. . . . The present Param Mahant is named Lal Giri. The two sects make regular tours to several different shrines, viz, Allahabad, Gaya Jagannath, Godavari, Rameshwar, Ganga Sagar, Hardwar, and a few other places. They complete their circuit in six years.

"They marked out for themselves ground in a somewhat tasty style; on this they ereted in two lines, little grass huts facing each other at a distance of about 50 paces. These were built in neat rooms. In front of each hut is a mound of earth about four feet high, having a little parapet, or wall of a few inches high, extending all round the top. This is neatly smoothed over with cowdung. On the top of these chabutras they bask in the sun during the day, and read their sacred books, or talk or sleep as they feel inclined.

"Near the centre of each encampment they have a rather splendid flag, suspended on a very high bamboo. . . . Alongside the flag staff is erected a kind of pyramid of earth about 20 feet square at its base, and 15 feet high, ascended by flights of steps on the four sides. On the apex of this are placed a few sea-shells (*shankh*), a dish of flowers, a small image of Mahadeo, and a few rather elegantly polished brass candlesticks.... Over it, at a well-adjusted distance, is a large awming, suspended by four corners. It consists of four separate awnings of beautifully fringed pink silk and crimson velvet; each one diminishing in size as its place is lower in the series, so as to suggest the idea of an inverted pyramid.

"When they go out on public days, &c., the principal man of the Nirvani sect go paraded on seven large and splendidly caparisoned elephants, over which are spread a number of splendid flags. Others are mounted on the finest; horses and camels, some of them armed. The whole is preceded by mace-bearers carrying enormous silver sticks, and much of the insignia of royalty; then all this is followed by the mass of the sect clothed in all their uncouth, and ashy . . . nakedness. . . . The other sect follows them in about equal parade, to the river side, where they all bathe.

"The Param Mahant of Abbot of a sect of Gosains whose head quarters are here at Allahabad, died a short time since, and the sect fixed upon the time of the *mela* to place another upon the *gaddi.* As a matter of course, or of etiquette, they had to invite the whole tribe of Nagas, Gosains, Udasis &c. to a feast. On the appointed day they all assembled on an elevation extending from the corner of the fort. They seated themselves naked as they were generally, two and two facing each other on the smooth ground. . . . They served out to each person two balls of a sweetmeat composed of flour and sugar, and one or two other ingredients, fried in *ghee.* . . . They had each a kind of platter made of leaves stitched or fastened together by wooden pegs. . . . They ate them together. Afterwards a portion of *dahi* (curd) was served to each in a cup made of the same kind of leaf. The next morning, the sweetmeats, &c. that remained from the feast were distributed as charity to the Brāhmans, Nagas, Gosains &c. There passed by our place 20 men with full baskets on their heads on their way to the quarters of the Nagas. These were preceded by mace-bearers and two men blowing trumpets. . . .

"Both parties of the Nagas prepare at certain intervals of time, or on certain occasions, what they call *hom* (burnt offering). In this they burn insense with various ceremonies and reading *shlokas* from their sacred books. The incense is composed of *ghee* and various kinds of grain and flowers &c., all vegetable substances. The ceremony of burning is performed by the Param Mahant, aided by others high in rank". (*Calcutta Christian Observer,* 1840, pp. 243-51, signed W.)

The Kumbh mela of 1882 is thus described by Mr T. Benson, ICS, in his report:

"To each corporation (*akhara*) of religious ascetics was assigned a space of ground, within which it erected a temporary village or town for the accomodation of its members, in the centre of which moved the standards of the guild on a lofty flag-staff. These encampments were orderly and well laid out, and of a comfortable description. . . . The various camps formed were,

(1) Nirvani Naga Gosains.
(2) Niranjani, with whom were associated the Juna.
(3) Vairagis, including three sects.
(4) Chhota Akhara Panchayati Udasi Nanak-panthis,
(5) Bara Akhara Panchayati with the Bandhua Akhara (Sikhs).
(6) Nirmala Sikhs, with the Vrindavani.

"On three great days (*Makar Sankranti*), *Amavasya*, and *Basant* (*Panchami*) each of the six sects went separately down to bathe in formal procession, the most noiceable features being the body of naked *faqirs* closing the procession of each of the first two sects (the *Nirvani* and the *Niranjani*), and the gorgeous silken banners and elephant trappings of the wealthier guilds.

CHAPTER 7

Householder or Grihastha Gosavis

The married members of this sect form a very important and wide-spread portion of it. They are known in south India under the name of *Gosavi*, which is a Marathi corruption of the Sanskrit word *Goswami*, meaning a religious leader, or etymological "a man who has acquired a complete mastery over all the organs of the senses". Similarly, among the Vaishnav sect of northern India the religious heads (i.e., gurus and priests) whether married or celebate—are called *Goswamis*, popularly *Gosains*.

Many of these married Gosavis of the south (like the Gosains of north India) still officiate as priests and religious teachers to their hereditary followers *shishyas*), but most of them have taken to lay professions in the course of centuries in consequence of the expansion of their families. Thus, in the census of 1911 it was found that only 37 Gosavis out of a hundred in Berar were priests and 47 per cent of this sect were cultivators by profession.

The Bengali Gosains do not form a separate caste, they are an integral part of the Brāhman caste and can lawfully marry with the Brāhmans of other sects in the province. But in south India the orthodox Brāhmans belonging to other sects, quite unreasonably try to run down the Gosavis by saying that they are no better than Shudras, as by the act of marrying they have fallen from their high spiritual ideal and have become impure or immoral (*vratya*).

This argument is absurd. Among the Hindus, from the earliest Vedic age, marriage has been regarded as a sacrament (*samskar*), binding upon every man who would live in the world. The Vedic

Rishis had their wives. Religious performances are incomplete unless the wife accompanies the husband.

In the most ancient Christian Church, the Council of Trullan (AD 680) allowed the marriage of priests, deacons, and all inferior clergy, but bishops were to be celibate, or if previously married their wives were to be separated from them and made to enter into a nunnery. This rule still governs the Eastern or Greek Church among the Christians. Similary, among the Dasnāmis if a man had been married before entering the order, he is disqualified for election as a *mahant* or abbot. Among the Roman Catholics, "at the end of the first thousand years after Christ, in Europe generally, . . . the marriage relation was still adhered to by large numbers of the Clergy, and the rule of celibacy, when enforced, gave rise to concubinage more or less flagrant" (Dr. G. Cross). In this branch of Christianity, celibacy of the priests was not enforced before the time of Gregory VII who was elected Pope in AD 1073.

In the Protestant Church the clergymen and even Deans of Cathedrals (whom we may consider as equivalant to the *mahants* of our *maths*) are allowed to marry.

Thus, it is opposed to history and opposed to the basic principles of Hinduism to hold that the Gosavis have become a degraded sect or caste by reason of their having married while discharging the function of religious teachers. In recent times, many *mathdhāri* Dasnamis have married (esp. in Gujrat and the U.P.) and become householders or *Grihasth Gosavis*. This is not a sinful act.

Today the Gosāvis are among the best merchants, bankers and businessmen, especially in south India. They have all along been the solid supporters or backbone of the monastic section of their community, namely the *mathdhāris* and the *akharas*.

The position of the community technically known *Gosavis* in Berar and the Bombay Presidency can be clearly seen from the following account of these people in Poona city. Out of a population of 1798 classed as religious mendicants, '527 are Vairagis and 956 Gosavis (figures from the census of 1881). The Gosavis live mostly in Gosāvipurā, a street called after them, where they own large mansions which they call *maths* or religious houses. They are beggars merely in name, many of them being traders and a few bankers. Except goldsmith, carpenters and other artisan classes and classes below Marathas, they recruit freely from all castes. They admit freely their children by their mistresses and children vowed to be Gosavis. They are divided into *ghar-baris* or householders and *nishprahis* or celibates, who eat together. . . . As a class Poona Gosavis are clean, neat, hospitable and orderly. Formerly Gosavis used to travel in armed bands pretending to seek charity, but really to levy contributions, and where they were unsuccessfully resisted, they plundered and committed great enormities. Later on (in 1789) they were first employed by Mahadji Sindhia in his army and afterwards by other great Maratha chiefs. Under the Peshwas they were great jewellers and shawl merchants and traded in varities. In 1832 Jacquemont described them as bankers and traders, all with a religious character. They had most of the riches of Poona in their hands. They came chiefly from Marwar and Mewar, and had adopted children of those countries' (Campbell's *Bombay Gazetteer*, vol. XVIII, pt. 3, pp. 301-2).

The residence and influence of the leading married Gosavis can be judged from some well-known instances.

Peshwa Baji Rao I built a temple to the Goddess Vajreshwari at the village of Vadvali and granted five villages for her worship. The priests in charge have been householder Gosavis for the last five generations.

CHAPTER 8

Hindu Fighting Priest: Their Early History

It is a general belief in Europe and India alike that the Hindu caste system has rigidly divided men according to their functions in life and that each caste follows one profession exclusively, with the result that Brāhmans cannot do any other work than serving as priests and teachers of sacred books, or that Kshatriyas must not do anything except fighting battles and governing kingdoms, and a violation of this rule would be a sinful encroachment of one caste upon the divinely ordained functions of another caste. But true oriental scholars know this popular theory to be false, and even the modern history of our country furnished many instances to the contrary of it. Thus, the priestly caste has produced warriors from the earliest age of the *Rigveda* down to the nineteenth century when the East India Company's 'Bengal Army' was mostly recruited from Oudh Brāhmans bearing the titles of Pandes, Chaubes and Dubes. Indeed, during the Sepoy Mutiny the British soldiers gave the sepoy mutineers the general name of Pandeys. We also know that the Maratha Brāhmans, whether of the Chitpavan section to which the Peshwas belonged, or the Karhares to which the heroic Rani of Jhansi belonged, or the Saraswat branch to which Sindhia's famous general Jivva Dada Bakhshi and Lakhwa Dada Lad belonged, were all soldiers as well as priests.

Similarly, the warrior caste of Kshatriyas is known to have

produced not only soldiers and governors, but also sages and teachers of God-knowledge (*Brahma-vidya*) like Janak and Gautam Buddha, besides numberless sadhus or wandering monks and even a world honoured female saint, Mīra Bāi. Hence, there is nothing incongruous to reason or opposed to the root principles of Hinduism, if a member of the priestly caste takes up arms in defence of faith and country or a member of the warrior caste by birth turns hermit and teaches religion. The Dasnami *akharas* are only one more illustrations of this elasticity in Hinduism as will be proved below.

The first indisputably historical evidence that we find of fighting Brāhmans occurs in the course of Alexander's invasion of India in 3 BC when after crossing the river Ravi (Greek name Hydraotes in pursuit of the Malava people (Greek Mallot), "he led his forces in person against a certain city of the Brāhmans, because he ascertained that some of the Malloi had fled for refuge into it. . . . He led his phalanx in serried ranks close up to the wall on all sides. The enemy being repulsed by the missiles, abandoned the walls, and having fled for safety into the citadel, began to defend themselves from thence. A few Macedonians having rushed in with them, they turned round and drove them out, killing 25 of them in their retreat. But the Macedonians scaled the walls by means of ladders . . . and the citadel was soon in their possession. . . . Most of the Indians were slain fighting. About 5,000 in all were killed, and as they were men of spirit very few were taken prisoners" (Arrian's *Anabasis*, Chinnock's translation, pp. 303-4).[1] This town was situated in the modern Montgomery district of the Panjab.

The Naga Sannyasis were called by the Greeks *Gymnosophists*, which literally means "naked philosophers". They are thus described by Arrian in his *Indika*: "The philosophers (i.e. Brāhmans) form the caste most esteemed in reputation and

[1] It is a mistake to suppose, as the Yeotmal Gosavi has done that the Glausoi tribe, whose territories lay immediately east of the kingdom of Poros, were Gosavis. Another form of this tribal name, Glaukanikoi, given by Aristobulus is more correct (Arrian, p. 276).

dignity. No necessity is incumbent upon them to do any bodily labour, . . . nor have they any compulsory duty except to offer sacrifices to the gods on behalf of the commonwealth of India. These philosophers pass their lives naked; in the winter, in the sun under the open sky, but in the summer when the sun holds sway, that live in the meadows and in the marshes under the great trees" (*Indika*, Chinnock's trans., pp. 411-12).

Alexander's dealings with the naked Brāhman sages are thus described by Plutarch and give a correct picture of these wise men in that ancient age: "In the course of this expedition (against the Malloi tribe) he took ten of the Gymno-sophists, who had been principally concerned in instigating Sambos (Shambhu) to revolt and had brought numberless other troubles upon the Macedonians. As these ten men were reckoned the most acute and concise in their answers, he put the most difficult questions to them that could be thought of. [At the end] the king loaded them with presents, and dismissed them. After which he sent Onesi-critus, a disciple of Diogenes, to the other Indian sages who were of most reputation and lived a retired life, to desire them to come to him. Onesi-critus tells us, Calanus treated him with great insolence and harshness, bidding him to strip himself naked, if he desired to hear any of his doctrine; "You should not hear me on any other condition", he said, "though you came from Jupiter himself". Dandamis (Dandin) behaved with more civility; and when Onesi-critus had given him an account of Pythagoras, Socrates, and Diogenes, he said they appeared to have been men of genius, but to have lived with too passive a regard to the laws.

As to Calanus, it is certain that King Takshashila prevailed with him to go to Alexander. His true name was Sphines but because he addressed men with the word *Cale* (*Kalyan*) which is the Indian form of salutation, the Greeks called him Calanus" (Plutarch's *Lives*, XXXIII)

The extant fragments of the account of India written by Megasthenes, the Greek ambassador at the court of the Maurya Emperor Bindusar, do not give us any new or striking information about the Brāhman ascetics of that age.

CHAPTER 9

Rajendra Giri Gosain (AD 1751-1753)

In the middle of the eighteenth century the Mughal Empire was crumbling to pieces. Two parties, the Iranis and the Turanis, swayed politics at the court and filled the country with unrest by their wranglings. The champion of the Turanis was Intizamuddaulah, and that of the Iranis Safdar Jang.

On 28 April 1748, the Emperor Ahmad Shah ascended the throne of Delhi. Three months later, he gave his confidence to Safdar Jang, the Governor of Oudh and appointed him Wazir, (chancellor of the empire). He had also won distinction by fighting against Ahmad Shah Abdali, in 1748. After the assumption of the *vizierate* he first surmounted the opposition of his Turani rivals. Intizam and Javed, and was then embroiled with the Bangash Afghans of Farrukhabad. Early in 1750 he seized their territory and appointed his deputy Nawal Rai in-charge of it. This high-handed action caused a general rising of the Bangash Afghans. They defeated and slew Nawal Rai in an action at Khudaganj, 13 August 1750, and beat the wazir himself at Ramchatauni, |23 September 1750. The victories let loose their pent-up fury, and they spread like a devastating flood across the territories of the Oudh Nawab. The city of Lucknow fell; prominent chiefs, e.g., Raja Hindu Singh Chandel of Chachendi; Rup Singh Khichar of Asothar, Balwant Singh of Benares and Prithwipat of Pratapgarh and Akbar Shah of Azamgarh transfered their allegiance to the

Bangash Nawab. Only the suba of Allahabad held out, but Ahmad Khan Bangash personally marched and reduced the whole of it, compelling Ali Quli Khan, the deputy governor, to take shelter inside the fortress of Allahabad, Febuary 1751. This holy site at the confluence of the three rivers became the scene of violent fighting. Ahmad Khan encamped at Jhusi, a mile east of Allahabad, and started a violent cannonade upon the fort from a battery erected on a mound called Raja Harbong's fort. Raja Prithwipat came and joined him with his forces. The Afghans used their artillery and terror tactics. They sacked the open city of Allahabad, set fire to houses and dragged away 4,000 women of respectable families into captivity. The report of the Afghan violence spread alarm in all directions. Thus, a Maratha letter of March 1751, states "Benares the holy city went without lights. It has been in fear for ten days. The bullock-cart hire from Kashi to Patna has risen to eighty rupees: Porters are not available. The residents are leaving the town and flying to whenever they can" (*First two Nawabs of Oudh*, p. 173).

During this period Safdar Jang stayed powerless at Delhi. He had no powerful army at his back, nor the support of the Emperor. The garrison of Allahabad could therefore count upon no succour from him. Yet upon the tenacious opposition of the fort depended not only the chance of his recovery of the Wazir's position but also India's deliverance from the prospect of Afghan tyranny.

It is hardly realised that the accession of a member of the Abdali clan to the heritage bequeathed by Nadir Shah in 1748, had given an unprecedented impulse to the Afghan race. The ambition of the Bangash and Rohela clans who had built up enclaves or their power in Rohilkhand and Farrukhabad flamed up. Hence the issue at stake in Allahabad was not merely the trial of strength between two rival parties, but also the possibility of the revival of Afghan rule over India.

Quite unexpectedly Allahabad did not fail; it held out from February to April and belied all the anticipations of the besiegers. This was due to the appearance of a strange body of men, viz., Naga monks.

From time out of mind, Allahabad has been a city sacred to the Hindus; here devotees came from all parts of India. In the winter of 1751, a body of Naga monks (estimated by *Siyar*, at 50,000 and by *Imad* at only 60) had assembled here for the practice of religious rites. They were very strange in their visage and bearing. They rubbed ashes on their person; wore matted locks upon their heads and had no other covering than a string of cloth round their waist. They were hardy and trained in arms, and their leader was Rajendra Giri. He had lived for many years at Moth, 32 miles north-east of Jhansi, built a fort there, and gained possession of 114 villages (*Jhansi Gaz.* 172-3). His power and position became a threat to Marathas in Bundelkhand, and so he was expelled from his possession by the Maratha vakil Naro Shankar in 1749-50. He then wandered with his followers to Allahabad and took up his quarters in the open space between the old city and the fort. He burnt with indignation at the sight of the atrocities committed by the Afghans and offered the aid of his arms gratuitously to the besieged garrison.

His intervention gave a new turn to the war. The dispirited Oudh troops were fired with a new spirit at the sight of the courage of the death-defying monks, who, refused to go to shelter and delighted to bask in the sun under enemy fusilade. They executed lightning attacks upon the Afghan camp and did daily killings there. As Ghulam Hussain says, "Every day he (Rajendra Giri) used to set out with the bravest of his people, all mounted on excellent mares, and to gallop about the Afghan camp; from whence he never returned without having killed several of the bravest of the enemy, and brought away both their arms and horses with him; so long as the siege lasted he did not miss a single day, and always did some execution."

As this inspiring example of the monks buoyed up hearts of the garrison to a stiffer resistance, Ahmad Khan altered his strategy of war; he decided to starve the fort into submission. About half a mile south-east of the fort there stands on the right bank of the Jamuna, a small town named Arail from which supplies were drawn by a bridge of boats to feed the Allahabad garrison. Baqaullah was the commander-in-charge of this important post. Every morning and evening he shuttled across the bridge with his force and kept the garrison well-supplied and in good cheer. This small town was now chosen by the Afghans for hitting at the enemy stomach. Mahmud Khan, son of Nawab Ahmad Khan, and Raja Prithwipat were deputed to execute this attack and when this news leaked out, consternation prevailed among the garrison at the apprehension of a two-fold attack simultaneously, one from the Jhusi and the other from the Arail side. The leaders met in deliberation to combat this danger, though it is not stated if the Gosain was present there. During this crises he proved, however, to be a tower of strength to the besieged. While Baqaullah went to action with the bulk of the forces at Arail, the Gosain faced the enemy from the other side "by drawing up in battle array from the Ganges bank to a point between the old city and the fort". The action that took place at Arail was sanguinary. The Afghans occupied the place but Baqaullah effected the retreat of his men across the bridge and then broke it down, Ahmad Khan did not follow up this success by striking from the Jhusi side. Yet the Gosain's firm stand on the bank of the Ganges without the cover of artillery was a great succour.

During this long interval the wazir retrieved his position at the court and marched to the neighbourhood of Farrukhabad. At once the lowering cloud that had hung over Allahabad was lifted, Ahmad Khan hurried back to the defence of his own realm. The mercenaries that had gathered round him in prospect of pay and plunder melted away and the insolent Afghan chief turned from a conqueror into a fugitive. Such a change was due to the heroic resistance of the Allahabad garrison who were sustained by the fearless fighting of the Nagas. Shortly after this even the Gosain was enrolled with his followers in the wazir's army and the Naga monks emerged as a factor in north Indian politics.

From April to June, Nawab Ahmad Khan fought hard to stem the tide of the wazir's triumph. The Ruhelas made common cause with him but their generals were outmatched and driven to seek shelter in the foothills of Kumaun, December 1751. Twenty-two miles north-east of Kasipur in the Moradabad district, there is an obscure place called Chilkiya which was favourably situated for fortification as well as defence. A dense forest surrounded the place on three sides and guarded it from attack; a rill near by trickled down the hill and offered a copius supply of water. The Afghans chose this site for their encampment. The Imperial chancellor came up in pursuit of them with the whole of his forces. The menace knit the Afghans together still more closely. But mutual cooperation and common exertions they fortified the exposed side of their encampment by a rampart and a moat which was filled with the water of the rill by means of an artificial channel. The earthen wall was so strongly built with bastions and towers that, according to the Afghan chronicler, "It looked like the fort of Daulatabad in the Dakhin" (*JASB*, 1879, p. 107).

From Lucknow and Allahabad, Singhirampur and Fatehgarh, the fighting now swung to the forest glade at the foot of the Kumaun range. For nearly eight weeks the military action was confined to an artillery duel and petty skirmishes. The wazir had an immense superiority both in the number of the forces and the strength of the artillery, but the volleys went beyond the target across the Afghan camp to the plains behind. In the meantime Abdali's invasion of the Punjab demanded the wazir's presence in the capital, but how could he go back, without concluding the war against his deadly adversary? He therefore summoned the Maratha chiefs, Jayappa Sindhia and Malhar Rao Holkar and his own commanders to a conference and consulted their opinion as to the course of action that should be adopted. Jayappa Sindhia who was intent on furthering the Maratha policy of expansion by keeping up an enmity among the north Indian powers, discountenanced the idea of a headlong attack upon the Afghan position saying, "we are used to fighting in the open not in entrenchment or fortress" (ibid.). The lukewarm attitude of the Marathas in the face of a grave emergency evoked a remonstrance from the Gosain. He interposed and said "the enemy is in the open; the only obstacle is the water," but this too, he pointed out, was non-existent at the eastern and western wings of the Afghan camp, which was therefore easy of approach at those points. At these words Jayappa fiared up and remarked, "you are also in the service of the Nawab-vizier. Why then don't you undertake the attack?" The Gosain readily took up this challenge. He declared that he would lead the attack next morning and bring Ahmad Khan alive a prisoner into the camp.

During the night the Gosain evolved his plan of attack. The wazir was to make a demonstration before the wing commanded by Najib Khan, keep him in play, while he himself would deliver the full-scale assault upon the wing of Ahmad Khan at the opposite moment. At day break the 15,000 troops of the Gosain were passed in review before the Nawab and then they marched towards the Afghan camp, they halted in a hollow at a certain distance from the point of attack and waited for the appropriate hour to strike. Another force under the personal command of the wazir headed towards the enemy camp in the opposite direction. The presence of the wazir in the field and the loud report of his guns produced among the Afghans the impression that the decision would be effected at that point. Excitement ran high in Najib's wing. Messengers rushed to Mulla Sardar Khan and Dundi Khan; Hafiz Rahmad [Rahmat] Khan came to Ahmad Khan, in order to draw off men to the threatened point. The Gosain's plan was about to bear fruit; but it did not. Ahmad Khan declined to reduce the strengh of his wing, and sent away the Ruhelas to their own post.

This unexpected conduct on the part of Ahmad Khan was due to perfidy in the wazir's camp. His resounding success against the Afghans had been won with the aid of the Marathas, but they were opposed to the annihilation of the Afghans and sought to preserve them as a counter-poise to his a scendency. Accordingly Jayappa had corresponded with Ahmad Khan after his flight from Aonla and urged him to take refuge in the hills. Again, when he was threatened with utter extinction at Chilkiya, the Maratha took steps to secretly communicate to him the Gosain's plan of attack. Of all these intrigues behind his back, the supine and short-sighted Safdar Jang took no account and this caused his own undoing.

From his position in the hollows, the Gosain scanned the Afghan position all day long. The Afghan battery which was his point d'appui seemed, however, always alive with men. A frontal attack upon an elevated position in the face of the withering fire of a watchful enemy was sure to smite his ranks; but the sannyasi's sense of honour was too strong to be damped by such a consideration. He therefore decided to fight. At the decline of the day, columns of foot and horse, in which a large element of swarthy monks presented a novel and incongruous sight were seen approaching the Afghan camp. Their leader was not the Gosain Rajendra Giri who kept himself in the hollow, but one of his *chelas*, who acted as his second-in-command. As they hove in fight of the battery, the sleepless nawab sounded the signal and his army drew up. In that hour of peril, he called upon his men to bend their knees in prayer; they recited the *Fatiha* and implored Allah. The guns boomed forth; the rockets exploded. The Afghans went forward under cover of fire and took up their position. The artillery duel continued for an hour after which the Afghans flung away their firelocks and made a rush with the bare sword. They were now swayed by an irresistible impulse to kill and die. In wave after wave they poured upon the enemy and swept all opposition aside. The Gosain army, composed of heterogenous elements, at first fell back and then broke. We do not know if treachery was at work and split up their ranks.

When the Gosain commander of the day saw his huge host flying away, he urged them to return to the fight. He was yet mounted and his colours were flying. To unite and inspire the scattered elements he got down and took his place among the ranks of the foot, attended only by his personal followers amid the yells of the surging enemy; swarms of them dashed upon him like breakers upon the shore.

The sun was going down at this hour and the western horizon was dyed with a crimson glow. Some of the Gosains were killed and others scattered, so that the commander was left alone in the field. He challenged, an Afghan that came forward. He long parried the enemy's sword and at last fell down.

This defeat at Chilkiya changed the whole aspect of the relations between the Afghans and the wazir. Faced with treachery and internal split, Safdar Jang was constrained to treat with the Afghans and hastily concluded peace with them.

Circumstances now recalled the wazir to the capital. The occupation of Lahore by Ahmad Shah Abdali caused panic in Delhi; and at the pressing invitation of the emperor, the wazir in the company of 50,000 Maratha troops reached the bank of the Jamuna opposite Delhi, on 25 April. A friction soon arose between him and Javed Khan, the leader of the Turani party, regarding the payment of the Marathas. Javed contrived to get out of the scrape by deputing them to the aid of Firuz Jang in the Deccan, but during the period of tension, the wazir had twice crossed the Jamuna in full force and made a demonstration of his strength by entering the palace in full military pomp. Among others, Rajendra Giri and Lutf Yar Khan attended on him to the grand public assembly-hall (Diwan-i-am) of the Mughal emperor.

Fresh causes of estrangement between the wazir and Javed Khan soon cropped up. In order to pique his rival, the latter fomented a disturbance in Sikandarabad, a privy-purse estate, 32 miles south of Delhi. At his instigation, Ballu Jat fell upon the place with his hordes, looted and made forcible extractions of money. A puny chief, Ballu was noted for his reckless daring and swiftness of attack. The conduct of operations against this audacious Jat was entrusted to the Gosain. The reknown of the military capacity and singular courage and fortitude of this monk had already spread far and wide. At the report of his approach to the Jat's hide-out at the fort of Dinkaur, Ballu slipped away with his forces and succeeded in covering his retreat to Ballamgarh by rear-guard fighting.

After the settlement of Sikandarabad, the Gosain joined the

post of faujdar at Saharanpur, about September 1752. It was a high post which was held formally by the Emperor's maternal uncle Mutaqaduddaulah, and after his death, by his minor son Atiqad. Here were settled many high families of Afghans, Gujars and Barha Sayyids, owning estates and claiming various exemptions and privileges. They had never entertained any respect for the authority of the local faujdar. The Gosain put them down, extracted revenue without any discrimination so that *Tarikh-i-Ahmad Shahi* laments, saying "the Afghans and Gujars and the Sayyids of Barha who had never obeyed any faujdar before, were totally ruined". He had been hardly eight months here when events called him back to Delhi.

In September 1752 the wazir had gained complete hold over the administration by causing the murder of Javed. But his selfish and shortsighted policy set in motion counteracting forces and brought about his expulsion from the court. His military and financial resources were then large; on the other hand the Government was virtually bankrupt; and the troops almost mutinous for arrears of pay. In the circumstances the wazir hit upon the expedient of manoeuvring his return to power by a threat of quitting the capital but his calculation went awny, the Emperor under the influence of his advisers, accepted the proposal. The wazir prevaricated, but the Emperor insisted and offered the aid of porters to expedite his departure. Safdar Jang was thereupon obliged to move out on 20 March. For more than a week he hovered menacingly with his forces around Delhi, yet no call came. He then made up his mind to coerce the Emperor in to submission by the demonstration of his armed strength. It was under these circumstances that he called in the aid of Rajendra Giri Gosain from Saharanpur, in the middle of April 1753.

At the instance of his master, the Gosain committed the first act of hostility by plundering certain villages along the Jamuna, on 22 April. On 4 May, he rendered another service by surrounding Salabat Khan the late Mir-Bakhsh when out on a pretended excursion to Shah Mardan's shrine, and then bringing him to his master's camp. On the following day he attacked Barapula, while another general Ismail Khan, pillaged Nagli, alarm spread in the capital. The emperor wrote with his own hand to the wazir ordering him to desist from violence. Under a false notion of his own power, Safdar Jang sent a haughty reply, demanding the immediate dismissal of Imad and Intizam and threatening an assault upon the palace-fort.

Mortified at this affront to his honour, the emperor sounded the call to arms. He ordered trenches to be dug in the sands below the palace and personally supervised the emplacements of the guns.

In the early period of the civil war that now ensued, the wazir maintained an offensive, on account of his marked superiority in men and materials. There hardly passed a day when his commanders did not swoop upon certain parts of the city and inflict destruction upon the inoffensive people. On 9 May the Gosain plundered the market (*mandavi*) and inhabited localities outside Shah Jahan's new city; on the day following the Jats roved across suburban areas like Sayyidwara, Bijal Masjid, and the first brush between the imperialists and the wazir's van commanded by the Gosain took place. While the Jats were out on the expedition, a party of the imperialists made a sudden sortie from their entrenchment on the advanced line of the wazir's troops and pushed the Gosain back. Thereupon the Jat attacks upon the old city mounted in violence. On 13 May, there was a complete rupture of relations between the Emperor and the wazir when the former publicly in vested Intizam with this office. Four days after the event, the ex-wazir achieved a signal triumph when the Kotilah-i-Firuz Shah, 3 miles south of Delhi was captured by his troops, Eighteen days later, 5 June, his commander Ismail Beg was forced out of this important vantage-point from which balls could be thrown into the imperial palace. It was no doubt a great set-back to his arms but the ex-wazir launched a vigorous efforts to regain the lost ground by breaking through the lines of imperial defences at the Idgah, off the Ajmeri Gate. The battle was joined at this point on 11, 12 and 14 June; on the last day the wazir personally attended the field in order to stimulate his troops. The casualties sustained by the imperialists on that day rose high and their defeat was averted only by the personal gallantry of the imperial Mir Bakhshi Imad-ul-Mulk. On the very day the Gosain who was charged with the conduct of operations on the Kalkapahari side, presumably to turn the imperial flank was shot (according to Imad) either by an assasin hired by Ismail Khan or by Najib Khan (according to *Gulistan-i-Rahmat*) and he died on the following day, 15 June 1753.

The Sannyasi's disappearance altered the aspect of the war and destroyed the ex-wazir's chances of victory. It sapped not only the fighting spirit out of his own immediate followers by rendering them leaderless, but also destroyed the initial impulse of the offensive on his side. As the *Tarikh-i-Ahmad Shahi* (599) says: "After the death of Rajendra Giri, Safdar Jang never went forth personally into any battle. When this fearless faqir died, none was left on Safdar's side eager to fight." His enemies steadily cornered him in the contest and drove him back to his own provinces, November 1753.

From the scanty materials at our disposal it is difficult to appraise the military stature of the Gosain, but one thing is clear; he was the principal support of the Safdar Jang, nay the moving spirit behind all his military enterprises. The *Siyar-ul-Mutakharin* pays him a fitting tribute when it says, "He had but a few bravoes with him, but all as determined and as invulnerable as himself, and so often did he come off unhurt from desperate engagements, that a notion prevailed that he had some piece of witchcraft about his body, or some talisman about his person; and this notion, which took hold of people's minds, rendered him still more formidable." By such matchless daring and leadership he had carved out a very high position for himself; Safdar Jang had conferred upon him the extraordinary privilege of not bowing before him in his presence and of beating his kettledrum while mounted— an honour enjoyed, only by the highest rank in the Mughal peerage (*Fall of the Mughal Empire*, I).

True, the historian cannot assign him the rank of a general; he rose only to the height of a divisional commander. He was not alive to the potency of fire-arm as an instrument of fighting, and bears resemblance to a paladin in his capacity for endurance, scorn of danger and fidelity to plighted word; but there is hardly any body who would deny the fact that he was a Sannyasi-warrior freed from the ordinary mortal ties and fortified in all his actions by the spirit of a devotee.

CHAPTER 10

Anupgiri *alias* Himmat Bahadur: Early Career

Anup and his elder brother Umraogiri were, according to one version the *chelas* of Rajendragiri, and according to another, the offspring of a Sanadhya Brahmin adopted by Rajendragiri. Of the two brothers, born in 1730 and 1734 respectively, the elder became more proficient in learning, and the junior in arms, receiving from Shuja the title of Himmat Bahadur in recognition of his prowess. After Rajendra Giri's death, Umraogiri was entrusted with the leaderships of the Naga Army. From July to December 1753 during which the civil war continued, both the brothers took an active part in fighting which is only casually mentioned in our sources (*Sujan Charita* and *Tarikh-i-Ahmad Shahi*). We learn from the former that the Nagas went into action on the first of July when the imperialists lost in action 500 on their side (*Sujan*, 191). A fortnight later, the imperialists mounted a counter-offensive; on the 16th a general action was planned when the Emperor Ahmad Shah and the new Wazir Intizam were to take the field in person. The report spread alarm in Safdar Jang's army, thinned by desertions. The Nagas, however, offered readily to fight, when others were lukewar. The action on that day took place at an unusual hour; it began an hour and a half before sunset and continued till two *gharis* of the night. A leader of the Nagas named Beni distinguished himself by fighting on that day; he bravely contested the ground against superior forces and kept up the fight until he was killed by the musket-shot of a Maratha Jamadar (*T.Ah.Sh* 64b). In two other actions, on 19 August and 23 September, the Nagas must have played their part, though this is not mentioned in any of the Chronicles.

After the conclusion of the civil war, the Nagas followed Safdar Jang to Lucknow. When the latter died in October 1754, they passed on to the service of his heir and successor Shuja-ud-Daulah. The author of *Shujauddaullah* has very much censured the Naga commanders for their part in abducting the Kshatri girl of the town of Faizabad (Ayodhya) Shuja's partisans allege that the agitation over this episode was a got-up affair, being engineered by Ismail Khan Kabali to supplant him and place his own nominee Muhammad Quli on the Oudh throne. The period from 1754 to 1764 is the hey-day in Shuja's career. During this period he secured his throne against the intrigues of enemies at home, the machinations of a wily diplomat like Imad-ul-mulk and the armed hostility of an invader like Ahmad Shah Abdali. Driven out of Delhi, he tried to turn the scales against his rival by promoting subtle schemes of territorial expansion in Bundelkhand and eastern India. He did not succeed due to the treachery of his allies; but it was chiefly due to the unswerving military support of the Nagas that Suja could make such a bid.

We can best show the part of the Nagas by unfolding the chief incidents of the period (1754-64). In the very beginning of Shuja's reign, the Naga leaders had to defend themselves from a covert attack made by Ismail Khan Kabuli. Second to none in influence in Oudh after the death of Safdar Jang, this Ismail Khan looked about for means to establish his virtual supremacy in the state. He found that the Nagas, being the loyal adherents of Shuja were the chief obstacle in his path and determined to root them out. The ruler of Oudh was a dissolute youth; struck by the beauty of a Kshatri girl of Faizabad, he sought to get possession of her and when others failed, employed the Nagas. At once the whole city was stirred by an agitation against the young ruler and his accomplices, the Nagas.

Ismail Khan entered into a league with the leaders of the

Mughalia troops; at his instigation Muhammad Quli Khan, governor of Allahabad marched towards Lucknow. The only body of men who stood by Shuja at this hour were the Gosain brothers with their followers. Ismail Khan now asked Shuja to absolve himself of the heinous guilt by dismissing the Nagas from their services. The latter understood the motive behind this seemingly just proposal and refused to disband them. A civil war seemed inevitable; but Shuja's mother brought her influence to bear upon the Diwan Ramnarain and weaned him from the rebel group. Ismail Khan and the Mughal sardars too there upon submitted, partly out of consideration for the sentiment of Begam Sadrunnissa and partly out of the fear of a clash with the Naga arms in which victory was not certain.

After the failure of this coup the Nagas gained a firm footing in the Oudh service, but could not feel secure until their arch-enemy Ismail Khan was removed by death in October 1755, and their fidelity was tested in the campaign against the Hindu Raja of Benares.

NAGA HELP AGAINST RAJA BALWANT SINGH

During the long period of Safdar Jang's absence from Oudh, the local feudatory chiefs, specially Raja Balwant Singh of Beṇares and greatly increased in strength. He had captured a chain of fortresses with a view to rounding off his dominions in the south. In 1765, he planned the capture of Chunar by bribing the Commandant of the fort. In the same year the unrest and resentment among the Hindus of Benares against the Nawab's authority, consequent on the destruction of the temple of Visweswara at the instance of the overzealous local Qazi gave the fillip to the Raja's ambition. As soon as Shuja felt free after the death of Ismail Khan, he struck against the Raja.

In this expedition the Naga troops formed the principal element of the Nawab's army, and materially contributed to its success. During the march from Jaunpur to Benares, Shuja was opposed at Pundurra by the mother-in-law of Raja Balwant.

This lady had well garrisoned the small fort and kept up a tough opposition even after a violent cannonade by the Nawab's army. In order to avoid needless loss of life and delay in march, the Nawab took recourse to diplomacy and deputed Anandgiri to effect a peaceful accommodation with the spirited woman. The Gosain executed his task skilfully and secured the surrender of the fort on terms honourable to both the parties. The lady was to make a show of submission by evacuating the fort and the time of his departure (*Shuja*, vol. 1, p. 2) the settlement with the Rani faciliated the capture of Chunar, and the reduction of the Raja of Benares before the storm of the Abdali invasion burst upon the frontier of his dominion.

NAGAS AGAINST ABDALI

At the end of 1756 the Afghan invader, Ahmad Shah Abdali had again appeared in India. The adversaries of the Nawab became active again; and organised a confederacy to compass his over throw under the pretext of recovering the imperial territory. They brought two princes of the imperial family, Mirza Baba and Hidayet Bakhsh, out of seclusion and put them at the command of two separate forces. Attended by Ahmad Khan Bangash, the Durrani general Jangbaz Khan, Sultan Khan (brother of Najibuddaullah), and the wazir Imad-ul-mulk, this army rolled towards Oudh in two different directions, in two divisions, one under Mirza Baba, and the other under Hidayet Bakhsh. In the first week of April (1757) Mirza Baba reached Qadirganj (40 miles north of Mainpuri) and Hidayet Bakhsh Etawah (30 miles south of it). The command of the army by the princes gave Shuja the character of a rebel and unsettled his position. His Mughalia troops wavered in their allegiance, but the Naga troops came forward and Anupgiri assumed the conduct of the campaign against this imperial forces. He so adroitly moved as to upset the plan of his enemies, he did not strike at either of the forces, but marched towards Farrukhabad. Alarmed for the safety of his own capital Ahmad Khan Bangash quitted the prince Hidayet Bakhsh.

The latter deprived of his guidance soon followed the Khan to Farrukhabad (6 May). The army under prince Mirza Baba also fell back on the Bangash capital.

In the meantime, Anup Giri advanced as far as Daraganj near Sangi and nipped in the bud the threat of a two-fold attack upon the capital of Oudh. He stood alone, a sentinal on the frontier for six weeks and held the enemy back until the Nawab joined him in full force at Sandi on 6 June. The imperial force too had by the time been strengthened by the adhesion of the Ruhelas and were eager for an encounter with the Nawab. As the contemporary authority Samin says "Every day the prince's audience was attended by all the leaders, including Jangbaz Khan, Hafiz Rahmad Khan, Mulla Sardar Khan Bakhshi and Nawab Ahmad Khan. . . . The (other) chiefs admitted that they were willing to obey the orders of the emperor and of the Shah; in whatever direction the princes might advance, they were ready to follow in their train and take part in the contest and battle-fray (*Indian Antiquary*, 1907, p. 67). On the other hand, the Nawab's army was filled with a despondent spirit owing to a prevailing belief in the superiority of the Afghan arms. As Samin says "When the regiment of Mimbashi Sadiq Beg was ordered out for parade, Sardar Khan, the leader of 5,000 Mughals attended, but of his whole command only 25 men put in an appearance at the muster. All the rest, out of the fear of the Afghan . . . had fled."

In this depressing situation, the Nagas showed a reckless disregard of life and a laudable fighting spirit. They engaged in skirmishes with the enemy (*Siyar*, in tran. 3-4, p. 351) cutting off once a number of Afghan foragers (Sam in p. 67) This audacious fighting did not prove in vain. As a consequence the Nawab got better terms and extricated himself out of the impasse by primising an indemnity contribution of Rs. 5 lakh.

During the same year a large body of Nagas had won martyrdom by fighting for their faith against the fanatical Afghans at Gokul, opposite Mathura. Ahmad Shah Abdali had issued that time a stern decree[1], ordering a general slaughter and burning of the whole country from Agra to Mathura. His faithful followers deluged the town of Mathura with blood. "For seven days . . . The water of the Jamuna (at this holy city) flowed of a blood red colour. The Sannyasis and the Bairagis were depapitated and their heads were defiled by being tied to a cow's head. The account of unopposed massacre and loot was relieved by the resistance of a body of 4,000 Naga monks. Of them 2,000 laid down their lives but saved the shrine of the Diety at Gokul from defilement (*Marathi Riyasat, Panipat Prakaran*, p. 77; Qanungo, *History of the Jats*, p. 102).

ANUPGIRI AGAINST THE MARATHAS

Finding northern India in a state of anarchy, the Peshwa Balaji Baji Rao matured his scheme for the conquest of the country. In 1757-8 the Punjab fell into Maratha hands; in the following year they swept down to Najibuddaulah's territory. Unable to match his strength against this vast army, the Ruhela leader split up his forces into two parts; with the larger one he shut himself up in the impregnable fort of Shukartal; while the residue was left in charge of his son Zabita Khan at the capital of Najibabad. When after a three month's seize, the Ruhela stronghold showed no signs of yielding, the Maratha general Dattaji set his lieutenant Govinda Ballal with a force of 10,000 light cavalry upon Najibabad. Destruction now threatened Najib; his Ruhela clansmen like Dundi Khan, and Sardar Khan were lukewarm, they were afraid

[1] Abali's order to Jahan Khan is thus given in Samin, ibid, p. 51: "Take Najib Khan with you and march this very instant. Move into the boundaries of the accursed Jat, and in every town and district held by him slay and plunder. The city of Mathura is a holy place of the Hindus, and I have heard that Suraj Mall is there, let it be put entirely to the edge of the sword, to the best of your power leave nothing in that kingdom and country. Up to Akbarabad leave not a single place standing."

to risk battle with the Marathas. Najib had therefore no friend upon whom he could count for immediate succour.

Such was the hour when a diplomatic revolution occurred in northern India by the burial of the hatchet between the Sunni Afghans of Rohilkhand and the Shia ruler of Oudh. Shuja; understanding the Maratha designs, considered the Maratha attack upon Najib's territory as one on his own, and dashed out to Bareilly with the pick of his force in November 1759. Shuja's intervention at a critical turn in the Maratha-Najib contest stirred up the Ruhelas; more than 4,000 of whom under Sardar Khan immediately marched to Najibabad. They reached the outskirts of the Ruhela capital in time to intercept Govinda Ballal baulked of the prey, the latter diverged into a south easterly direction towards Shukartal, spreading terror all along the way by his ravages. Najib was now in imminent danger of being trapped between two fires.

This calamity was averted by the adroit military leadership and daring of the Naga commanders, Anupgiri and Umraogiri while Shuja encamped at Haldaur, 18 miles south-east of Bijnor, hc placed the van of his army consisting of 10,000 men under the Gosain leaders, and directed them to engage the Marathas whenever they could be found. The Naga leaders wound their way under cover of nocturnal darkness through forests and defiles along the trackless route and suddenly burst upon Govinda Ballal, when he was resting his weary troops in a glen after his lightning marches and pillaging. The Marathas taken completely by surprise, could make no stand. The Nagas made a slaughter of two to three hundred men, taking many others captive and looting the booty (*Siyar*). After routing Govinda Ballal, Anupgiri crossed over to Shukartal by Najib's bridge and set up his camp at a distance of only half a *coss* from the Ruhela encampment. Within a short while Shuja too finding the way clear joined Najib at Shukartal. This dramatic turn caused by Shuja's diplomacy and the military enterprise of the Nagas upset all the calculations of Dattaji counter-balanced in strength and alarmed by the renewed invasion of the Abdali, he came to terms with Najib and departed from Shukartal, December 1759; while the Nagas with their ruler marched back to Lucknow.

NAGAS AT PANIPAT

As a natural sequel to the diplomatic revolution during the seige of Shukartal, Shuja cast die against the Marathas on the occasion of the fighting at Panipat. He knew the Moslem, aversion to the naked Naga monks, yet he chose to take them with him to the vast assembly of the Afghans at Panipat. We know, however, that their ungracious visage accentuated by nudity acerbated the feelings of the Durrani Shah himself. Having caught sight of them once in the course of his daily peregrination of the entrenchment, he said, "how could the *Kaffirs* have so much liberty as to walk with their things and buttocks exposed (*peshopas barhana Kardah*) before the Moslems (*Imad*, p. 80) and demanded of Shuja their removal from his encampment. The Nagas had to comply with this edict by removing to a distance with their tents. On the fateful, 14 January 1761, when the violent contest of Panipat occured, they stood firm in their position and fought in support of the Afghan ally unconcerned with the fate of the Marathas. Anupgiri assisted by Kashi Pandit discharged the duty of giving Hindu cremation to the last remains of the Maratha generals, Viswas Rao, Sadasiva Rao Bhau and Santaji Wagh. The bodies were bathed with the holy Ganges water; mounted on pyres made of sandal-wood and then set alight; Anupgiri standing guard during the performance of the funeral rites (*Imad*, 201-2; Sarkar, *IHQ*, 1934, p. 272)

ANUPGIRI AGAINST THE BUNDELAS

Bundelkhand especially the south-eastern part of it, cut up by low mountain chains, has been the hearth of freedom for centuries. At integral part of the Mughal empire from Akbar to Muhammad Shah, it was granted to Safdar Jang in 1748, but neither he nor his successor Shuja dared to challenge the Maratha rule over this territory until the debacle of the latter at Panipat threw Bundelkhand into a ferment, 1762. This was the year when Shuja was united in arms with the Emperor Shah Alam II and felt strong enough to recover the territory which formed a part of his ancestral heritage.

In encouraging and partially realizing this design, Anupgiri was his chief instrument. Of the two persons Balaji Govinda and Ganesh Sambhaji, governors of Kalpi and Jhansi respectively who represented Maratha authority in the region, the former was more greedy and self-seeking. He had already trimmed his sail with the favourable wind by opening hostilities with the Marathas loyal to the Puna Government, and commenced overtures for entering the Mughal service. The go between in this clandestine negotiation was Anupgiri; he arranged the trems of the compact between the two parties; as a consequence Jhansi fell like a ripe plum into the wazir's mouth, and was opened for the attack on the heritage of Chhatrasal, now represented by two rival lines headed by Ghuman Singh and Khuman Singh, the ruler of Jaitpur, and by Hindupati, that of Panna.

Shuja's first tussle with the Panna ruler was (March-April 1762) abruptly terminated owing to the outbreak of rebellion in his own dominions and Hindupat's compliance with the demand for an annual tribute (March-April 1762). The Bundela Raja however made no attempt to pay the stipulated tribute; the Nawab-Wazir who considered him a minor chief was mortified at this insolence and decided on curbing his pretensions once for all. Here again, the Gosain leader became his guide and pointed out the way by which the wooden horse could be introduced into Bundelkhand and the country reduced to obedience.

There was an Afghan named Keramat Khan who had grown up like a blood brother of Hindupat in the Bundela country. Having quarrelled with him over a dancing girl, he had quitted the Bundela service in disgust and was then living at Fatehpur within the jurisdiction of the pargana of Kora-Jahanabad.

This Pathan was a man of immense size and strength; and was endowed with warlike capacity. He knew the country throughly well. The Goswami now induced him to enter the wazir's service and lead the forces against his inveterate enemy under his supreme command.[2] Undismayed Hindupat accepted the challenge. He

[2] fn. p. 10.

was the ruler of a considerable territory yielding a revenue of Rs. 90 lakh annually; owned a gold mine which was estimated to produce an additional income of more than Rs. 1 crore. His rustic clansmen untouched by civilization, supplied him with a body of excellent soldiers. At the report of Anupgiri's advance with a force of only 25,000 men, he joked to his courtiers saying "What measure of pride has puffed up this naked man (*naga*) that he dares to get to grips with me? I shall depute such and such a person that would bring the *naga* before me as a prisoner" (*Imad*, p. 87). Yet without making light of his adversary, he leagued with Ghuman Singh, chief of collateral lines and stood ready with a force of 80,000 men.

The contest took place at Tindwari in the Banda district (Pogson, 113 (*Himmat Bahadur Birudabali*). Anupgiri and Rahim Khan Pathan (uncle of Keramat Khan) who commanded the bulk of the Oudh forces closed with Hindupat. While Keramat encountered 12,000 Bundelas of Karachal denomination (*Shuja* I, 149). Though out-numbered the Gosain fought obstinately. But the mounted Bundela spearsmen signally defeated (*Imad*, p. 88). Anupgiri and pursued him with slaughter as far as the Jamuna, while Karamat died fighting on the field (Pogson, 113, *Himmat Bahadur Birudabali* and *Imad*, 88).

In the mean time while Anupgiri was engaged in the fight with the Bundelas, he was overtaken by another calamity. His brother Umraogiri had long chafed under a sense of his merit not being properly recognised. In the midst of the Bundela war, he had left the Nawab's service and entered that of the Bangash chief Ahmad Khan. This unfortunate event very much compromised the position of Anupgiri; he became importunate in soliciting Umrao to return to the path of fidelity; but the latter was intractable. Shuja who had long watched the hostile proceedings of Ahmad Khan issued an ultimatum demanding the expulsion of the Naga on pain of war. Hostilities seemed imminent, the esteem in which the fighting qualities of the Nagas were held is revealed by Ahmad Khan's statement to Umraogiri, in reply to hit request for leave in order to avert the hostilities that impended, "If you stay on and a hundred Shujas arrive, I shall never separate you from me my place is your own (*Khana-i-man Khana-i tuast*). If on the other hand, you choose to depart, I have not put fetters on your feet. God is the protector and helper."

For sometime the war clouds rumbled on the frontier of the two territories; the storm did not burst owing to the judicious restraining of Shuja and the intervention of Najib. Umraogiri having quitted the Bangash territory, returned to Agra.

ANUPGIRI AT PANCHPAHARI (PATNA) AND BUXAR

After the death of Nawab Alivardi Khan, there was a succession of kaleidoscopic changes on the masnad of Bengal owing to the establishment of the supremacy of the East India Company. In November 1763, the deposed ruler Mir Qasim came, a fugitive to the Nawab wazir's camp with a vast amount of treasure and the trained battalions of Samru and the clash which had been deferred since 1759 between Shuja and the English now took place.

In the two battles of Panchpahari and Buxar that changed the whole complexion of affairs in northern India, a vast army consisting of Qizilbashes, Turani Mughals, Pathans and Rajputs fought on the side of the wazir, but none responded with so much enthusiasm to the wazir's call as the Nagas. It is wellknown that the Nawab wazir's allies like Balwant Singh and Mir Qasim and a trusted Diwan like Beni Bahadur remained indifferent and inactive; but when at about 2 p.m., the battle was renewed, after an ineffectual cannonading in the morning, the Nagas who had taken their position by the side of the Ruhelas inspite of a brush with them on the way from Maner to Patna, were the first to head the charge upon the English right wing. There were five to six thousands of them in the field; they were armed with the outmoded weapons of sword and arrow; they were no steel helmet or coat of mail, which could protect their person from the bullet, yet they went joyfully to the attack; with all the fury of which they were capable; but swords could not score over gun-powder and the Nagas had to fall back beaten.

At Buxar too (23 October 1764) the palm of bravery was carried by the Nagas. They, allied with the Mughal cavalry, suddenly bypassed the village of Jagdishpur and the morass that lay north-east of it, and flung themselves upon the English rear and flank in impetuous assaults. By means of swift evolutions the English received the ferocious Nagas and the Mughals in front. Grape and musket fire slowed down their assaults on the rear, but the flank was pierced it would have been shattered to pieces, and the English would have lost the day, if as Col. Harper wrote, "one or two thousand of the enemy's cavalry had behaved as well as those that attacked the grenadiers", The Englsh did not lose the day. Leadership and unity of purpose were wanting on the side of the wazir.

The Gosains had played their part well. But they could not stand the hail of bullets from the English line which poured with such a deadly effect upon them.

CHAPTER 11

In the Jat Service, 1764-1766

In the middle of the eighteenth century, the Jats under Suraj Mal stepped into prominence as a leading power in north India. In 1763 he pitted his strength against that of Najib-ud-daulah and in the fighting that ensued, Suraj Mal was shot dead on 25 December 1763. His son and successor Jawahir Singh tried to transform the tribal headship into the pattern of a full-fledged royalty and to plant the Jat standard in the imperial city of Delhi.

Umrao who had entered the service of Suraj Mal after resigning from Farrukhabad, and Anup from Oudh, rendered conspicuous work during this Jat-Ruhela contest. When Jawahir Singh's first offensive against Delhi city (15 November 1764) was rendered infructuous by Malhar Rao's refusal of the necessary support, Jawahir planned an assault from the eastern bank of the Jamuna, but the indiscreet plunder of the Patparganj mart on the way, and the clouds of dust raised by the Jat cavalry on the other bank forewarned the wary Ruhela dictator Najib-ud-daula of the coming storm. He met the danger by a wise disposition of his troops and by the use of the art of ambuscade in which his clansmen were past-masters. As a consequence, not only did the expedition miscarry but the entire corps of Jat troops was threatened with annihilation. As Nuruddin Hasan, a contemporary chronicler and eye-witness of the battle, reports, "Sewairam, with 150 horsemen fell in a hand-to-hand fight. . . . The other Jat sardars such as Balram, and (Ram) Kishan Mahant, with all their soldiers took to flight. The Ruhelas began to pursue and the Mughalia horsemen who had run away (at the first shock), came back and joined in the pursuit. The Jats were placed between the galloping Ruhels in front and the water of the Jamuna behind, without any prospect of succour. Jawahir, mounted on horse-back, espied the scene from the other bank and was filled with alarm. He wanted to rush across the water forthwith to their rescue. It was a task involving risk to his life and he was prevented from executing it by Imad-ul-Mulk.

In this critical situation orders were issued to Umrao Giri to extricate the fleeing Jats from the jaws of the Ruhela horsemen. Racking little of the consequence, the intripid warrior plunged his horse into the river with a band of followers numbering six to seven hundred men (ibid., 80a). By a lucky accident he discovered fleeing Jat troops; and under his inspiration they turned round and engaged. The struggle continued till nightfall, when the Ruhelas retired to the city; while the Jats got across the river between two rows of torch-bearers lining the Jamuna bed from one bank to the other. The Jat Raja's sense of relief was great; he appreciated the Gosain's devotion and bravery by lifting him to the howdah of his own elephant and riding round the camp to visit and comfort his wounded soldiers.

The Jat-Ruhela tussle was in full swing for more than a month after this event. Jawahir replenished his strength during this interval by summoning the Sikhs to his standard, yet he failed to win any decisive advantage over the enemy.

In these circumstance he planned to mount a still greater offensive by taking into his pay the contingent of Anupgiri. This Naga leader had followed his master Shuja through all the vicissitudes from the battle of Buxar to his exile in the Ruhela country, but when he failed to feed his risala any longer for want of money and his stored up wealth (such as tents, carpets, camp-equippage and lakhs of coins) was taken away from the fort of Achalgarh by Najaf Khan (*Ibratname*, II, 150), he bade a reluctant adieu to his master and transferred his sword to the service of Jawahir Singh, end of December 1764. For sometime after his junction the war did not undergo any material alteration in its fortunes. Najib cooly endured the privations caused by the scarcity of supplies and animated his troops by his own reckless courage. This spirited resistance in the face of overwhelming odds filled the Jat Raja with dejection. One of his allies, Imad who had been living upon the hospitality of the Jat State for years, was supine, while the other Malhar Holkar who had taken large sums from him was playing fast and loose. Jawahir muttered in despair. "The Maratha has taken a large sum from me but is not giving his heart to the fight". Anupgiri who was standing near, took the hint and responded with alacrity, "Today I shall go forth with the Nagas and do what can be done by us" (ibid., 86 a). The Gosain acted according to his word. On that very day he led his followers and some of Jawahir's men across the river and occupied the mansion of Hafizuddin outside the city-walls. Jawahir had hitherto pursued what is termed by the well known writer, Liddel Hart, the strategy of "Direct Approach". That is to say, he had endeavoured to overcome the enemy by a preponderance of strength and a frontal attack. Anup wisely altered the scheme and attempted to encompass his opponent's downfall in an indirect way. He split up his infantry armed with musket and sword into several groups, and ordered them to infiltrate into Delhi city in the fashion of guerrilla bands, Behind the cover of their artillery fire came the corps of cavalry. In the beginning the onset was well under way, causing casualties to the Ruhelas and dragging Najib to the scene. The Afghan genius in war could not be outwitted. After surveying the situation he called his men away from the fighting. The Nagas then began to advance slowly when all of a sudden Najib launched his Ruhela Soldiers from different directions against them. By a single stroke the Naga plan of battle was deranged. The encirclement of the infantry columns immobilized the Jat cavalry which depended for its advance upon the artillery curtain and Anupgiri had to pull his men out after a heavy bloodbath, January 1765. The see-saw battle dragged on for some time more. The spectre of famine and increasing desertion from the Ruhela ranks betokened the doom of Najib; but he was saved by the support of Jawahir's own allies Malhar and the cowardice of the Jat leaders, who could not subordinate their pretty family advantages to the overriding consciousness of their national interest. Jawahir's grand scheme failed; the Gosains, however, had acquitted themselves very creditably, amidst the puny Jat chiefs such as Balram Ramkrishna Mahant and others with their narrow selfish intersts and the perfidious allies like Malhar and Imad.

The Maratha authority in north India after the debacle of Panipat was represented among others by Holkar. In the beginning of 1766 he lent the services of his arms to Nahar Singh, Jawahir's rival for the throne. This stirred up the hostility of the Jat raja who attacked and signally defeated the Marathas taking many of their commanders captive (13 and 14 March 1766). Flushed with success, Jawahir swept away the Maratha authority fron north Malwa and threatened to wipe it out of Bundelkhand as well.

Such was the turn of affairs when the Peshwa's brother Raghunath Rao appeared in north Malwa. The contingents of Mahadji Sindhia and Malhar joined him near Bhander, 24 April, and his force of cavalry swelled to 60,000 men and artillery to more than 100 pieces (Wendel, Sarkar's tr.). With this host he battered the fortress of Gohad in vain for more than six months and then turned to settle accounts with King Jawahir. The rival forces moved towards each other for a trial of strength, but the reported Abdali invasion cooled their ardour and led to the initiation of discussions for peace.

Springing from the Vindhya ranges, the river Chambal flows across Rajputana and Malwa to unite with the Jamuna east of Etawah. Below Dholpur it winds in a narrow course southward; there down the steep banks extended patches of plain soil marked out from the whitey-grey of the stony earth, and broken by a labyrinth of ravines. In November 1766 on this rough edge of the Chambal, a canvas city sprang up from the assembling of the Jat and Maratha armies. For days together negotiations went on with an exchange of vakils, e.g. of Harji Chowdhury on the side of the Jats and Dewan Nandram on that of the Marathas, and an atmosphere of perfect friendship and cordiality prevailed among the various elements of people gathered here, which was illustrated by an inter-change of visits by Jawahir, Umrao Giri and Naru Shankar (10 and 11 December) and the reciprocal offer of gifts. On this occasion the Gosain in his turn sent Rs. 500 and 10 maunds of provisions to the Maratha chief, Naru Shankar (*C.P.C.* II, 12 B.C.D.E.)

In the midnight of 22 December, when the inmates of the respective camps were sunk in profound sleep and the lights glowed feebly under the blanket of the deepening fog, Jawahir ordered some of his loyal corps to advance and deal destruction to the Gosain camp. They executed the order with efficiency; they poured upon the unsuspecting sleepers from all directions, and cut to pieces 5 to 7 hundred of them. Umrao, Anup, and Mariehgir fought their way through the ranks of the Jat troopers with only 300 men and sought asylum across the Chambal in the Maratha camp.

Such was the cowardly attack made upon the Jat raja's most sincere and steadfast followers and the responsibility, curiously enough, for arousing Jawahir's frenzy and provoking this shameful outrage has been fastened upon the very victims of this cruelty. Harcharan Das, who completed the work *Chahar Gulzar-i-Shujai* in 1784 first put out the story current in his time that the two Gosain commanders had conspired to betray the Jat raja into the Maratha hands in return for the grant to them of Moth and other fiefs on the Kalpi side[1] (Sarkar Ms., fl. 473-4).

This statement has coloured the opinion of modern historians (vide, Qaunngos, *History of the Jats*, 189-90). From the contemporary Jesuit father Wendel's account, and Maratha records (S.P.D. 29, O 164) it becomes apparent, however, that Jawahir committed this crime, on the mere suspicion of the Gosain having entered into an understanding with the Marathas.[2] We know farther from

[1] In har du baradar az Jawab-sawal-i-muamalat, Jawahir Singh garhi Moth. Ghayera ke tarat-i-Kalpi ast baraye khud az Maratha maqarrar sakht (*Chahar Gulzar*).

[2] Having been informed of a treason, which two of his chiefs secretly

the *P.P. Akhbarat* dated 3 February 1767 (recently explored by Sir Jadunath) that this suspicion was inspired in Jawahir's mind by his religious guide and political adviser Ramkrishna Mahant.[3] This was the man who had shared power with Umraogir ever since the young raja's accession but he had presumably been overshadowed by the latter in consequence of his superior diplomatic and military ability. Tormented by his jealousy of the alien fighting monk, Ramkrishna must have brooded over the means for his ruination. He accomplished it, when the junction of a body of 20,000 Nagas under Balanānda Gosain from Gohad, made Jawahir independent of Umraogir's support.

By this reperehensible act Ramkrishna Mahant gained his personal end, but the Jat State was made poorer by being deprived of the services of a very loyal and efficient fighting force and the moderation and wisdom of their leaders; for after their exit, there remained at Bharatpur hardly one sage and disinterested counsellor who could bridle the caprices of this Jat Don Quixote. His armed march across the Jaipur territory to Pushkar lake that followed the expulsion of the Gosains was disastrous to the Jat raja and hastened the downfall of the Jat power in Bundelkhand.

---

in the party of the Marathas were thinking of practising or suspected to be so, he was obliged to come to an accommodation with Raghunath but was avenged afterwards on the traitor (Sir Jadunath's trans.).

[3] By the instigation of Ramakrishna Mahant, Jawahir had alineated Umraogir and other sardars and looted their camp (*P.P. Akh.* A 4a).

CHAPTER 12

In Bundelkhand and Oudh Service

Raghunath Rao accorded a cordia reception to the Naga commanders in his camp and provided for their urgent needs such as tents, clothing elephants and horses. This kindness was reciprocated by loyal exertions on their part on his behalf. As the *P.P. Akhbarat* records (March 1767) Umraogir constantly attending on Dada (Raghunath), raising troops and offering to cross the river (Chambal) and plunder the Jat territories. But the Maratha was in no mood to cross swords again with Jawahir and therefore restrained him. Shortly after he left for the Deccan, and the Nagas now became free-lances again, subsisting by the plunder of Bundelkhand, which had now become a no-man's land, on account of the antagonism between Ghuman Singh and Khuman Singh and the insurrection of the vassal chiefs. In June 1787 Anupgir wrested Samthar from the Gujars and put Umrao in possession of Jhansi (*S.P.D.* XXIX, 185). The two commanders roved across this taluq with their bands and completely ruined 29, out of its 42 villages (ibid., 195). But by this time the staggering Nawab of Oudh had risen to his feet; the Congress of Chapra had restored him to his territories; he drafted the Gosains back to service. They were given the rank of *four hazari zat*, and *three hazari* troopers, with the extraordinary privilege of *Mukhtari-i-dasthhat*), i.e. enlisting troops in their contingent without reference to the Nawab; each of them was assigned an yearly pay of Rs. 49,000 and thus put on the same rank as that enjoyed by the other commander Gopal Rao Maratha, a member of the Peshwa's family in Shuja's service (*Imad.* 102).

During this period of renewed service in Oudh from 1767 to 1775 they played their part in the field of warfare and diplomacy and their faithful and honest exertion was one of the factors that contributed to the Nawab's astonishingly quick recovery of his old position in the political chessboard of India.

IN SHUJA-UD-DAULAH'S SERVICE, (MARCH 1770-1775)

Early in 1770 the Peshwa's agents reappeared in India at the head of a mighty force. In June-July, Umrao was deputed to the Maratha Camp at Aligarh in order to workout a secret entente for the division of the Ruhela territory, but the English suspicion of Shuja's design and their opposition obliged the Nawab to recall the Gosain in August. When the Maratha depredations in the middle Doab in the following months and their capture of Etawah, 15 December, menaced the safety of Oudh, the Nawab again posted Umraogiri at the head of his corps at the frontier outpost of Kanpur to watch the Marathas, January 1771 (*C.P.C.* III, 562, 564, 579). In April 1771, the Emperor, Shah Alam, weary of English protection at Allahabad started for returning to his capital. The Nawab escorted him as far as Jajmau and then bade him good bye. On 3 June, leaving the Gosain brothers with 5,000 horses and 5,000 foot and 5 pieces of cannon to accompany him (*C.P.C.* III, 998).[1]

On arriving near Farrukhabad, Shah Alam provoked a conflict by demanding the succession fee or tribute from Muzaffar Jang, the son of the deceased Nawab Ahmad Khan Bangash. In desperation he summoned Mahadji Sindhia to his aid. The prospect of the junction of the Emperor with the Maratha chief

[1] According to the *P.P. Akhbarat* they were left with only 3,000/4,000 troops.

and of Sindhia acquiring dominance over the affairs of the empire caused profound irritation and disgust among the adherents of the Emperor, the Bangash and Ruhela Afghans. A letter of the *P.P. Akhbarat* dated 7 November thus depicts the situation, "The Afghan and Ruhela sardars are saying that when the lord of Hindustan falls into the hands of the Decannis, it will become impossible for the country to enjoy a little safety and ease. It is therefore better that we should all go to the emperor and from such a combination that the Maratha may not gain control over the affairs of the empire."

In this posture of affairs Shuja sent his Prime Minister Elich Khan to the Emperor. The latter refused to retract from his determination of proceeding to Delhi. With an instinctive sense of reality, Shuja now endeavoured to regain his lost position in the Emperor's court by becoming the medium of negotiation with Sindhia and appeasing the growing resentment of the Afghans against him. This delicate task of wire-pulling in a manner which seemingly favoured a union of interests between the Emperor, Sindhia and Shuja but left the real direction in the hands of the Oudh Nawab, was confided to Anup Giri. He met the Emperor in November and was sent to Sindhia's camps which was then separated from his by a distance of 25 *coss*. He coaxed the Maratha chief and declared to him his master's intention of facilitating the interview between Sindhia and the Emperor, but neither he nor Shah Alam was deceived by the tissue of halftruths, and untruths. On 18 November they affected their junction at Nabiganj before Shuja could arrive. Eight days Shuja recalled the Gosain to Faizabad.

In February 1772, Shuja's capital was rocked by an explosion arising out of an armed conflict between two different corps of his army. Sabit Khanis and Ihilangis. In response to Shuja's order, the Gosains marched with a body of 5,000 troops to the residential quarters of the insurgent regiments and by ruthless violence and destruction to their property and houses quelled the mutionous troops (*Harcharan*, 507 a & b, *Imad*, 105-6).

In the same month the Marathas backed by the Emperor invaded Rohilkhand. The fortresses of Shukratal and Pathargarh were captuered in the sweep of their victories; but the emperor quarrelled with his allies over the share of the booty that had fallen into their hands. Shuja chose the occasion for sending Anupgiri to the emperor's court, along with Sindhia's envoy Bahirji Takpir. The Gosain worked upon the common points of interest between the two chiefs and induced in Sindhia's mind such a feeling of respect and friendship for Shuja that there now occurred an exchange of turbans between them in sign of full brotherhood.[2] In July 1772 the Gosain in concert with Elich Khan succeeded in settling contribution of the fugitive Ruhela chiefs, payable to Shuja and effecting the release of the captive wives and children of Zabita Khan (*P.P. Akh.*). Hardly nine months had elapsed after this event when, by a curious turn, the Marathas, in the absence of Sindhia in the Deccan, planned on attack upon Shuja's dominion. The Nawab personally marched his forces on 3 March 1773 and engaged the Marathas. The Gosain contingents took part in this fighting, and their action so impressed Col. Champion, the conqueror of Rohilkhand, that he called them the best cavalry in the Oudh service (Macpherson, *Soldiering in India*, 203). Simultaneously, a detachment commanded by Umraogiri, with the assistance of another Gosain Sinhagiri considerably shocked the Maratha authority in Bundelkhand. The former attacked Jhansi, while the forces of the latter operated in the Kalpi side. The situation became so critical in November that the local Maratha commander wrote, "If 5000 troops came from your place, then the fort (Jhansi) can be saved, otherwise I do not see how it can remain in our possession" (*S.P.D.* 29/274). In November-December, Shuja took advantage of the dissolution

[2] Sir Jadunath humourously remarks on this episode, saying "It was done in absentia, the turban without the head having travelled from Fyzabad to Sindhia's camp for being exchanged with the Maratha's cap (*pagoti*), *Fall*, III, 58.

of the Maratha Government at the centre, to reoccupy the Middle Doab. Anupgiri took an active part in this expedition and in the capture of Etawah, of which territory he was appointed faujdar (*C.P.C.* 704, 712, 731; *Shuja*, II, 236). In April 1774 occurred the conquest of Rohilkhand by Oudh. It appears from the Maratha despatches that Anupgiri was present in the action of Miranpur Katra on 23 April. His service were rewarded with the conferment of the privilege of beating the *naubat*, gift of an elephant and other marks of honour; he was granted the lease of a vast tract in the Doab yielding Rs. 51 lakh (*S.P.D.* 29/280). In November he was again deputed with a force of 10,000 to 15,000 troops, against Etwah which had slipped out of Shuja's control after Naim Khan's defeat in Bundelkhand.

April 1774 (ibid., 29/282), after the death of Shuja, January 1775, his son and successor Asafuddaulah planned a campaign against Bundelkhand and placed Anupgiri at the head of an army in March 1775 (*C.P.C.* IV, 1693) but invasion had to be put off; mounting expenditure and the financial dislocation of Oudh soon forced the Gosain to seek service under Mirza Najaf Khan, the regent of Delhi.

CHAPTER 13

In the Emperor's Service

The disorganisation of the Central Government of the Empire of Delhi in the eighteenth century was followed by the rise of a few soldier-statesmen to the helm of affairs at the imperial court. Foremost among them was Mirza Najaf Khan, a Persian who became the steward of the Delhi empire, after the fall of Hisamudaulah in May 1773. His successive contests with the Jats, in 1773, 1775 and 1777-8 fill a large space in his advent to power he found the Jat fortresses of Maidangarhi, 13-14 mile distant from the Qutab Minar and Dankaur across the Jamuna, aimed like uplifted pistols at Shahjahanabad, and that the Jat troops were roving across Ghaziabad and Shahdara, so near the capital.

In 1773, the Jat ruler Naval Singh was no doubt a weak man, but he was buttressed by the warrior monk Balanand and his Gosain contingent. It was Balanand who in concert with Dan Shah Jat had put Naval Singh at the head of affairs in 1776 in preference to Ranjit Singh. It was mainly under his influence and inspiration that Jats tried conclusions with the Marathas hired by Ranjit at Sonkh-Aring on 4 April. Notwithstanding the reverse sustained here, Balanand maintained his position of ascendancy and the spirits of Jats remained high. Hence the Gosain troops formed the core of opposition during Najaf's repeated tussles with the Jat power. When Nawal Singh cowered under the terror of Najaf's arms, these Gosains barred the Mughal's path at Barsana. In the action that was fought here on 30 October 12,000 of them (*Ibrat*, i. 236) armed with muskets took their position on the Jat left under the command of Balanand, while opposite their ranks stood the Ruhelas under Rahimbad. The Nagas began the action by a fusilade from their firearms, but it was not effective. The mass of charging Ruhela infantry rose and fell before them like the waves in a tempestuous sea and by didging the bullets, bore down upon them in a tumultuous rush. The wall of the Naga line held for a time the surging billow of the Ruhela attack, but broke after a thousand of the Nagas had laid down their lives. The position could yet have been retrieved for the Jat right under Samru had scattered the Mughal left; but at last the Jats went down for lack of grit and commanidng ability in their generallissimo, Nawal Singh.

During Najaf's second offensive, 1775-6, Balanand must have done his part in frustrating Najaf's swoop upon the Jat Raja on 10 June 1775, in the course of Rajah's pilgrimage from Dig to Govardhan (*Fall*, III, 114-15). His greatest service to the Jat State was to liberate Dig from grip of Rahimabad Ruhela. The latter had seized the occasion of general mourning on the death of Nawal Singh to make himself master of thc fortress city. But it was wrested from him by a bold coup organised by the monk. Allied with a body of 2,000 Maratha horse under Jaswant Rao Bable the Gosain marched under cover of darkness in the night from Kumbher and fell upon the Ruhela camp under the fort-walls at break of day. Attracted by the uproar, the Ruhela chief hastened out of the city, when Ranjit Singh who had already entered the city, displayed himself to the people "like the rising sun" and was greeted with enthusiastic acclamation, August 1775 (*Ibrat,* i. 271). In the December of the same year the Gosain took a conspicuous part in the defence of this fort against the multitudinous host of Najaf Khan. He anticipated attack from the western side and stationed himself with his contingent in the gap of one-third of a mile between Shahburj and Gopalgarh on the western face of the fort. After skirmishing for the first three days, he engaged Najaf on the 4th day and repulsed the assault and began to sally forth upon the Mughal trenches, to rove behind their lines and to cut off their grain convoys (*Ibrat,* i. 273). Unable to cope with them

Najaf summoned his lieutenants Muhammad Beg Hamadani and Najaf Quli to his side and then drew the monks into a regular battle in the open ground between the two camps. The Gosain put up once again a tough fight; they assailed the enemy with a shower of rockets which brust in scores over the heads and among the ranks of the Mughal troops, causing heavy casualties among them. In the end Najaf's generalship triumphed; they had to retreat inside the fort; yeilding ground to the Mughal troops, January 1776 (ibid., 274). But the capture of the Jat capital remained as remote a possibility as before. The Jats defended Dig with fanatical enthusiasm and devotion; Najaf's position worsened again, with growing discontent among his troops, supplies failing, and enemies at court planning his overthrow.

ARRIVAL OF ANUPGIRI TO AID MIRZA NAJAF

In these untoward circumstances help came to the Delhi General from an unexpected quarter; The effete government of Oudh under Asafuddaulah had dismissed the Naga from service and 20,000[1] of them were now welcomed by Mirza Najaf into his service, not on any regular pay but with the right to live by plunder (*Bengal Past* & *Present,* 1936, p. 123). Their leader Anupgiri, by his ability, discreet counsels and constant attendance[2] upon the Mirza gained such an ascendancy in his darbar, that the Delhi Regent considered him as one of the well-wishers of the state and never decided any thing without reference to his opinion (be istiswab i-rai) (*Ibrat.* I, 279). This reinforcement with their 30 to 40 guns altered at once the fortune and the strategy of the war.

[1] Comte de Mohave merely states that Najaf ably profited by this reinforcement to change his plan of operations against Dig. . . . He turned in some sort this siege into a blockade and communication was rendered so difficult that provisions there became very dear (*Bengal Past & Present,* 1936, p. 123).

[2] Khairuddin remarks about the Gosain's attachment to Najaf saying Hargaj az state Judah namimand.

With the bulk of the Jats couped up in the fort, and the Mughals in their distant camps and the near trenches, there had ensued a deadlock. Into this stalemate the Nagas after their junction introduced the character of a moving war by their boldly scouring the country for supplies, and attacking and plundering the grain convoys from Kumbher to Govardhan. The tactics of raids upon the enemy troops in the open country that was now adopted to end the war of attrition bore fruit in the capitulation of the fortress on 30 April 1776. On the preceding night Ranjit Singh whether by chance or design issued out by the very side where Anupgiri was entrenched. The Gosain pursued him for some distance, but the Jat Raja scampered off to safety (*Ibrat.* I, 284). As the star of Anupgiri rose, that of Balanand[3] set.

AGAINST MURSAN

As the glory of Jat power departed in the Vrajabhumi, another Jat, Phup Singh of the Tenwa sect unconnected with the Bharatpur House, endeavoured to rehabilitate it in the fertile tract of the Doab. By means of his organising ability and skill in the use of arms, he had turned his small ancestral estate into a principality and consolidated his authority by fortifying his seat of power at Mursan, 33 miles east of Agra. His resistance to Afrasyab and rejection of all demands for payment of revenue brought Najaf before Mursan in December 1776. The Mirza attacked him in full strength. Phup Singh, however, commanding only an armed peasantry, could not stand before the disciplined battalions of Najaf; he was forced to seek the shelter of his small fort. From inside it he kept up a fight by means of a well directed fire, hitting Anup in the thigh. His strength wore out after seventeen days, when he fled to Sasni and sued for peace. He could expect only the severest terms for the loss and suffering caused to the imperial

[3] He quitted the service of the Jat Rajah presumably after the fall of Dig and entered the service of the Jaipur State (Br. Mus. or 25020, Sarkar Ms, f. 312 a).

troops. But the interests of political stability and peace weighed with the Gosain who recommended clemency for the beaten foe. Najaf, out of regard for the feelings of the Gosain left the Jat chieftain undisturbed in his possession, confiscating only Mursan to Afrasiayab's jagir (*Ibrat.* 1.291).

AT GHAUSGARH AND MACHERI

The next great military enterprise in which Anup Giri wielded his arms was one against Zabita Khan, the proud and irascible son of Najib-ud-daulah. The partition of the Ruhela dominions between Shuja and Najaf had left him master of a small block of territory with only the strong fort of Ghausgarh in his hands, yet the embittered rivalry between Abdul Ahad Khan the Kashmiri favourite of the emperor and Najaf had led him into thinking that he could dictate his will to both. His audacity exceeded all bounds. He had defeated and slain Abul Qasim, brother of Abdul Ahad and sent his corpse in a draped coffin to the Delhi Court (*Fall,* III. 133-4). In the violent conflict that blazed out, the Gosain bore his part. With great foresight Najib had planted there colonies of Orkzai, Afridi and Umarkhel Pathans in the tips of the triangle forming the fort of Ghausgarh.[4] Campaigning was the very breath of these Pathans and the salt of their life. Anup fought them. His part in the long-drawn fighting is not specifically stated in any of our sources. Munalal offers us a glimpse by stating that he was appointed to the command of the rear-guard (*chandal*) in the assault of 8 June (Sarkar Ms.). He endured passively all the sufferings of the rains and contributed to the final victory on 14 September.

Before the autumn and winter had passed, the Gosain was summoned by his master to a new theatre of war. During Najaf's absence in Rohilkhand, a new foe had raised his head between the Jat and Jaipur territories. This was Pratap Singh belonging to the Naruka branch of the Kachhwa clan, who in alliance with

[4] Read Sir Jadunath's charming description of the topography, *Fall.* III.

the Jat Raja Ranjit Singh tried to oust the Mughals from their newly acquired possessions. In obedience to Najaf's call, the Gosain crossed into Pratap Singh's territory and laid siege to the fort of Lachhmangarh in March 1778. The Rao Raja's own force was contemptible; his real strength lay in the pedatory horde of Ambaji Maratha hired out by him. With his instinctive grasp of the situation, the Gosain reduced the Naruka chief by trick rather than by force. He made secret overtures to Ambaji and seduced him from the Macheri side by a higher bid. A single stroke laid low the haughty Rao Raja who made peace by promising an indemnity of Rs. 33 lakh in July 1778.

Shortly after this, the Macheri Raja went to war against Jaipur and the Gosain was again deputed against him on behalf of the Kachhwa king. Pratap Singh made a pretence of submission and announced his intention of visiting Najaf in his camp. He rallied under his standard Nawal Singh of Nawalgarh and other Shaikhwati chiefs and advanced towards the Mughal camp with the air of an independent chief rather than a loyal vassal. Anupgiri performed the delicate task of ushering in this insolent chief before the pay-master general of the empire. The interview took place in an atmosphere of apparent cordiality; but outside the canvas palace of Najaf, the Raja's retainers thronged and made a row. The Raja himself browbeat the officers who raised the question of the tribute, how could the Mir Bakhshi of the empire subject himself to insult at the hands of a Raja who ten years back could not step into the presence of the Jaipur king? The Gosain again extricated him from an embarrassing situation by his diplomatic finesse. He won over Ambaji with another bait of Rs. 4 lakh and then organised a coup with great skill and secrecy for avenging the insult of his master. In the dim foggy light of a December morning, 1778, when the sun was about to rise, the Marathas from one side and the imperialists from the other fell like a thunderbolt upon the Macheri camp and threw it into utter confusion. As Khairuddin says, "Some were yet asleep on their beds; some had gone away to a distance for attending to nature's call; the Rao Raja himself, after the morning ablution, was engaged in the worship of his tutelary deity",[5] when a tumult as of a doomsday arose. With extra-ordinary promptitude and pluck Pratap Singh formed up in battle array with a body of his devoted adherents; he cut his way through the enemy ranks amid a welter of confusion. By chance, Anup crossed his path at the time he was trotting away in military formation. Out of commiseration for his misfortune the Gosain shrank from engaging him and allowed him to gallop away to his citadel of Lachhmangarh (*Ibrat.* I, 352).

IN THE KACHHWA STATE

In January 1779, Anup Giri followed Najaf to Amirnagar, in the vicinity of Jaipur; he was presumably present at the ceremony of investiture when the emperor put the *tika* mark with his own fingers on the forehead of the Jaipur Raja, Sawai Pratap Singh. On 26 February, the imperial cortege started for return to Delhi, but the Gosain remained behind as Najaf's agent for collecting the tribute promised by Jaipur.

By the middle of November, a palace revolution gave Najaf unfettered authority as the emperor's regent; his rival Abdul Ahad Khan was expelled from the Court. This triumph of Najaf was due no doubt to the soldiering and devotion of his able lieutenants, Afrasiab, Shafi, and Najaf Quli; but the military and diplomatic services of the Gosain cannot be lightly set aside. He had restrained Najaf from dissipating his strength in unnecessary fighting and accomplished by fineses what others did by means of the sword. He thus aided in Najaf's rise to the height of greatness.

A work of a greater value was performed by him under Najaf. It was the preservation of the fabric of the heritage of Mansingh

[5] We cannot accept Khairuddin's statement that the Gosain recoiled from an encounter out of fear of Pratap Singh (*Ibrat.* I. 851). Such an act of temerity is difficult to reconcile with the Gosain's fearlessness and reckless disregard of his personal safety throughout his careers.

and Sawai Jai Singh. It is a story fraught with dramatic interest and would be unfolded here.

We have seen that Anup Giri was commissioned with the task of collecting the tribute of Jaipur. The Maratha and Jat ravages and the insurrection of its vassal chiefs had so dried up the wealth of this kingdom that the Jaipur government was virtually bankrupt. The State had therefore always been in default of payment. During 1779 its unwillingness to pay any contribution had increased owing to various factors, such as the persistent intrigue and hostility of Abdul Ahad against Najaf, the failure of the emperor's Patiala expedition October 1779, and disturbances in his own territory and the Hissar-Rohtak region (*C.P.C.V.* 1568). After one year's ineffectual attempt the Gosain was compelled to report to Delhi his failure to collect any sum, by peaceful means about March 1780. Distressed for want of money, Najaf appointed Mahbub Ali Khan, recently resigned from Oudh service, to reinforce the Gosain and reduce the refractory Raja to terms as quickly as possible. The Moslem warrior had in his train four *paltans* (regiments) of flint lookmen under Captain Lewis, one paltan of Najib sepoys under Nasirullah and a large body of horse recently recruited after his admission to the Delhi service. He met Anup at Bayana; at once differences arose between them as to the precedence in rank and the question of command. The Gosain, on account of his acquaintance with the country and commission from the regent, wanted Mahbub to submit to his directions, but the latter could not reconcile himself to this inferior position and was supported by the captains under him (*Ibrat.* II, 18). He therefore marched away one night with his troops and launched operations on his own initiative. Disregarded and baulked in his plan, the Naga incited the Raja of Mahewa, through his brother Rai Singh, the Jaipur vakil in his camp, to oppose the Moslem general in his march. He did so, but Mahbub swept his opposition aside by the strength of his artillery. Places like Hindaun, Lalsot, Deoli and Chatsu fell before him one after another. On 20 October he stood before the Jaipur capital. About the same time, another Moslem general Murtaza Khan Barech had worked his way through the Shaikhwati country to Sri Madhupur, 40 miles north of Jaipur. The Jaipur State had now practically dissolved into fragments, as revealed in the Maratha despatch of 10 October (*Fall* III. 209). The city of Jaipur where Sawai Pratap Singh had shut himself up remained the sole relic of the State. With the advance of the northern prong of the Muslim pincer, it was also doomed to fall and the Kachhwa heritage to roll and crumble in the dust. Alas the unbridled rapacity and brigandage of the Moslem soldiery revealed from day to day by the priceless newsletters (Sarkar Ms.) did not set the spirit of the Rajput chiefs on fire. How then was the Kachhwa state saved from disintegration, nay extinction? It owned its salvation to the Gosain.

When Mahbub's and Murtaza's operations were in full swing, Anup had relinquished the command, but instead of joining the court-party against Najaf, he had retired to his jagir in his *dera* (villa). Meanwhile the Jaipur Raja had approached Najaf and Mahbub for terms in September, but when after a month-long waiting, his minister Khushhali Ram was dismissed by the over-confident Moslem general, the Rajah as a sinking man caught at the straw of the Gosain. He sent agents to Vrindavan renewing the offer of a large sum as tribute (*Ibrat*, II. 21) and pressed the Gosain with solicitations for saving the State. In his retreat Anup had kept up his old relations with Najaf who had visited his *dera* in Vrindavan on 10 October. Heat once proceeded to the task. Hence, after the arrival of Jaipur agents, he went to Delhi and met Najaf's financial agent, Shiv Ram Kashmiri. He greased this man's palm with Rs. 50,000 and entered into a pact for the settlement of the Jaipur tribute (ibid., 22). How the matter was adjusted is not detailed in our *akhbarat,* but the subtle wit which the Kashmiri wizzard brought into play can be glimpsed in a letter. The Jaipur offer of an immediate payment of one lakh in cash and Rs. 1 lakh more on the restration of the occupied mahals and the recall of Mahbub, and the balance of Rs. 1¼ lakh to be paid in two instalments, was kept standing before the regent for sometime;

but the latter had been insisting on the cash payment of Rs. 2 lakh. When he would not consent to lowering the demand, Shiv Ram smoothly said 'Under Mahbub and Murtaza's command there is a force of nearly 20,000 horse and foot. Where from would the money come when they would return?" Najaf fumbled and said "Oh ! brother you will see the tamasha of what happens, because parleys have been going on for long and nothing so far settled", 14 November 1780 (Or. B.M. 383 a).

In the weeks that followed, the Gosain succeeded through Shiv Ram in winning Najaf's acquiescence in the terms offered by him. By March 1781, the pendulum had swung so completely to the other side that he was reappointed agent for the collection of the Jaipur tribute. Frantic with rage, Mahbub came away from Jaipur territory to the Regent for pressing his case 3 March (Or. 25020, 54 b). His appeals were piteous; "My troops, encamped near Dig are going away for want of pay; if such be your wish, say so clearly so that my soldiers may not perish". Najaf asked him to accept the settlement of the Jaipur tribute as a *fait accompli;* he met him in private and entreated him to agree to it, out of consideration for his personal sentiments for the Gosain, but how could the proud soldier sign with his own hand his own humiliation and the victory of a naked sannyasi? In the end Mahbub's army broke up for want of pay; his camp was looted; and he sought solace for his tormented spirit by a pilgrimage to the Kaba (*Ibrat.* II. 23 Or. B.M. 78 b) while the Gosain again went to Jaipur. By his personal influence and exertion he freed some of the parganas from the control of the refractory vassals, and fought to stem the depredation of the Macheri Raja, (167 a). In the middle of April he was encamped near Malarna. On 25 March he had an audience of the Raja of Jaipur when his son Kumar Gangagii was also introduced into the presence of Pratap Singh by the minister Khusali Ram, (1888 b). Two days later, in the course of another interview, he swore by taking the Ganges water in his palm that he would always befriend the Raja and stand by him in sunshine and adversity. The Raja in his turn made over to him mahals calculated to yield Rs. 12 lakh a year, one half of which was to be remitted to Najaf Khan and the other spent in maintaining the troops deputed for revenue collection (ibid., 221 b). Before, however, the Government could regain its feet, Mahadji Sindhia's agents, Ambaji and Gangaram Sathe, appeared and demanded *chauth*, 8 May (ibid., 246 a). Anup who had gone to Vrindavan, hurried back to Jaipur (250 a). In the beginning of June, he was called upon to lead the Jaipur forces against the Maratha freelance Jaswant Rao Bable (May 1781). The latter made an announcement of his Solanki pedigree and claimed possession of the Malpura and Toda parganas on the ground of their having been Solanki territory. Anup met him in an engagement and vanquished him, killing his son and seizing all his war eqipment and valuables (308 b, *Vamsa Bhaskar* 3889). By his exertions, measures of pacification, Anup succeeded in realising a sum of Rs. 75,000 and remitting a draft of the amount to Delhi 15 June (335 b). On the following day Kumar Jagatgir, son of Umraogir was conferred the title of Jagatendra by the emperor and, Created a 5-hazari (342 a). The Gosain continued his work of rehabilitating the Jaipur territory, but before the year had ended, there was another turn of the kaleidiscope with the death of Najaf and he was back again at the centre of the political dream in Delhi.

CHAPTER 14

Later Service under the Empire: Anupgiris Diplomacy, 1782-1784

Mirza Najaf Khan, the virtual dictator of Delhi, died on 6 April 1782 and a bitter scramble for power ensued among his four lieutenants, causing the annals of Delhi to be stained with blood. First arose Afrasiyab Khan to prominence. He was driven out by Shafi, who in his turn was overthrown and Afrasiyab returned to power again, to fall a victim to the treachery of his colleagues. The way then remained open for Hamadani to mount to power, but in his stead a Hindu chieftain sprung from the Maratha race became the arbiter of the central government at Delhi under the title of waqil-i-Mutlaq (Regent-plenipotentiary). This dramatic political development was not the natural working out of the forces that were released by Najaf's death but was brought to pass in a large measure by the steady and persistent diplomatic manoeuvre of a Hindu monk. In the course of his chapter, we shall trace an outline of Anupgiri's diplomacy, leading to Mahadji Sindhia's supremacy at Delhi.

After Najaf's exit, his favourite Afrasiyab Khan was appointed regent on his promising large financial contributions, to the Emperor. When he failed to meet the heavy obligations, the emperor plotted to supplant him by Shafi and buttress himself up with the aid of the English battalions. At this critical turn in Afrasiyab's career, the Gosain befriended him by Canvassing support for him from all influential quarters (*C.P.C.*) and endeavoured to put him at the head of an army by taking a son of Shah Alam out on an expedition to Agra. This plan, however, miscarried and the emperor, taking umbrage at the insult to royalty, publicly censured the regent's councillor. Anupgiri (DY. 79). Afrasiyab mortified, in his turn at the disgrace of his adviser, took retaliatory steps which ultimately forced him out of office and raised Shafi to the supreme direction of affairs.

Shafi's elevation was primarily due to the armed aid of Hamadani. He now alienated him by disregarding the terms of their covenant. The irresistible Mughalia leader, thereupon, broke into rebellion; leagued with the Jaipur and Macheri Rajas, he ranged in the region round Agra. Shafi met this challenge to his authority by making accommodation with his erstwhile opponents, Afrasiyab and Anupgiri. He also set on foot negotiations with the English, with a view to securing their military assistance. As it took a long time for the Governor-General Warren Hastings to define his attitude, the Gosain seized the occasion to propose a counter-alliance with Sindhia as an effective means of doing away with Hamadani (*Ibrat* II, 57). Thus under his impulse was intiated a new policy which was destined to profoundly affect the Delhi politics.

Mahadji was then engaged in hard fighting at Gwalior with the Jat Rana of Gohad. At the instance of Shafi, Anup Giri proceeded on a visit to his camp in order to mature the project conceived by him. By a strange irony, more than twenty years previously, the selfsame Jats had assisted a union of interests between the Sindhia and the Gosain by pillaging the latter's camp and forcing him to seek the protection of Mahadji. The Maratha chief had then offered him a hospitable shelter and forged endearing ties by exchanging turbans with him (Dy. 79). From such friendly connections subsisting between them, it might be presumed that the Gosain had an easy task before him when he undertook the mission, but such is not the fact. Shortly before his errand, his brother Umraogiri, who had been deputed on a similar task by the emperor, with a personal missive from Prince Jawan Bakht, had returned in disappointment. To the Prince's proposal for a visit to the Maratha chief's camp, the latter had sent a cold reply saying, "you should not come to me; I will go to you" (*Satara History*, Sec. 1, 69 *New History of the Marathas*, III. 139).

No doubt, in the beginning of February, immediately after his arrival at Gwalior, the Gosain found Sindhia inclined for a combination with Shafi, on account of Hamadani's menacing presence at Gwalior and his secret overtures to Rana Chhatra Singh. But when as a result of "a kind of reconciliation betwixt Mahadji Sindhia and Hamadani the latter marched away towards the Rajah of Jaypore" (*P.R.C.* I, latter no. 1). Sindhia's sentiments underwent a change. He advanced fictitious claims of Chauth over on the territories conquered by Najaf Khan and "of a kind protectorate over such Hindu princes" as the Rajahs of Bharatpur and Jaipur, so that the British Resident in his camp, deemed the conclusion of any "close or great alliance" beyond the range of possibility. To the credit of the Gosain the apparently insuperable barriers in the way of an alliance were overcome; Shafi and Mahadji met on the banks of the Chambal, near Dholpur at the end of June and cemented their friendly ties by an exchange of turbans.

During the interval of the Gosains stay at Gwalior, February-June, the Delhi politics had assumed a complexion with the advent of James Browne, who was deputed by the Governor-General Warren Hastings to manifest to the world . . . 'the attachment of the English nation for the Emperor Shah Alam and to promote his interests" (Forrest, *Selections from Records in the Foreign Department*, III 1025). Starting from Calcutta in August 1782, he had reached Farrukhabad on the Oudh frontier in November. Here he was obliged to half for nearly three months owing to the imperial rescript forbidding his visit to the court and ultimately gained an audience of Shafi at Agra, on 26 February, through the exertions of his secretary, Khan Salihuddin Muhammad. By means of his unusual keenness and ability, Browne soon became a force in Delhi politics. He was introduced to Sindhia in the conference on the Chambal, and after the retirement of Shafi to Dig became the Jat Rajah's intermediary in his negotiation with the Mir Bakhshi. He thus began to sway Shafi's council and promoted, by his exertions, a comprehensive treaty of mutual assistance in peace and war, (*C.P.C.* VII, 110-13; Forrest, *Selections in the Foreign Department*, III, 1087), but before he could bring about a ratification, of the treaty or subvert the alliance formed with Sindhia, he was removed from the stage by conspiracy in which the Gosain had a hand. This is indicated in a letter of the *Akhbarat*, dated 30 October 1784. Mahadji having demanded the surrender of Shafi's property seized by Hamadani, the vakil Lachhmi Ram declared the complicity (*dastawez*) of all men in the affair (murder of Shafi). Mahadji then made a rejoinder saying "among all men, was Raja Himmat Bahadur too?" At this the Gosain who was present on the spot, made a caveat saying "I had given advice for arresting Shafi, and not for killing him" (B.M. Ms. Or. 25021, 300).

Shafi's murder caused a new alignment of political parties. Abdul Ahad Khan who had been driven to a corner by the late Mir Bakhshi, now backed Afrasiab and promoted him to the position of the Regent. The secret entente between the two foremost Mughal peers and their antagonism to Sindhia's influence, drove Anupgiri to a voluntary exile in his retreat at Vrindaban. From this refuge he watched the proceedings of the Delhi court and issued out in time to tear asunder the cob-web of intrigues spun by the indefatiguable British agent, Browne.

The early period of Afrasiyab's regency lasting for only thirteen months was signalised by successes against the Sikhs, pacification of such recalcitrant chiefs as Zain-ul-Abidin Khan and Zabita Khan, and active negotiation for a subsidiary alliance with the English. After Shaft's assassination James Browne who shifted his activity to Delhi in November 1783, became the axis round which the emperor and the foremost nobles, like Abdul Ahad and Afrasiyab Khan revolved. They had sickened of the revolution and counter-revolution in the court, and were keen on putting the administration on a stable footing with the English aid. The swing in favour of the English had been so complete that Warren

Hastings hastened to Lucknow in March 1784 and at a hint from the Emperor, Prince Jawan Bakht escaped from the palace, on 14 April with a view to binding the Governor-General to his side. Sindhia's influence at the Delhi court seemed irretrievably lost when the gosain brought about an extraordinary turn in the situation.

Sindhia's agents at the court had been filled with alarm at the sight of the growing Anglophile sentiment but they found no way of combatting this tendency and performed their duty to their master by resuming representation after representation to Mahadji. It was at this juncture that the latter with all his energies directed to the siege of Gohad, addressed the Gosain to effect the recovery of his lost influence at the Court (*Ibrat*, II, 68).

As early as November 1783, Anupgiri had perceived the coming change in the direction of the court-policy from Brownes removal to Delhi and Afrasiyab's visits to his camp at Mathura *en route* to the capital. The Gosain had then invited the new regent to a banquet in his retreat at Vrindaban and whispered into his ears words designed to excite suspicion of the emperor, (B.R. Ms. Or 25,021, 30 a). But they failed to produce any effect whatsoever; for Afrasiyab frisked before Browne with the same jovialty as marked Abdul Ahad Khan and pursued actively negotiations for an alliance on the old basis of mutual aid for offensive and defensive purposes (*C.P.C.* VI. 1123, 1128).

The task of effecting a reversal of this policy was one that baffled ordinary diplomatic resources. The Gosain therefore formed the sinister resolve of dividing and overthrowing the cabal that now ruled the state. An event now occurred which gave him the whip-hand. On 12 May, five miscreants armed with lethal weapons were detected hiding in the very office-room of Afrasiyab, with a view evidently, to despatching him. The murdered Mir Bakhshi's brother Zain-ul-Abidin was suspected to be the prime-mover behind this plot, but the Gosain trumped up accusations against Abdul Ahad Khan and denounced him as having promoted this affair. During the same month, the gosain improved his position by leading a force against the Raja of Bhadur and quelling him (B.M. Or 25,021, fol. 130 b). He next proposed to Afrasiyab to take the Emperor to Agra, in order to stamp out the unrest seething in the region. This proposal caused a sharp cleavage of opinion between Abdul Ahad and Afrasiyab. The former opposed this measure, as tending to excite hostility with Hamadani and provoke a civil war, and recommended instead the appeasement of the Mughalia leader. He declared in unmistakeable terms his preference for the sahiba as against the Deccanis" (Ghulam Ali, 208-9). After having put him out of the way, the Regent made preparation for a march to Agra which provoked Hamadani to arms. The latter had carved out an almost independent principality in the Agra-Dholpur region and regarded the emperor's march as an infringement of his cherished privilege. He set the imperial authority at defiance and committed terrible atrocities at Kama. The Gosain found in this fresh fuel for kindling hostilities between the two leaders (*Ibrat*, II, 81). Almost simultaneously (10 July) Mahadji announced his desire to meet the emperor at Agra (B.M., op. cit., 34 a). While the Gosain was busy at work, creating the condition for renewed overtures to Sindhia, James Browne who had gone away to Lucknow in May on the plea of bringing back Prince Jawan Bakht, returned to the court with the draft of a treaty of alliance at the end of July. The Gosain seemed to be outmatched in diplomacy and Sindhia's cause to suffer a set-back, but Hamadani now launched upon vigorous hostilities. He allied himself with the Jat and Macheri Rajas and attacked Zulfiqar Khan, the vassal chief of Alinagar. The bellicosity of the Mughalia chief converted Afrasiyab to the Gosain's view of alliance with Mahadji who promptly deputed, at the Gosain's instance, his general Ambaji Ingle with a force of 6,000 cavalry to the regent's assistance, August 1784. Events now took almost that same course as in October 1783, foreboding the same fatal consequence. But it did not follow as a matter of course Sindhia himself altered his view of juncture with Afrasiyab, when he received from Ambaji the report of his rough temper and the want of discipline in his army. He was prevailed upon the recommence his march in September, but a fresh cause of dispute arose when he conquered Dholpur-Bari on his way and refused to yield it to imperial control. Afrasiyab deputed the Gosain to Sindhia's camp cancelling the proposed interview at Rupbas, in case of his non-compliance with the demand for the delivery of the disputed districts.

The edifice which Anupgiri was laboriously trying to erect was now about to topple down, and a new one fashioned by the English Agent seemed likely to take its place; for by this time Browne had again drawn up terms stipulating the conditions for the "loan of the British battalions and fixing their monthly allowances while employed in His Majesty's Service (*C.P.C.* 1286, 1305, 1321). They were finalised in a new treaty that was ratified on 1 November (ibid., 1471) but only a week before, Afrasiyab and Sindhia had met at Rupbas on 23 October, and on 2 November the day following the ratification of the Anglo-Mughal treaty of friendship, the man upon whom rested the superstructure of the engagement had perished by the hand of an assassin.

This astonishing turn was brought about by the diplomatic agility and resourcefulness of the Gosain. After his return to Sindhia's camp in September, he found Mahadji opposed to the idea of intervention on behalf of Afrasiyab, without any compensating return for his service (*Ibrat*, II. 86) and consequently to the cession of the conquered districts. The Gosain then made proposal for an accommodation of the matters at issue by a friendly interview. Mahadji rejected it as well, where-upon Anupgiri felt so hurt that he declared his intention of renouncing the world and taking to a life of mendicancy. It was apparently an innocuous idea of self-abnegation, of voluntary retirement into obscurity, but Sindhia took into account the public stigma as well as the impiety which such a threat, it excuted by a member of the priestly caste, would impose on him who was *marathi* (Shudra) by caste. He therefore yielded and proceeded to Rupbas where the interview with the Regent took place on 23 October; the disputed possesion of Dholpur-Bari remained as yet the impediment to a cordial understanding Mahadji's personal prestige hinged on the maintenance of his authority over them; this was clearly expressed in his statement to Anupgiri, "If I withdraw my posts from Dholpur and other places, I shall be made light in all the country up to the Deccan. Tell him (Afrasiyab) to supply me with money soon" (B.M. Or 25,021, 28a). In the course of the interview, however, Afrasiyab, imposed apparently by the personality and prowess of Mahadji called him his father in the same way as Shafi had addressed him (*Fall*, III, 25c). The Gosain promptly proposed to close the controversy by suggesting to Afrasiyab the plan of making a present of the disputed districts of Sindhia's wife, henceforth his mother. This was done, and Mahadji's advanced division of cavalry now marched to the vicinity of Hamadani's camp, on 31 October. On the following day the treaty with the English was ratified which solemnly "declared and affirmed in writing that the forces waiting on prince Jahandar Shah shall be placed under the order of His Majesty" (*C.P.C.* VI. 1471). Next day, on 2 November Afrasiyab was fatally stabbed in his own tent, and the treaty of alliance with the English made infrutuous, before the ink was dry upon it.

Thus two of Najaf's lieutenants fell one after another but the most capable and energetic Hamadani stood at the head of an army, facing the Marathas and the leaderless Delhi army. The emperor melted in kindness towards him and wrote to Sindhia saying, "Hamadani is a good soldier. Do not destroy him. He will prove useful in an expedition in some quarter" (B.M. ibid. 29a). Would he now coalesce with Afrasiyab's troops and instal himself in the regency? Or would Mahadji overawe the hostile elements by the demonstration of his military force and step into the seat vacated by Afrasiyab Khan? Opposition against him was so strong and prejudice against the Maratha troops as deep-rooted that he disavowed any ambitious design of his own to impose his control over Delhi. "If I had any desire for the Emperor's ministry" said he to Hamadani's vakil, "how often in the past had I not had the chance of it? Even now I have no such greed" (*H.P.* 606), but hardly had six weeks elapsed after this utterance, when the office of Vakil-i-Multaq was conferred on him, the emperor becoming a willing pensioner of his. No doubt, Sindhia's uncommon insight and singular selfpossession aided him largely in attaining to this exalted position, but the ground upon which he stood in November was so slippery and the men with whom he had to deal were so unreliable that a single stumble might have ruined him. At this critical hour, the Gosain held him firmly by the hand and steered him clear of the shoals that beset his path.

Afrasiyab Khan was assassinated at 11 o'clock on 2 November; within four hours, of this occurrence, Mahadji arrived in the Gosain's camp and remained closetted with him for some time. It was in the course of this meeting that the plan of action was presumably outlined against Hamadani, leading to his overthrow. For on the very day of Afrasiyab's murder, it was under the Gosain's direction that Mahadji took the step of putting a force of 2,000 cavalry round the imperial camp and thus screened it from rejuncture with the Mughalia leader Hamadani who had raised the communal bogey to seduce them to his side (*Fall*, III, 285). Next the Gosain reinforced Mahadji's army by his own contingent and that of Narayandas, the Kashmiri diwan of the deceased Afrasiyab; while his intimate knowledge of the state of affairs in the imperial army, and connexion with such men as Bayazid Khan, commander of the artillery, accounted for the coalescene of the Mughal-Maratha army, that is, of the late Afrasiyab's and Sindhia's army. It was by means of this formidable array of forces as well as by the weight of the Gosain's artillery placed at Mahadji's disposal that the rapacious free booter, Muhammad Beg Hamadani, was coerced into surrendering on 10 November.

After this formidable antagonist was got rid of, the Gosain concerted those measures that eliminated other rivals and cleared the way for Sindhia's dominance in the state. The most formidable of them was Abdul Ahad Khan who was released from Aligarh prison by order of Shah Alam. As a counterpoise to his measure, Sindhia announced, at the instance of the Gosain, his intention of securing the Mir Bakhshiship for Khadim Husain Khan and of personally retiring to the Deccan (B.M. Or 250,21, 33a). The prospective elevation of this infant induced his grandfather Shujadil Khan, qiladar of Agra, to take Abdul Ahad captive, as soon as the latter arrived at Agra on 5 November. The emperor felt so shaken by this blow as well as the support of Prince Sulaiman Shukoh's candidature by Khadija Begam (*CPC* VIII) and Prince Jawan Bakht's intrigues with the British Agent at Delhi, that he decided to surrender his own interests into the hands of Sindhia. Thus was laid the foundation of the *entente Cordiale* between the Emperor and Sindhia which led to the investitude of the latter with the office of Wakil i-Mutlaq on 1 December 1784.

Needless it is to state that in making the ceaseless exertions and diplomatic manoeuvres the Gosain was not inspired by purely disinterested motives; his own desire for aggrandisement was dovetailed into that of Mahadji Sindhia. Naturally, after the fall of Afrasiyab, the Gosain became the virtual director of the affairs of Delhi holding Mahadji in his leading-strings. As a letter despatched to the Governor-General says "A minor son of Afrasiyab Khan has been appointed Bakhshi, but in fact, the Gosain Himmat Bahadur is in absolute control of that office (*C.P.C.* VI 1423; *Ibrat*, II, 91). The period from the beginning of November 1784 to about the middle of March 1785 marks the hey-day of the Gosain's career; but as early as on 16 November when Sindhia and the Emperor met for the first time, the former showed his distrust of Anupgiri by warning Shah Alam against the latter (*Ibrat*, II, 92). This was the first symptom of the parting of ways between the two allies which with its attendance consequences, we shall set forth in the following chapter.

CHAPTER 15

Mahadji Sindhia and the Gosains: Anupgiri's Rupture with Mahadji Sindhia and Recovery of Power (November 1784-October 1788)

"Hamadani has been defeated, Mahadji's interview with the Emperor has taken place and all the control has come into our (Sindhia's) hands; all this has been done by Anupgiri Gosain; because of his peristence all this has been achieved so quickly." In this concise sentence the Maratha ambassador Hingane summoned up the work of the Gosain in promoting the glory of the great representative of the Maratha race in northern India. Such sterling services naturally raised the Gosain to the position of the Chief Manager, and Adviser of Sindhia in administrative affairs, and secured for him new jagirs, out of the late Afrasiyab Khan's estate, yielding an income of Rs. 10 to 12 lakh and a few other mahals, such as fort Mursan in the Doab and Mau-Mohini belonging to the Raja of Samther, villages near Jhansi, taluq Bhander and Mot in Bundelkhand (*H.P.* 351, 408).

In this new role, the Gosain became Sindhia's chief instrument in stabilising the unsettled country. He stood by Mahadji in wresting Dig from Malik Muhammad Khan, and mediated in respect of his claims for tribute on the Jaipur Raja. His intimate knowledge of Delhi enabled Sindhia to effect the peaceful transfer of the fort and city to Sindhia's lieutenants Ambaji Ingle and Ladoji Deshmukh, from the hand of a haughty and able warrior like Najaf Quli Khan, subahdar of Delhi. Similarly, the

Gosain's understanding with the Sikh chiefs and his personal exertion accounted for an accommodation of terms with them, securing thereby the immunity of the imperial territory north of Delhi from the levy of *Rakhi* (*Ibrat.* II. 103; *C.P.C.* VII, no. 41). Under his directions, Sindhia carried out the renovation of the Diwan's Secretariat by the introduction of Deccani officers. This ascendancy, however, did not last long. The emperor, under Sindhia's dictation, administered to Anupgiri the first rebuff by declining his proposal for an interview, about 14 November (*Ibrat,* II. 92); simultaneously, he was superseded as the intermediary in the negotiation with the emperor by Appa Khande Rao (*P.R.C.I.* letter nos. 7 & 9). On the other hand Sindhia began to press the Gosain for effecting the peaceful transfer of the forts of Agra and Aligarh, held respectively by Afrasiyab's partisans Shujadil Khan and Jahangir Khan. Mahadji felt that the high sounding title conferred upon him by the emperor was a sham and pretence, so long as he did not command these two fortresses. The gosain, on the other hand came to realise that Sindhia's victory over these two chiefs, with whom he was bound by party ties, would be followed by his own downfall.[1]

Such a posture of affairs was precipitated by Mahadji's resort to arms for the capture of Agra and Aligarh. In January 1785 he rejected the Gosain's recommendations in respect of the jagir of Karim Quli Khan, who had sided with Hamadani in the late contest, in order to win British sympathy on his behalf in the

[1] Such premonitions were supported by Sindhia's statement to the British Resident in the Court who thus wrote to the Governor-General, "He (Sindhia) declared the necessity he was under availing himself of this man's (Anupgiri) assistance who had possessed himself of a complete knowledge of affairs and that his connexion with him should cease from the moment he could do without him" (*P.R.C.I.*, no. 10). This letter was most probably not a forged document. It was natural for Anupgiri, in his bitterness against Sindhia, to instigate resistance to the Maratha authority and contrive a union of all hostile elements against Sindhia, as a consequence of which the English brigade under Sir John Cummings moved from Anupshahar to within 10 miles of Aligarh (*P.R.C.I.*, letter no. 16).

impending conflict with Shujadil Khan. In May he administered another shock by confiscating some of the Gosain's Jagirs (*P.R.C.*, no. 16). The estrangement was completed when during the hunt for the fabulous accumulations of Afrasiyab Khan, Sindhia's agents, Naubat Rai and Saif Khan, Haider Ali and Vishvanath forced out of the widowed Begam and her brother Jahangir Quli; a pair of documents (*qaulnamah*) bearing the seal of the Gosain. These letters purported to incite resistance to the arms of Sindhia during the siege of Aligarh in such words as "You must never bend your head in submission; and flinch from tenacious opposition. I shall seduce the Hindustani and Mughalia nobles to your side and . . . get yourself nominated as the deputy (of Khadim Husain Khan) with the support of the Emperor" (*Ibrat* II, 153).

On the discovery of this treasonable correspondence, Sindhia first of all demanded from Anupgiri an explanation of his conduct in the open durbar, on 4 January 1786. Anup at once declared it to be forged document, and was commanded to submit a, written statement in the tent-court nearby. Some of his friends, such as Kurji Beg and Khairati Khan, who happened to be present there, suspected foul play on the part of Sindhia. All of a sudden they excited a faked brawl with the Gosain in respect of their pay and allowances (*tankhwa*) and threatened to murder him on the spot, in the event of Sindhia approving the step. But the Maratha chief disguised his real feelings beneath the armour of impenetrable reserve and directed them to keep the Gosains in their custody, pending the adjustment of their dispute with him. In consonance with Sindhia's command, Kurji Beg along with his friends dragged the Gosain out of the court, mounted him on an elephant and then led him away. Happy at the idea of being rid of an nuisance, Sindhia dissolved his court and retired to his inner apartment. His bewilderment therefore can be imagined when the news reached him of the Gosain having been set at liberty by the miscreants. In disgust and indignation, he now planned his arrest by resort to force. At his command, the famous captain Rahim Beg Khan surrounded the Gosain with a very large force.

Finding the latter determined to fight and die rather than give in Mahadji desisted from the extreme step of an open clash of arms and recalled his forces. Such a generous step moved the Gosain to again, assert his innocence to Sindhia through his friends saying, "I am a faqir and the begging bowl is enough for me; whenever the Maharaja desires, I shall, of my own accord send away horses, elephants, and valuables and retire to the forest with a rag tied round my waist and a piece of cloth on my head." This representation elicited no reply from Mahadji. The day following the incident Marichgiri Gosain came with reinforcement from Firuzabad to Anupgiri's camp at Dig. In fear of arrest, the Gosain now gave up attending Sindhia's court and voluntarily suffered political *nirvana*. His jagir and that of his brother Umraogir were confiscated, middle of January 1786 (*H.P.* 432). For more than a month he remained at Dig negotiating terms for his retirement. But no material alteration occurred in his lot; he got a cash sum of Rs. 20,000, out of the monthly allowance of Rs. 10,000 only, also Moth taluqa and Vrindaban with permission to keep only 100 horse as his retainers, while the rest of his army was to serve under Sindhia for which again a contribution of Rs. 5 lakh was to be paid by the Gosain himself out of the income of his estate (*D.Y.* 149).

The Kachhwa state of Jaipur, which had been the nursery of soldiers and statesmen and a centre of liberal influence had, by this time, reached the last stage of decadence. "Hindustan" wrote the Maratha news-writer in a letter to Puna "has become Kshatriya less" (*D.Y.* 1.181; Raj XII, 139). Internal factions and party-rivalry had bled the state which was still farther paralysed by the enroachment of chiefs like the Rao Raja of Macheri and Najaf Quli Khan. At the end of February 1786, Sindhia marched into the heart of this state and coquetted with the scheme of virtually overthrowing the ruling dynasty by installing a nominee of his own, the minor Man Singh, an alleged son of Raja Prithwi Singh. From such a danger, the state owed its redemption to two circumstances, one of which was the armed rising of the Gosain brothers in the Doab. The initiative in the matter was taken by Umraogiri, the real steward of the jagirs who opposed their delivery into the hands of Sindhia's agents. Allied with two other zamindars, Dayaram of Hathras and Phup Singh of Mursan, he led a rising which enveloped a large part of the Doab in flames. Umrao's *chela* Agangir looted many parganahs and took many Maratha *amils* captive. To quell this rising Sindhia deputed a force under one of his captains Kesho Pant, under the secret of Anupgiri. They first marched to Mathura and made a halt. Here the Gosain first sent his family, artillery and valuables across the Jamuna, and then personally crossed the river with his force and applied for asylum in the Oudh territory. Kesho Pant, after landing in the Doab, engaged Umraogiri but was slain on 10 March. Rebellion against Sindhia now spread like wild fire; Maratha outposts were expelled from such places as Atrauli, Charra Bhamuri and other mahals. Reinforcements were expeditiously sent under Abhaji, son of Jaswant Rao Bable, but they shrank from an engagement when they found after their arrival at Koil, that Umraogiri was encamped on the Kalinadi with a force of seven to eight thousand men. In a light engagement, two Companies of their infantry were worsted and two guns wrenched away from them. The alarm spread to the city of Koil. In the meantime Anupgiri attacked Firuzabad and made himself master of it. The situation was retrieved by the pouring in of fresh Maratha reinforcement under Devji Gauli and Muhammad Beg Khan. Umrao unable to match this huge army, retreated to the Wazir's territory and took shelter in the fort of Kachhura[2] previously built by himself, belonging to Raja Udikaran (*Ibrat, A.S.B.* II 476; *P.G.* no. 574; *P.R.C.* I, no. 39, while his brother Anupgiri gained the protection of Almas Ali Khan the Oudh Nawab's governor of Etawah.

This Gosain insurrection is no doubt, a minor episode, but it had important consequences for the Jaipur state. The Maratha's distraction was the Kachhwa's opportunity. It put the brake to

[2] The Grosavi family was settling in Kachchaura as late as December 1787 at P. C., VII, no. 1829.

Sindhia's ambition and enabled the Jaipur Raja to obtain better terms (*P.R.C.* II, nos. 56 & 59).

BALANANDA MAHANT

It has been stated that Mahadji had already marched into the Jaipur territory. Renewed parleys for the adjustment of the tribute brought again into prominence the Gosain Balananda Mahant, who after his flight from the Jat land, had been leading a secluded existence as the Guru of Sawai Madho Singh of Jaipur and after his demise, that of Pratap Singh. In the face of Sindhia's threat to overthrow the Kachhwa monarchy, the monk exchanged his bowl for the diplomatist's wallet and set out with the Dewal Khush-hali Ram Bohrah (about 5 March) to negotiate with the Maratha lord, outside Jaipur. On arrival near the Maratha camp, he was honoured by Sindhia personally kneeling down at his feet and laying down a gift of one hundred gold coins and receiving one necklace of pearls and four doshalas, one for himself and the rest for his high officers, as a token of blessings (*Ibrat, A.S.B.* II. 481).

On the 10th. commenced the negotiations in the course of which Sindhia's preposterous demand of Rs. 3 crore and 40 lakh as the arrears of tribute was whittled down to Rs. 63 lakh (*D.Y.* 163). When, owing to Jaipur inability to pay, Sindhia brandished his sword again, Balanand returned to Jaipur; he brought back some money, stood personal security for Rs. 2 lakh (*D.Y.* 165; *H.P.* 476) and finally led Sindhia out of the state.

SINDHIA'S EXIT, ANUPGIRI RE-ENTERS

From June to July 1787, northern India enjoyed comparative calm, but it was the lull before the storm. The, Jaipur envoy, Daulat Ram Haldia at Lucknow and the Gosain Anupgiri in Etawah carried on, during this period, skilfull negotiations under the seal of absolute secrecy, resulting in the formation of a confederacy of Rajput states and a sort of armed neutrality between the Ruhelas and the Nawab-wazir of Oudh to resist Sindhia. The

Gosain Anupgiri's correspondence with Faizullah Khan, with the Oudh court through Almas Ali Khan (*C.P.C.*, no. 930), Khadija Begam (*P.R.C.I.*, no. 72). Umraogiri's coquetting with the Sikh leaders (*C.P.C.*, VII, 1093, 1158, 1093) consolidate the evident indications of a deeply-laid scheme to enmesh all the leading chiefs together in one diplomatic net agains Sindhia. Into it even the English were enticed by such seductive offers of the Gosain as are contained in his words to Col. Harper, the Oudh Resident "Passing days under this asylum for the last seven months, the writer is yet willing to serve his master the vizier by ousting Sindhia from Hindusthan and Bundelkhand, if the wazir can only equip him with an army, equal to a *brigade* for that purpose" (*C.P.C.* VII, 1, no. 931). Such overtures led to the political isolation of Sindhia and a general desertion from his ranks of his Hindusthani and Mughalia leaders on the eve of Lalsot on 28 July 1787. The action was prevented from turning into Sindhia's Waterloo, by the disciplined valour of De Boigne's battalions and the unstinted sacrifice of his Naga troops.

In this historic battle the latter bore the brunt of fighting. Five thousand Naga musketeers, probably of the Vairagi Gosain order took their stand in the right wing of the Rajput army, while two thousand Naga monks under Motigir Gosain confronted them along with De Boigne's battalions on the Maratha left. In the clash that ensued, the Rajput cavalry swept like a whirlwind upon the Maratha. Left hundreds of Naga Gosains fell in trying to stem this violent onset[3] (*P.R.C.I.*, nos. 135-7) but they were thrown back along with thereat of their comrades. Promptly reinforced they reformed, returned to the fray along with the rest of the army and helped to roll back the flood of the enemy cavalry. On

[3] The intelligence conveyed to Poona in the letter no. *P.C.I.* 1, no. 137 about the Naga chief (that is to say, Motigir) being killed, is contradicted by the Delhi chronicle. This Motigir, along with a large following, proceeded as far as Murshidabad in course of a pilgrimage; but he was hustled back, on account of his long halt at the place and frequenting the houses of the people on the plea of arms (*C.P.C.* VII, nos. 32, 46, 179).

14 August, Motigir along with his comrades was discharged from service by Sindhia, with the gift of robes of honour and a sum of Rs. 4,000 in cash and bills of exchange (*D.C.*, vide Sarkar Ms., *Ibrat* III; *A.S.B.* 19-20).

The action at Lalsot was followed by a change in the political chess-board of India. The Mughalia and Hindusthani, Ruhela and Rajput, all now rose, as if by a common impulse for the recovery of their lost authority. The Gosain brothers now left their asylum for winning back their jagir by arms. Umraogiri attacked the fort of Firuzabad with a force of four to five thousand men and continued his fight until the whole of Bhow Bakhshy's possessions was annexed, (August-September), *P.R.C.I.*, pp. 250, 259; *C.P.C.* VII, 1771), while military adventurers and old-established monarchs swung towards Delhi to fill up the vacuum caused by Sindhia's eclipse. Raja Pratap Singh sent a force under the command of Gaur Mohant, Maharaj Jograj (*P.R.C.I.*, no. 199) but the Ruhela Ghulam Qadir forestalled all his rivals by forcing his way to the palace six months earlier on 26 August, and getting himself nominated as the Regent, on 5 September. About this time the Gosain was summoned to Delhi by the emperor (Munna Lal, 315-16). It is not known if he took any part in fanning the antagonism between Begam Samru and Ghulam Qadir and causing the latter's eventual retirement from the capital in September. The Ruhela, however, returned to the fray with renewed vigour early in October and continued an intermittent firing of the city during the whole of this month. From the menace of his re-entry, the city was delivered by a turn in the political situation mainly brought about by the Gosain.

Prince Jawan Bakht Jahandar Shah had made many a furtive effort to seize power at Delhi, but failed. He was now living in Benares as a British protege. All of a sudden he burst into the town of Jalesar in the third week of October, in response to the invitation of Anupgiri, who immediately placed his own contingent and that of the local jagirdar at the prince's disposal. Greatly honoured and encouraged, Jawan Bakht played the royal role by confirming Malik Muhammad Khan in his jagir and was then conducted to Mathura on 1 November. Here the prince met Ismail Beg in a cordial interviews. The reveberation caused by these events and the threatened march of the prince drove away the Ruhela storm-cloud from the environs of Delhi; while Anupgiri took quick possession of places like Saadabad, Vrindaban and Mathura (*Ibrat*, *A.S.B.* III, 77-8). The scheme engineered on behalf of the Jaipur Raja to use the prince as a puppet on the throne failed, for he joined Ismail Beg and after many adventure quitted Jalesar with a broken heart on 16 January 1781 (ibid., p. 11).

In December 1788 the report spread of the emperor's march to Ajmer in order to instal Prince Akbar Shah on the vice-regal seat of the place. This was a fresh threat to the newly-won freedom of the Rajputs. They had not watered the field of Lalsot with their blood to wear chains again. But they were too exhausted to draw their sword again; hence recourse was had to diplomacy, the conduct of which again was assigned to the skilled hand of Anupgiri. Here again the Gosain's wit and ingenuity, though unscrupulous, secured the Raja's ends and baffled their enemies. He first flattered the emperor with the compliance of the Rajput Raja as to his demands for financial contribution and encouraged the idea of a royal march by sending his favourite Khanahzad Khan. Allured by the prospect of financial relief, the emperor, started on 4 January 1788, and took the route across Rewari which was then owned by Najaf Quli Khan, the adopted son of the late Najaf Khan. The emperor occupied Rewari and marched 5 miles south of it, when he was met by the Jaipur minister Daulat Ram Haldia, the Jodhpur Bakhshi Bhimraj and Gosain Anupgiri on 28 January. Five days later (3 February) he granted an audience to the Jaipur Raja with the observance of traditional usages and rites. On the 10th. began the negotiation for the pecuniary contribution. Amid claims and counter-claims, the Jaipur vakil set a fresh breeze blowing by proposing a lump payment of Rs. 9 lakh in return for the grant to his master of the usurped crown-lands. In sore strait for money, the emperor agreed to the proposal, to give up the idea of a further march, on payment of the sum. But as soon as the Gosain demanded payment of the sum in the presence of the emperor, the Jaipur vakils "rolled their eyes wide in astonishment", to quite Khairuddin's words, and confounded the whole court by saying that all their funds having been exchausted in the last war, they were unable to make any payment before reaching their capital. After a month's stay with the emperor, Raja Pratap Singh finally bade Shah Alam adieu, by paying a sum of Rs. 25,000 only.

While the emperor fluctuated in his plan of action, after the departure of the Jaipur Raja, the Gosain fanned his feelings against Najaf Quli and set him against this arch rebel who was only seeking an opportunity to play the regent at Delhi. Under his inspiration, the emperor suddenly orderd an attack upon him as he was proceeding to Rewari. Najaf Quli fled to a fortalice, 5 miles north of Rewari, where he was pursued and closely besieged by the imperial army. In the course of the siege, Najaf Quli contrived a hold night-attack upon the emperor's camp, when Major Hess from his side, and Ghulam Husain Khan from the fort of Rewari fell like a thunderbolt and swept on towards the emperor's tents by cutting down all who came in their way. At this juncture the Gosain rushed towards Major Hess with his followers and threw him back after a sanguinary fight. He then hastened to the emperor's side, who had by this time escaped to the square of Begam Samru's infantry (*Ibrat,* III, 198-200). Influenced by her, the emperor granted pardon to the rebel and confirmed him in his possessions; in disgust Anupgiri parted from the emperor and retired to Pataudi. Finding his councillors divided among themselves, the emperor relinquished the idea of a march of Ajmir and returned towards Delhi.

During this interval of January-March 1788, Umraogiri lost all his possessions in the Doab to the Ruhela Ghulam Qadir who had launched renewed efforts for the increase of his strength with a view to the conquest of Delhi. In the beginning of April, he wrested the fort of Firuzabad from the Gosain, compelling him to seek service with his contingent of 700 horsemen under Ismial Beg at Agra. A violent contest was now in progress between Sindhia and Ismail

Beg Hamadani in the course of which the Maratha general Rana Khan brust upon Hamadani's besieging army at Agra left under the command of his old father and Gosain Umraogiri (Ghulam Ali, 260). On this occasion the Gosain was surprised in his camp on the bank of Jamuna facing the fort, during the worship of his tutelary deity after night-fall. His sons Kumar Jagat Bahadur and Uttamgiri put up a fight, receiving sword-cuts, while their father, finding the situation desperate, plunged into the waters of the Jamuna to escape, but was taken captive (Chhakan Lal, Bankipore Ms).[4] The Jat Raja Ranjit Singh led him to Sindhia's presence, who accorded him honourable treatment and allowed him to escape (Ghulam Ali, 260).

From this inerlude of Umraogiri's career, the historian's eyes are drawn to a new scene that was now unfolded at Delhi, with Anupgiri in the very centre of it. In June Sindhia shattered Ismail Beg's strength, who as a consequence joined hands with Ghulam Qadir. At this new political alignment, the emperor deprived of strong military backing, again trembled for his safety. His apprehensions were deepened by intrigues in the bosom of the place, by his own sister who plotted the enthronement of her own husband (*P.R.C.I.*, letter no. 220). With chicken-hearted followers and perfidious plotters around him the emperor found none so faithful as the Gosain and sent Ahmad Ali to call him (possibly from Brindavan) as early as May 1788 (ibid). The Gosain responded to the call of the sovereign in distress and was deputed along with Ram Ratan Modi to negotiate with Ghulam Qadir. Nothing is known about the result of this mission. On 1 July, however, the Ruhela cloud moved to Shahadara; ten days later (11 July) Ravloji Sindhia and Bhagirath Rao reinforced Anupgiri who was now vested by the emperor with the conduct of the defence of Delhi. In pressing need of money, the Gosain imposed a military levy upon the citizens of Delhi. The resistance

[4] According to Chakkan Lal, the news-writer of Shikohabad, he was rescued by a body of two hundred Chandela warriors despatched by his sons (*J.B.O.R.S.*, September-December 1951, p. 86).

offered in collecting the tribute led to the arrest of some leading Moslem merchants, such as Rahim Beg from which followed by a violent communal outbreak. The emperor, however, remained an onlooker, without taking any step to keep the agitation in control and the mob in order. He snubbed the Gosain's appeal for the grant of money out of his private funds by saying, "Where can I find money? If you want the ornaments of the Begam, I can offer them". But Anupgir pushed on his preparations for the defence of the capital. The enemy drew up in files on the opposite bank. Owing to the communal feeling that yet raged high in the city, the Mughalia troops who were sent to oppose the enemy's landing on an islet in midstream made common cause with the Ruhela. Thus disowned by the city, deserted by his own troops, and opposed by the Nazir and the Diwan, the Gosain found no other course open to him than to cross the river at night and retreat to Faridabad, 7 miles south of the capital (Munna Lal, 336). Then occurred those unparalleled diabolitical outrages upon the emperor and the members of the royal family of which a moving account can be read in Sir Jadunath Sarkar's third volume of the *Fall of the Mughal Empire.*

Mughal Empire

From the abyss of suffering, the monarchy was again lifted to the pedestal of grandeur by Mahadji Sindhia in alliance with Anupgir. He was instrumental in seducing Ismail Beg to Sindhia's side (*P.R.C.I.*, no. 234; Dy. I, 342, 345), forcing thereby Ghulam Qadir out of Delhi. It was Anup who with Ravloji Sindhia engaged the Ruhela at the time of his exit out of it, on 11 October. He took the lead in getting the gateway of the palace opened from inside, and was the first to enter the Red Fort and usher in the Maratha rescuers.

With the fall of Ghulam Qadir, a new epoch in the history of Delhi empire begins, and a new chapter in the history of Anupgir Gosain opens.

CHAPTER 16

The Last Stage 1789-1804 Rupture with Mahadji Sindhia and Migration to Bundelkhand

Anup Gir Gosain had taken an important part in achieving the establishment of Sindhia as Regent of Delhi, but hardly any reward for all his labour was forthcoming from the Maratha lord of Hindustan. He therefore retired from Delhi to Mathura in 1789, expecting in time to get at least a suitable jagir; but in the course of this year, he was charged with the diabolitical crime of attempting Mahadji's life by black magic and witchcraft and was threatened with fatal punishment. The irrepressible monk, however, surmounted this danger with the same resourcefulness with which he had cut many a gordian knot in his career before.

Summoned to Mahadji's durbar, he gave the slip to his *chobdars* on the way and having entered the tents of the Peshwa's agent, Ali Bahadur, took sanctuary under the *jatrin-patka* (the golden standard) of the Peshwas as a refuge from Sindhia's vengeance. This incident precipitated a political crisis of the gravest import. Mahadji demanded of Ali Bahadur the delivery of the alleged criminal into his hands. Ali Bahadur found it inconsistent with his sense of chivalry and the Peshwa's honour, to comply with Sindhia's demand. Mahadji therefore took recourse to force and besieged Ali Bahadur's camp from 21 to 24 July. This hostility between the Peshwa's deputed caused a profound stir, and Tukoji Holkar who had now come to Maratha lent the weight of his support to Ali Bahadur on 31 July. A Sindhia's lately-won ascendancy, loomed on the horizon. The astute minister Nana Fadnis saught to avert it, by decreeing the administration of the monk's estate and contingent by the Maratha state and his detention in the Jhansi fort, pending the final determination of the issue. These terms were, however, denounced by Mahadaji as being a clever subterfuge to set the monk at liberty. So the sword of Sindhia was kept suspended over Anupgiri's head. In January 1790, his doom seemed imminent when Ali Bahadur, starving with his troops by reason of Sindhia's suspension of all grants, proposed to hand him over to the latter. But the Gosain non-plussed his host by threatening to kill himself rather than be dishonoured. He was attended by a body of three hundred desperate *chelas* (disciples) who were ready to lay down their lives for him. So Ali Bahadur relented and negotiated the refugee monk's release, on condition of his imploring pardon by appearing as a penitent in Mahadaji's durbar. The Gosain yet clung to the Peshwa's standard, with the same tenacity as before, and refused to budge an inch from his present post. His inexorable resolution ultimately forced the mountain of Sindhia to move to Ali Bahadur's camp and make it up with him by liberating the monk's family from internment and presenting him with a robe of honour, a horse and elephants on 6 February 1790.

Thus, the monk triumphed again over the virtual lord of Hindustan. For more than a year after this event, Anupgiri lingered in Mathura scanning the political horizon; but Sindhia's resounding victories at Patan (20 June) and at Merta (10 September) defeated all hopes of his ever regaining any influence either in Rajasthan or the Doab. He therefore joined the cause of Ali Bahadur and proceeded along with him to Bundelkhand to navigate in the troubled political waters there which we propose to delineate in the following chapter with as much lucidity as the scanty materials would allow.

ANUP GIR'S DOINGS IN BUNDELKHAND AND THE CLOSE OF HIS CAREER (1791-1804)

Nature has designed Bundelkhand into two parts, of which the eastern portion lying between the Betwa and the Paisuni *nadi* has been famed in history as being the seat of royalty and the home of chivalry. Low-lying spurs of the Vindhyas sprawl over his country and break it up into fragments. In the last quarter of the eighteenth century, the heritage of Chhatrasal Bundela partitioned after his death into the two kingdoms of Banda and Panna, was rent by a civil war between None Arjun Singh, regent of Banda and Khuman Singh, Raja of Charkhari, and between Dhokal Singh and his uncle Sarnet Singh of Panna, supported respectively by the Chaube brothers, Beni Chaube and Khemraj Chaube. This internal strife had prompted Mahadaji to lead his forces into this kingdom, in 1786. Five years after this event, the gosain Anupgiri, baulked in his ambition of wielding authority at Delhi, resolved to retire to this remote region and plough in insolation, the furrowed land of his birth.

Lacking the necessary military and financial resources, he bound himself in an agreement with Ali Bahadur, the Peshwa's deputy in northern India and conducted a force of forty thousand men across Datia into this country. The Bundelas had no strength to meet them in pitched battles, and adopted the guerrilla mode of warfare favoured by the geography of their country. Hence the story of fighting on the part of the Gosain and his lieutenants is one of sharp isolated engagements in widely scattered places.

The first blow of the combined force under Ali Bahadur and the Gosain was delivered on the Banda regent, None Arjun Singh Pawar. He met the mighty army in an action near Ajaigarh, in the course of which many eminent adherents of the Gosain, e.g. Mandhata, son of Sabsukh Rai Khazanchi (treasurer), Hindupat, nephew of Arjun Singh, and Khuman Singh fell, while others like Kumar Gangagiri and Rajgiri were wounded. Unperturbed by these mishaps, Anupgiri directed his forces with superb skill and seconded by his lieutenants, such as Swarupgiri *alias* Sundargiri, Uttamgiri, Dilip Singh and Surjan Singh rolled up the enemy army in a final assault in which he personally challenged Arjun and cut him to pieces.[1] After this victory the Gosain pursued a body of Banda warriors for nearly 30 miles up to Charkhari. While he was encamped in the course of this expedition on the summit of a ridge with only one thousand cavalry and four guns, the Bundelas made a surprise night attack on him. The Gosain who had taken precautions against such a contingency, met the enemy with the discharge of grape and in the resulting confusion, charged and routed the enemy with the slaughter of three hundred men including Vijay Singh, the new Raja of Charkhari.

After the death of Arjun and Vijay Singh, the spirit of resistance spread among the common folk and the Gosain was hard put to it to quell the hydra-headed rising, Sugaram, a commander of Ali Bahadur dispersed at Maudaha, about 30 miles North-West of Bandah, a Bundela force commanded by Puranmal, son of the deceased Charkhari Raja Vijay Singh and two other chiefs, Jiwan and Ananda. Undaunted by the reverse, another body of Bundela horsemen numbering one thousand assembled at Jaharpur under the leadership of the Dawa[2] and by marching 14 miles, under cover of darkness made a night-attack on the Gosavi camp at Murwal. The Gosain commandant Kumar Durgagir getting intelligence of such a design, had quitted his tents with his troops and lurked in the bushes nearly with their muskets loaded. As soon as the unsuspecting Bundelas burst into the Gosain camp at dead of night and found it deserted, Gangagir opened a withering fire upon them, and under cover of this artillery attack charged and louted the Bundelas with heavy slaughter. The record of victories won by the Gosain and his lieutenants was tarnished by a single reverse in which the Dutch Colonel Mieselback in his services was defeated and narrowly escaped death. The next enagement at Durgatal, near Tirwah in which Beni Chaube the Panna regent

1 Himmat Bahadur Biradabali, 26-42.

2 Brisingh Deo of Pogson seems to be a mistake for Vijay Singh Deo.

received a crushing defeat, wiped out the humiliation of the previous reverse and practically stamped out all opposition in Bundelkhand (Pogson, *History of Boondelas*, Chapter IV, 119-21).

There was, however, a renewed flare-up of hostilities when Jaswant Rai, general of Ali Bahadur, was beaten back from Rewah, with heavy carnage. The Bundelas kept up a vigorous opposition for a period of two years, after which they were quelled by Ali Bahadur with the assistance of the Gosain. The Nawab next planned an offensive against the Baghela Raja. The last defeat suffered by his general at Rewah had rankled in his heart; in sorrow and grief he had cast off the turban and declared that he would not do it, until he had hoisted the victorious standard on the Baghela capital. The Gosain took the lead in the expedition that was organised and forced the Raja to sue for terms. Moved by the Raja's entreaties, Anupgir interceded with the Nawab on his behalf and arranged terms for the evacuation of the invading army on payment of Rs. 12 lakh. Ali Bahadur rewarded the Gosain's services in effecting the conquest of Banda and the submission of the Rewah Raja, by granting him a jagir of Rs. 13 lakh which won for him a high standing among the petty chiefs of the region. His influence and authority in the administration of Bundelkhand was further extended when after the Nawab's death in 1802 a council of Regency was formed with Ghani Bahadur, brother of Ali Bahadur, at its head (ibid., pp. 104-6).

The political situation in this country, however, took a new complexion when the Peshwa signed the Treaty of Bassein on 31 December 1802 and submitted to the British yoke. The Maratha chieftains Sindhia, Bhonsal and Holkar, stung to humiliation, became bent on war against the British and planned to make Bundelkhand the base of operations against British territory. Such a project first matured by Lakhwa Dada, as early as 1796 (*P.R.C.* VIII, 1. 30) threatened to take practical shape when 5,000 Pindaries and 3,000 horsemen were reported in June 1803, to be in motion to join the Gosain and Ghani Bahadur (ibid., IX, 1, 156, 200). The prospect of this joint Maratha enterprise became not merely a matter of concern to the British but endangered the security of the Gosain's possessions in Bundelkhand. He therefore set on foot a train of counternegotiations with Ahmutty, the British Collector of Allahabad, through the medium of Colonel Mieselback in his service (ibid., 1, 155). Enemity to the advancement of British interest was the keynote of the Gosain's career, but for the maintenance of his own position and jagir; he now practically sold himself to them. By the Shahpur treaty concluded with them on 4 September 1803, he was promised a jagir[3] of Rs. 22 lakh for his assistance in the occupation of Bundelkhand, and an additional territory in the British dominion for his cooperation with the British army during the pendency of the war (Thorn, *Memoir*, 241).

Two days following the conclusion of the treaty, the British detachment led by Lt. Col. Powell crossed the Jamuna at Rajapur Ghat, and being joined by Kumar Kanchangir, the *chela* and adopted son of Anupgir Gosain, marched to the bank of Paisuni *nadi*, near Tirwah. The penetration of the British force into the interior greatly alarmed Shamsher Bahadur, eldest son of Ali Bahadur, who had now become master of Bundelkhand by overthrowing the regency. He quickly raised the siege of the fort of Kalinjar and fell back at Kunwara, on the Ken River, about 4 miles north of Banda, while the British advanced to Kalinjar and effected junction with the Gosain.

After skirmishes for a few days to probe each other's strength, Powell and Anupgiri crossed the Ken on 10 October and engaged Shamsher Bahadur at Kupsa. There was at first an exchange of fire from a distance of 1,200 yards; but as it did not produce much effect, the British moved forward to within 500 yards, when Shamsher Bahadur's army was overcome with panic and vanished from the field in an instant. The fugitive soldiers were pursued for nearly 3 miles by Captain Webbe, attended by five hundred horsemen from the Gosain force and his own squadron of cavalry.

[3] Growse says that nearly all the territory on the west bank of Jamuna from Kalpi to Allahabad was assigned to Himmat Bahadur (*Mathura*, p. 175.)

Utterly shaken in power by this defeat, Shamsher Bahadur kept dangling before the English terms of submission for a period of two months. The triumph of the British arms at Kalpi, the capitulation of its qiladar Nanda Govinda in December 1803 and increasing desertion from the ranks of Shamsher Bahadur's army left him no other alternative than to surrender to the British on promise of a jagir of an annual revenue of Rs. 4 lakh. His entry into the British camp, on the 18 January 1804 set the seal to the British conquest of Bundelkhand. The Gosain was recompensed for his active cooperation, in the expedition with a jagir of Rs. 20 lakh, and the authority to maintain a force of ten thousand cavalry with a complement of other rank in proportion. Thus the Gosain completely overshadowed the ruling Nawab of Banda both in military strength and material resources alike; without the kingly feather on his turban he became, as a matter of fact, the ruler of a considerable extent of a territory in Bundelkhand under the suzerainty of the British (Thorn, *Memories of the War*, 240-5). He did not live long to enjoy this power; in the very year of the conclusion of the war in 1804, he died at Kunwara and his earthly remains were deposited in a tomb at a distance of 2 miles from Banda[4] (H.B. Birudabali, p. 27).

[4] A *ghat* or landing steps for bathing into the Jamuna commemorates the Gosain's name (Grrowse, *Mathura*, 175).

CHAPTER 17

Military Services under our Princes

In this book the history of Gosain Rajendragiri and his disciples has been told in full detail because they played a long and distinguished part in the history of Hindustan as feudal barons, like Samant Rajahs, and were recognised as such by the Nawab of Oudh, the Emperor of Delhi, and the Marathas king. But no other Dasnami leader attained to such a high position and power. Many bands of Naga Sannyasis and their *mahants* did important military service to the Rajas of Rajputana, Gujrat and other States, and they were rewarded with grants of land and yearly money allowance, as the records of these States prove. Though they did not rise to the rank of barons like Himmat Bahadur, their loyalty and heroism in dafence of the right cause may be totally forgotten in their deeds are not included in this general history of the Ten Orders. Our only disadvantage is that these acts of heroism and loyalty were done in many scattered States and at different times, and detailed descriptions of these fights are not available, because the records of the feudal States of India have not been searched and indexed for the use of historical research scholars.

Many other orders of Hindu religious warriors took part in these wars of Rajputana and Malwa along with the Dasnamis. But the exact proportion of Naga and non-Naga fighters in those old half-forgotten battles and the names of their captains cannot be clearly distingushed now for want of detailed records. The only information that we get from the Persian, Marathi and Hindi manuscripts in that Gosain and Vairagis (and some called

Ramanandis and Vishnu-swamis), under the general name of Maha-purushas or Gosains fought in defense of our Rajahs, and only the general result of their actions is given in our old history. I have included all such Hindu religious warriors in this volume. However, the readers must remember that some of these heroes were outside the Ten Orders. But that does not matter; the Hindu religious and martial spirit is the same, whatever the monk's title and the colour of his dress.

IN RAJPUTANA

The Gosains of Rajputana are thus described by Tod:

"There is a numerous class of Gosains who have adopted celibacy and who yet follow secular employments both in commerce and arms. The mercantile Gosains are amongst the richest individuals in India. . . . The Gosains who profess arms, partake of the character of the Knights of St. John of Jerusalem. They live in monasteries scattered over the country, possess lands, and beg, or serve for pay when called upon. As defensive soldiers they are good . . . In Mewar they can always muster many hundreds of the Kanfora Jogi or split-ear ascetics . . . The poet Chand Bardai gives an animated description of the bodyguard of the king of Kannauji which was composed of these monastic warriors" (Tod's *Rajasthan*, vol. I, Mewar, Ch. 19).

IN JODHPUR

Maharajah Abhay Singh died in 1749 and his young and reckless son Ram Singh succeeded him. But next year the new Maharajah of Jodhpur was deposed by the nobles whom he had insulted and the throne was taken by Bakht Singh the younger brother of Abhay. When Bakht died in September 1752 and his son Bijay Singh ascended the throne, Ram Singh hired the Maratha to fight for him. In June 1754 a vast Maratha army under Jai Apa Sindhia invaded Marwar. At the call of Bijay Singh ten thousand Gosain troops, forming nine regiments (*bera*) each under its separate flag, came from Kumbhalgarh to defend him. Near Merta Bijay Singh was defeated after fighting a severe battle with the Marathas, but the Gosains helped him to reach his ancestral jagir of Nagor in safety. The Marathas next laid siege to Nagor, which was defended by Rajputs and Gosains.

The siege of Nagor dragged on for a year. The Maratha of Udaipur sent a pious Gosain named Bijai Bharati to Jai Apa's camp to negotiate a peace between the two parties. But on 26 July 1755, two assassins employed by the Marwar darbar treacherously murdered Jai Apa and the infuriated Maratha soldiers massacred every Rajput in their camp, including the innocent Gosain Bijay Bharati. Out of these nine regiments that had come to defend Bijay Singh four remained in the permanent service of the Jodhpur State—namely, the Bharati flag in Nagor, the Puri flag in Fathsagar, another branch of the Puri flag in Jalor, and another in Thambla. Of the other five regiments, some went to Jasalmir and some to Mewar where they still remain.

Later in his reign Bijay Singh became initiated as a follower of the Vaishnav *mahant* of the Nathdwara temple. He used to make long visits to this holy place, where the Mahapurusha soldiers were the hereditary defenders of the god. He greatly liked these Gosain troops for their valour and fidelity and took delight in improving their equipment and drill. About the year 1780, he enlisted a large body of these Gosain in the regular army of his kingdom. The Marwar State history declares that—"The Mahapurushas formed the cheapest, hardiest yet most trustworthy fighters. They used to get rupees three to three and a half per month as pay for each soldier, and fodder and corn for their horses as well as ammunition free from the Government." Some of their useful deeds are described below.

Between 1784 and 1793 they fought many battles in bringing under subjugation the many wild and criminal tribes in Godwar and the Aravali border on the south-east of the Marwar Kingdom. They also helped Bijay Singh in checking the predatory tribes of the western desert and conquering the fort of Amarkot and some territories from the Rao of Jasalmir. In fact the Nagas helped to remove two grave defects of the Rajput clan army, because they supplied the steadiness which the impetuous Rathor horsemen lacked and the use of fire arms which the Rajputs neglected and despised as unworthy of heroes.

In 1787, when Mahadji Sindhia invaded Jaipur and took post at Lalsot, the Jodhpur Maharaja sent a strong body of Gosain troops to aid the defence of his ally the Kachhwa Raja. In the battle of Tanga that followed, these Gosain fought most bravely, fired 35 rockets (*bans*) and prevented the advance of the Maratha cavalry. At the end of the day Sindhia had to retreat in disappointment. Naga monks also fought on the side of the Jaipur Raja against De Boigne and Jiva Dada (the generals of Sindhia) at the battle of Patan, in the left wing of the Jaipur army (20 June 1790). They checked Holkar's cavalry during the engagement. Ramanandi and Vishnu-Swami monk also fought for the Jodhpur Raja at the battles of Merta on 10 September 1790 (see Jadunath Sarkar's *Fall of the Mughal Empire*, vol. IV. Ch. 38 for details).

In November 1791, Bijay Singh, having become an old and half crazy man in weak health, wanted to please his concubine of the Jaiswal caste by seating his heir on her lap and forcing the nobles to salute her. At this a rebellion broke out in Marwal. All the nobles with their contingents, numbering it is said to 80,000 Rathore, left the court and assembled at Jamwar, wishing to set up another prince, Bhim Singh, as their Maharajah. But Bijay Singh was supported by the Mahapurushas who fought the rebel nobles; guarded the rear, and escorted him safely to his capital.

When Bijay Singh died (on 8 July 1763) Bhim Singh sat on the *gaddi* of Jodhpur as his successor and took up arms against Man Singh of Jalor. In Bhim Singh's attack on Jalor, Mahant Gulab Puri rendered signal service, for which his *chela* Moti Puri was rewarded by the grant of Lambabhala village in Metta pargana.

In November 1804 Bhim Singh died and Man Singh gained the throne of Marwar. But his chief vassal, Sawai Singh of Pokharan turned against him, and formed a conspiracy to murder him by treacherously inviting him to the Gigauli pass. But the attempt was foiled by some loyal nobles. The Mahapurush regiments under Mahants Budh Bharti, Daulat Puri and Moti Puri along with a few loyal nobles, fought the rebels and thus enabled Man Singh to retreat through the ring of his enemies to Jodhpur in safety. Moti Puri also saved his standard (mahi-o-maratib) and the elephant carrying his puja materials and idols from capture by the enemy and brought them to Jodhpur. For this service Mahant Daulatpuri received a parwana of honour stamped with the Maharaja's personal seal. This *mahant* led repeated expeditions against Sirohi, by order of the Jodhpur Raja.

In 1815 the Mahapurush regiments were sent to Desuri and they ably suppressed the disturbances there. Mahants Karan Puri (Bara. Corps), Sukhdev Puri the disciple of Moti Puri (Akhara Corps) and Santosh Puri, the disciple of Bhagwan Puri; were granted Rs. 7,000 per month from the treasury of Desuri for maintaining 3,500 men (August 1815). Their later services need not be detailed here.

In the Mewar State, a Gosain force was stationed at Kumbhalgarh and supported by a grant of land.

IN JASALMIR

In the wars of this State with its neighbour Bikaner, in the early nineteenth century, a Gosain force under Mahant Bhairo Puri (Suraj Prakash flag) and Mahant Sawant Puri defeated the Bikaner attack on Kot Vikrampur, at the cost of losing their two brave leaders and fifteen common soldiers (1829). In 1840 a Gosain Jas Giri was appointed commander of the Jasalmir forces, and he controlled the Pathan, Sikh and Gosain contingents in the State service, for thirty years.

IN BARODA

Nana Fadnis, the regent of the Peshwa of Poona, sent his own agent Aba Shelukar to Ahmadabad to collect the Peshwa's share of the tribute of Gujrat. This man began to extort money with great rigour and injustice, and to act in defiance of the authority of Govind Raj Gaikwad the Raja of Baroda. In fact, Aba Shelukar overthrew the regular government and filled the province with tumult, plundering many places. He collected a band of 15,000 infantry and 7,000 cavalry, mostly lawless robbers, and at last occupied the city of Ahmadabad. Govind Rao Gaikwad had to fight against him and in this he was greatly helped by his faithful Gosain contingent. In April and May 1800 two battles were fought in which the Gaikwad was victorious and captured two guns from the enemy. How these monks shed their blood for their master is proved from the Baroda State records, which tell us that in one battle, in a single regiment (*bera*) of Gosains seven wounded (all Giris, 31 May 1800), and in another battle next month eight were wounded (five Giris, with two Puris and one Baba), and so on. When Aba roved about looting the country near Borsad, Muhammadabad &c., the Gaikwad's forces (including Gosains) attacked and drove him away (April 1800). He was next attacked in the city of Ahmadabad, and taken prisoner (July 1800) with Gosain help.

In August 1797, the Gosains formed a part of the force sent by the Gaikwad to put down the rebellion of Kanhoji Rao and his Bhils at Songarh, and they greatly distinguished themselves here also (*Historical Selections from the Baroda State Records*, vol. VI, pp. 884, 872-4; Bana-ji's *The Gaikwads of Baroda, English Documents*, vol. III, pp. 225, 226, 243; letters of Govind Rao Gaikwad to Governor Duncan). The Baroda Govt, records give the names of 12 regiments of Giri *mahants* and their fixed money allowances. These were originally brought there by Pilaji Rao Gaikwad from Jhansi.

IN CUTCH

A Naga force did good service to Maha Rao Bhar Mal II of Cutch-Bhoj (reign 1813-19), and their descendants were retained permanently in the State army. Their place of honour is the fifth in the line of procession of the Maha Rao on the Nag Panchmi day. They were regarded as very brave soldiers.

When the chief of Morvi hired the armed aid of Sarbuland Khan the governor of Gujrat (1725- 30) and bringing a contingent of the Khan's nephew captured Bhuj city from his elder brother Maha Rao Prag Mal, the latter had to flee away from his capital. But next day a Naga force came to his rescue, and assisted by the Jareja Rajputs (the native of Cutch) they defeated and killed Sarbuland Khan's nephew and restored Prag Mal to his throne (*Bombay Gazetteer*, vol. V. *Cutch*, chaps. 3 and 7).

IN MEWAR

In 1628, the Maharana of Udaipur dismissed Nathu Koka and placed the management of temple of Nathdwara under Swami Ramanand Saraswati, who was formerly the Āchārya of the Dasnami Akhara in Benares. Since then the god has been under the guardianship of these sannyasis. The Maharana's guru since 1729 has been a Giri Gosain (see the record-books of the *math*).

IN AJMIR

The holy city of Pushkar had been taken possession of by the wandering robber tribe of Gujars. But in the Diwali night of 30 Kartik Badi, Vikram Samvat 1214 (AD 1157) Naga Sannyasi troops defeated and expelled the Gujars and restored the city to the Brāhmans. They planted the Bharatis in the Varaha temple, the Jnan-Naths in the Vaidyanath temple, and the Puris in the temples of Brahma and Savitri— where they are still in possession.

IN JHANSI

Jhansi was the chief centre of the Nagas in the early eighteenth century, and Gosain Rajah used to rule over this small State, which was at first very inferrior to the old Bundels Kingdom of Orchha. When the Peshwa was granted a large portion of Bundelkhand by Chhatrasal, his Subahdar Naro Shankar (governor of Jhansi 1742-56) was at first defeated and denied possession by Indra Gir Gosain the qiladar of Jhansi assisted by Ganga Puri. But Naro Shankar won the Puri over to his side and with his help established his own rule over Jhansi. But his recall and the battle of Panipat upset Maratha rule there.

Raghunath Hari Navalkar, Subahdar of Jhansi from 1770 to 1794, firmly established himself in Jhansi by his ability and good administration. The Gosain militia (*sebandi*) continued to live there and to serve the new masters of that State, up to the time of the Sepoy Mutiny. They formed the bodyguard of the heroic Rani Lakshmi Bai, when she fled away from the fort of Jhansi during its siege by Sir Hugh Rose in 1858.

The military services of the Gosains in many other States cannot be mentioned here for want of space.

CHAPTER 18

Gosains in Banking Administration and Civil Administration

The Gosain who took to the work of bankers enjoyed great respect in Rajputana, Hyderabad and other States. They proved very useful to the rulers of these States by standing security for the tributes imposed on them by the Marathas and other conquerors. Many of them acted as ambassadors and peace-makers, being aided by their holy character as priests. The case of Vijay Bharati of Udaipur, who went to Jai Apa Sindhia's camp before Nagor to effect a peace with he Raja of Marwar and was killed in 1755, has been given in the preceding chapter. The work thus interrupted was done by Mahant Amar Puri, who was sent by the Jodhpur Raja and effected a compromise with the Marathas.

When Warren Hastings sent British envoys to the Tisu Lama of Lhasa (George Bogle in 1773-5 and Samuel Turner in 1784) in order to secure the kingdom of Kuch Bihar from the attacks of the Rajah of Bhutan and also to promote trade between Bengal and Tibet, he employed a Gosain named Puran Giri as his agent. This holy man had connections with Bhutan and Tibet and the information that he gave and the personal contacts that he established proved of great service to the East India Company. Lieutenant Turner fully acknowledges the value of Puran Giri's help in his report to the Governor-General. This Gosain had a monastery at a place near Calcutta, called Bhot Bagan, and the East India Company rewarded him with grants. The Raja of

Burdwan was the Zamindar or superior landlord of the jagir of Bhot Bagan. During the absence of Puran Giri, the manager of the Raja of Burdwan forcibly dispossessed his *chelas* from Bhot Bagan and confiscated the land. But the English Government compelled him to restore the jagir to the Gosain (see Turner's *Embassy to the Court of the Teeshoo Lama*)

The Gosain bankers proved very helpful to the Indian princes in conducting their government, both in war and civil administration, by their loans and also by standing security for the due payment of the war indemnity imposed upon them by invaders like the Marathas. They thus saved the country from devastation. We find in our history that India like Europe had to depend on loans in carrying on wars. Thus, when Raja Shahu began the conquest of Bassein from the Portuguese in 1737, he took a heavy loan from some bankers at 36 per cent interest per annum and promised to mortgage a district to them if he could not repay the amont at the end of the war. Similarly, after the death of Peshwa Baji Rao I (1740), it was found that the Peshwa's Government had a debt of over Rs. 20 lakhs still unpaid, out of which Rs. 1 lakh and 69 thousand had been borrowed from Gosains, whose names are given in the Peshwa's account books. (See also Baji Rao's letters to Brahmendra Swami.)

Pantaji Shivdev Soman, the Governor of Maval under the Sachiv in the region of Rajaram (1690-9), conducted his master's administration by taking large loans from the Gosains out of which Rs. 10 lakh were still unpaid in 1727.

The Bhonsle Rajahs of Nagpur were still more heavily indebted to the Gosains for money help in running their government. Udepuri Gosain was always assisting Janoji Bhonsle in this way; he paid down Rs. 1 lakh at once when Janoji was helpless as his troops were starving being unable to buy grain. His loans to Janoji's brother Mudhoji Bhonsle, reached the total of Rs. 50 lakh. These Gosain bankers were not stony-hearted, Baijnath Puri excused a loan of Rs. 12 lakh to Janoji Bhonsle, when that Raja pleaded his present poverty and helplessness.

The Government of the Nizam of Hyderabad was most heavily indebted to the Gosain bankers, who were very numerous and enjoyed the highest honour in that State for their wealth and influence. Asaf Jah the first Nizam about the year 1740 gave many rewards jagirs and honour like a first class omra to Jogendra Giri who had helped him in this way. The Nizam's Government afterwards from time to time took loans from the Gosain monasteries (*math*) in that State, which totalled more than Rs. 1 crore. Thus, we find Rs. 60 lakh as due to the *math* of Bansi Giri, 22 lakh to Gyan Giri, 8 lakh to Bhum Giri, and so on. Unable to pay the original, the Nizam's Government granted to one Gosain jagirs yielding nearly Rs. 20,000 a year, and promised jagirs to others. The province of Berar was mortgaged to the Gosains for five years for the recovery of the loans advanced by them.

No history of the Dasnami Gosains can be complete unless it does justice to the activities of this sect not only in war but also in the fields of education, religious administration, charity, building works of public utility, and civil administration. For lack of space only a short general summary can be given here, and many important *maths* and great personages have been left out. The another hopes that this explanation will save him from the charge of partiality. Any one who wishes to know more about this aspect of Sannyasi history will be best served if he reads the Marathi book, *Gosavi wa tyancha Sampradaya*, by Goswami Prithvigit Harigir, 2 vols. (Yeotmal, 1931). In it will be found a mine of invaluable details collected laboriously from many scattered sources and places and very conveniently published for the use of future scholars. The book was printed after the author's death, and hence his slips of the pen and the printer's mistakes will have to be carefully corrected by the readers.

The temples and monasteries of the Gosain sect (both Sannyasi and Gharbab) are spread all over India, and their total number must exceed several thousands. Maharashtra, Berar and Hyderabad are the provinces most rich in Gosain *maths*, temples and ghats, all of which are for the benefit of the public only a few are mentioned here by way of illustration. Even Goswami Prithvigir's book does not give an exhaustive list.

The world-famous temple of Bodh Gaya marks the place where Buddha attained to the supreme truth by meditation (sambodhi). It was standing in a broken and neglected condition in the midst of jungles and unattended by men, when a Dasnami named Ghamandi Giri came there in the course of his travels (about AD 1590) and established his Shaiva *math* near it. Thus the place was rescued from total desolation and became a safe centre of pilgrimage. The temple was repaired from time to time with his help. The *mahant's* estate now yields six lakhs a year.

In AD 1754 the famous Aran Buwa Math (at Tulzapur, the most sacred *tirtha* in all Maharashtra) was founded by Keshav Aranya Avadhut, a Dasnami, who had come from Benares. His successors are buried there. There are in the same city the Bharati Math, Garibnath Math, &c. near the Bhawani temple.

In the city of Poona, more than 40 *maths* were counted when the British rule began (1818). Many hundred tombs of their *mahants* are still to be seen in all parts of this Maratha capital. Narpat Gir Buwa built a wonderful Vishnu temple. Nageshwar Giri, the *mahant* of the Kalyan Gir Math was famous for his charity from Benares to Rameshwar. He also built 21 dharmshalas or free rest-houses for pilgrims, and made large donations repairing old temple.

The free distribution of food (*bhandara*) held by the Poona Gosains was one of the wonders of the past. Sometimes ten thousand Gosains were fed for ten days together in communal seating arrangement.

Hurnam Giri, a householder Gosain and jewel merchant, built the fine *ghat* on the Sangam at Poona.

The parent *math* (*mul math*) of the famous Raja Bahadur Gyan Gir of Hyderabad was in Poona. In memory of this fact, Raja Narsingh Gir has founded the Raja Gyangir Vaidic Ashram on the Fergusson College Road of Poona.

Bholagir Buwa, who died in 1873, was a disciple of the Mangir

Math, and played an influential part in the local administration. His tomb in the Somwar Peth is worth looking at, and his charitable donations are worth remembering.

The Bansa Puri Math belongs to a famous banker family of Satara, who had often helped the kings and nobles with loans and exerted influence on politics.

In the Hyderabad State, the famous Bansi Gir Math was founded by Jogendragir who had come the Anandgir Devgir Math of Poona (about AD 1725). He had exercised great influence on the Nizam's government ever since the days of the first Asar Jah. One monk of the Ashram founded the *math* at Kalyani (midway between Gulbarga and Bidar), which enjoys a large *jagir*.

In Hyderabad, Raja Gyangir's disciple Raja Narsinghgir is famous for the good use he has made of his vast wealth for the public benefit. He is a rich mill-owner and industrial capitalist. One of his disciples Pratapgir mostly lives in Bombay on business as a mill-owner &c. Among his public donations may be mentioned large sums to the Benares Hindu University, the Matunga Hindu Orphanage, and many other good institutions. The other disciple of Gyangir, Raja Dhanraj Gir, has been equally liberal for the good of the public. They have been the main props of modern Hindu improvement.

Some other Gosain *maths* of Hyderabad are very rich and their heads occupy the same position as noble? in the political life of that State, but their records have not been made available to us.

It must be remembered that the Dasnami Gosains have not been lazy, selfish and idle in the modern age. They have harmonised themselves to the advancing needs of the present civilised age, by founding schools of Hindu learning and moral life at Benares, Allahabad and many other cities, where the monk-teachers are honoured by the public for their deep Sanskrit learning and pious character. The Maha-Mandaleshwars of this sect, whom we may liken to the Bishops and Deans of the Christian Church, are among the best Sanskrit scholars and efficient teachers of the present day. They do not keep themselves selfishly shut up in their monasteries, but travel over the country and give thousand of people in our towns the benefit of their pious teaching and moral example of life. Such teachers play an invaluable part in the modern materialistic age.

CHAPTER 19

A Short History of Akhara Mahanirvani (Contributed)

In the spiritual sphere as well as political field the Dashnami monastic orders, detailed in every corner of India, placed an important role in moulding the currents and cross-currents in the channels of our country's history. We read a good deal of their multifarious activities during the later Moghul period.

It wears an unique character and is an efficient organization based on democratic principles with strict, disciplined life, impassioned zeal of sacrifice to radiate Vedic religion and Āchārya Shanker's monism which serve the good of the vast body of Hindu society.

Even today there exists a long chain of these monasteries which are playing their part well in the spiritual, economic and cultural life of our country and each of them has its own contribution to make; amongst them Mahanirvani Akhara ranks first. It was established in the year 805 vs on the tenth day of Agahan (by Hindu calendar month) with its centre at Allahabad located in Muhalla Daraganj on the bank of the holy river Ganges. It's branches are spread all over Onkareshwar, Nasik, Hardwar, Kurukshetra, Udaipur, Jwalamukhi, Kashi, and Bhar (Akola). The chief deity (*upasyadeo*) of the Akhara is Sri Kapil Mahamuni.

The monks pertaining to this Akhara own a peculiar tradition; the nagas—weird unclothed sadhus—have become warriors of repute. The acts of chivalry of Sarvashri Rajindragiriji, Raja

Anupgiriji alias Himmat Bahadur, Mukundgiriji of Jhabua, Daulatpuriji of Jodhpur, Bhairopuriji of Jaiselmer, Nilkanthgiriji of Udaipur, are worthy of note and have been recorded in the pages of history. The annual grant given by erstwhile princely states of Poona, Gaikwad, Jodhpur Udaipur, Jaiselmer and Nagpur, etc., is the fruit of their chivalary. In these places the symbols of these *akharas*, which are in the forms of spears, "Surya Prakash, Bhairo Prakash" are held in high esteem still to day.

If we throw a glance on the history of this monastery we find that upto AD 1857 the cardinals of *akhara* took part in contemporary politics. In the war of independence AD 1857 they showed an example of chivalry by offering services to the Peshwa Nana Saheb and the great Rani of Jhansi. But like other leaders of the princely states the sun of their military glory set for ever in the even year. In other words the monks changed their outlook and vowed to spend their life in social service through the propagation of Vedic religion. Ever since then till date the monks of this *akhara* limit their activities to the spread of Hindu religion, pilgrimage, and holy worship.

In the later Mughal period these Dasnami monks shared fortunes in mercantile activities along with their fighting activities. They then established their monesteries in important trading centres like Udaipur, Nagpur, Mirzapur, Benares, Mandavi (Kutch), Poona, Mysore and Hyderabad, etc., and bound their activities to business only. The managers of such *akharas* are known as Dangali Mathadhari.

The fighting section saved holy places of Palanpur, Punjab, Ahmadabad, Kutch, Marwar, Udaipur and Somgarh in Gujrat, on the point of their swords along with the forces of erstwhile princely states. Thus the monks of these *akharas* have rendered valuable services to the commercial as well as political field. Still they have been exerting for spread of religion and social service. There is a big Goshala (dairy) in the vicinity of Hardwar and at Allahabad in Daraganj there is Ved Nirvan Maha Vidyalaya where Sanskrit education is imparted to hundreds of students. Fatehpuri ji who by dint of his merit wiped away the scarcity of water from Jaiselmer.

Even today the monastery is not barren of such torch bearers. A number of Mandaleshwars, who are the senior members and men of letters are appointed by the *akhara* to propagate Vedic religion. The trio of Swami Krishnanandaji, Swami Vidyanandaji and Swami Maheshwaranandji is worthy of note. Swami Krishnanandaji who is head of Sanyas Ashram of Ahmadabad founded by Swami Jayendrapuriji Maharaj is a great propagator of Acharya Shanker's ideals and Vedantic phiop.

For the facilities of the monks who braving various odds visit holy places devoid of any approach, situated in interior of Himalayas Swamiji has opened a dharmashala in Uttarkashi. He has also opened Sannyas Ashramas and Sanskrit Pathshalas in Bharoch and Benares.

Swami Vidyanandji, another Mandaleshwar of the *akhara* and a man of imposing personality, a well-known preacher of *Gita* is leaving no stone unturned in the noble cause of the propagation of *Gita* philosophy. He, giving a novel conception of *Holy Gita* has established Gita temples in Ahmadabad, Benares, Bardwan, Karnal, Delhi, and Nagpur. Recently he visted Burma, South Africa and some other countries of Europe for acquainting persons of these foreign lands with the lofty ideals of *Gita*.

Swami Maheshwaranandji a man of attractive personlity a reknowned scholar of Sanskrit is also doing his best to propagate Shanker's philosophy. He has opened Sannyas Ashram and Sanskrit Pathshala in Villey Parley, Bombay. He is the head of Kankhal Ashram.

There are not a few but many examples of such monks who are still held in high regard by the masses and classes alike of this land of religion.

Index